SCAM-PROOF
Your Life

SCAM-PROOF
Your Life

377 SMART WAYS

To Protect You & Your Family
From Ripoffs, Bogus Deals
& Other Consumer Headaches

BY SID KIRCHHEIMER

AARP'S "SCAM ALERT" EXPERT

STERLING PUBLISHING CO., INC.

AARP Books publishes a wide range of titles on health, personal finance, lifestyle, and other subjects to enrich the lives of older Americans. For more information, go to www.aarp.org/books

AARP, established in 1958, is a nonprofit organization with more than 36 million members age 50 and older.

The AARP name and logo are registered trademarks of AARP, used under license to Sterling Publishing Co., Inc.

Library of Congress Cataloging-in-Publication Data Available

2   4   6   8   10   9   7   5   3   1

Published by Sterling Publishing Co., Inc.
387 Park Avenue South, New York, NY 10016
© AARP 2006

Distributed in Canada by Sterling Publishing
c/o Canadian Manda Group, 165 Dufferin Street
Toronto, Ontario, Canada M6K 3H6

Distributed in the United Kingdom by GMC Distribution Services
Castle Place, 166 High Street, Lewes, East Sussex, England BN7 1XU
Distributed in Australia by Capricorn Link (Australia) Pty. Ltd.
P.O. Box 704, Windsor, NSW 2756, Australia

Sterling ISBN-13: 978-1-4027-3041-2
          ISBN-10: 1-4027-3041-1

For information about custom editions, special sales, or premium and corporate purchases, please contact the Sterling Special Sales Department at 800-805-5489 or specialsales@sterlingpub.com

To my parents . . .
and the lovely Christine Jane.

CONTENTS

INTRODUCTION

I HAD JUST FINISHED speaking with another scam victim—a retired salesman from Georgia bilked out of $4,500 in a fraudulent work-at-home scheme—when my telephone rang.

"Hello," said a pleasant voice. "I'm calling from your mortgage company. And I see from our records that you may qualify for a lower loan rate."

Interestingly, she did not mention the name of the company that gets my monthly mortgage check. Even more telling was the fact that I had refinanced just two months earlier—and mortgage-interest rates had climbed since then.

"Really?" I replied, glancing at the caller ID gizmo on my desk. "Tell me more." The incoming call was marked "Private." It was about 8 in the evening, a time when most mortgage-loan officers are home digesting dinner.

"Well, sir," she said, "based on your excellent credit history, I think we can save you hundreds of dollars a month with our much more attractive rate."

"Is that right?" I encouraged her. "What's the rate?"

"Before I can answer," she replied, "I just need to verify some information—your Social Security number and bank-account numbers—to make sure they match our records and that you really qualify for this great mortgage rate."

Hmm. "Do you know my name?" I asked her, since she hadn't used it yet.

She gave the one listed in the phonebook—which is not Kirchheimer. To spot telemarketers—who continue to phone my home, despite my enrollment on the National Do Not Call Registry—I use a pseudonym as my White Pages listing.

"Seriously," I said, "do you expect me to fall for this?"

She gave a harsh little laugh. "You'd be amazed how many people do," she sneered. And then she hung up.

Actually, I wouldn't be amazed—and neither should you. Every year, tens of millions of Americans are cheated in a range of scams:

There's the artist in Pennsylvania whose car literally fell apart two weeks after she bought it. The vehicle had been damaged by hurricane flooding, but its title was doctored to hide that fact—from both the car dealership and the buyer.

There's the self-employed insurance agent in New Hampshire whose bank account was emptied in a debit-card "skimming" scam a week before she had to pay her quarterly income taxes. The 88-year-old retired teacher in Florida who lost $8,000 in a sweepstakes scam. The soldier's wife in California victimized by a perfectly legal scam—an additional $300 per month in credit-card fees because her payment arrived a few days late. (The reason for the delay: She was saying goodbye to her husband, deployed to Afghanistan after 9/11.)

These are not stupid people. Rather, they were simply unaware of the numerous cons—and their consequences—that occur every day, whether they originate in boiler rooms or boardrooms, in some back alley or right at their front door.

This book aspires to spare you their fate. In these pages, you'll get specific advice from nearly 100 reformed scammers—and those who tirelessly fight them—to sidestep scores of scams, ripoffs, and costly consumer headaches.

In Section 1, you'll learn how to protect your money when making or using everyday goods and services. This includes fending off those who would separate you from more than their rightful share of your dollars when you buy, refinance, or repair a car or home. You'll learn how to save money on credit cards and phone service. I'll cover the art and science of traveling to more places for less—without sacrificing luxury or convenience. I'll even show you how strong-but-not-stellar high-school students can score merit scholarships.

Section 2 explains how to protect your health—and minimize the costs surrounding it. This includes practical and proven tips from doctors and other experts on how to prevent medical errors. You'll learn how to halt hospital and drug overcharges and block other health-care ripoffs. You'll unearth the secrets of getting high-quality, courteous care and preventing everyday illness. And you'll glean inside information on the best ways to choose a doctor or a hospital, find where to buy top medications for less, and even uncover some of the surprising health risks that may lurk in your home.

Section 3 pinpoints scores of easy steps you can take to protect your identity, your job status, and yourself from some of the most notorious scams—everything from classic charity cons and door-to-door dupes to the newer "phishing," "pharming," and work-at-home swindles born of the Internet age. These schemes steal billions of dollars annually from their victims (to say nothing of their self-esteem).

All quoted advice comes directly from our Panel of Experts (profiled on pages 326-329), each of whom I personally interviewed. Their counsel is buttressed by the nearly 1,000 studies, surveys, and other documents used to research this book. All material was fact-checked by AARP-trained researchers and in-house consumer advocates and policy mavens. The data were accurate and up-to-date as we went to press.

The book you hold in your hands may not shield you from every attempt to defraud you. It will, however, give you more insight—and foresight—into cons, ripoffs, and costly maneuvers, leaving you better equipped to protect yourself, your family, your money, and your peace of mind.

And who knows? It may just scam-proof your life forever.

—SID KIRCHHEIMER

PROTECT YOUR MONEY

CARS
Don't Get Taken for a Ride

CAR OWNERSHIP can be a rough ride. After buying a home or funding a college education, a set of wheels is the largest single expense that most Americans must confront. In December 2004, the average price of a new model topped $30,000 for the first time. Then there's the psychic cost of dealing with car salespeople, who ranked at or near the bottom of a 2004 consumer survey in perceived "honesty" and "ethical standards." Along with auto mechanics, they trigger more consumer complaints than any group but home-repair contractors.

Maybe that's why the "no-haggle" concept of buying new and used cars has taken off—at least in popularity. Despite this method's lower stress levels, experts estimate that a no-haggle car sale typically costs $500 to $1,000 more than a purchase made from a dealer who engages in old-fashioned on-the-spot bargaining. And those discount programs in which automakers offer you the same deal as their own employees help clear the lot, but in some cases the incentives translate to a higher let-go price: In July 2005, for example, a PT Cruiser convertible cost $17,299 under Chrysler's employee-discount-for-everyone program, whereas the *Kelley Blue Book* indicated that Joe Consumer could have negotiated the same vehicle, with rebates, for $16,455.

No matter how you buy, financing ploys can also needlessly inflate a car's cost. That 0 percent interest rate is usually awarded only to buyers with the best credit histories—and even for them, it requires a financing period of three years or less. Borrow $20,000 to finance a new car, and a no-interest loan still translates to monthly payments of more than $555.

The hemorrhaging continues after you take ownership: Car insurance premiums average close to $1,000 a year nationwide, says the National Association of Insurance Commissioners. Drivers in the costliest auto-insurance cities—Detroit, Philadelphia, Newark, Los Angeles, and New York—can easily pay three times that amount. From 1999 to 2003, car insurance premiums jumped nearly 25 percent overall.

You know about soaring gas prices, but did you know that the Environmental Protection Agency (EPA) mileage estimates posted on every new car are usually inflated? According to *Consumer Reports,* the actual mileage on some tested models was 35 to 50 percent lower than the EPA estimates—especially in city driving. After testing 40 vehicles, the American Automobile Association said these estimates are typically overstated 10 to 15 percent—and may be off as much as 30 percent. The reason: EPA mileage estimates do not reflect real-life driving conditions. Instead, they are based on a lab simulation in which vehicles are placed on rollers that mimic highway speeds of only 48 miles per hour and city speeds of only 20, with the air conditioner kept off the entire time.

Nor can you overlook mechanic-mandated repair and maintenance costs (these can scam even the best-informed gearhead) and the triple-digit fines you're likely to pay for traffic violations.

Read on to discover how to buy and maintain a car without being taken for ride.

Buying New

Dealerships typically buy new cars from manufacturers for 10 to 15 percent less than what appears on the MSRP sticker—the "selling" price to consumers. (Commonly known as the

---

Hybrid cars are hot sellers, but are their higher prices justified?

Edmunds.com reports that compared with traditional models, gas prices would have to top $9.20 a gallon to justify the $3,800 higher cost of a hybrid Honda Accord. They would have to top $5.60 a gallon to justify a hybrid Ford Escape.

"Manufacturer's Suggested Retail Price," MSRP actually stands for "Monroney Sticker Price," named for the Oklahoma senator who sponsored federal legislation requiring its posting.) But with high-end luxury models and some other vehicles, you can expect a markup of 30 percent. The dealership is looking to sell most cars for at least 7 percent more than the invoice price it pays the manufacturer to buy that vehicle.

Although the wholesale-to-retail markup may seem low on a percentage basis, the high expense of new cars means a dealership still stands to make a $3,000 profit on the typical $30,000 car sold at sticker price.

"Most car salesmen are paid strictly on commission, usually 25 to 30 percent of the profit margin," says Peter Humleker, a former car salesman and dealership general manager who wrote a book on the topic, *Car Buying Scams: Auto Dealer*

▶ A BETTER WAY

When Is the Best Time to Buy?

Mark your calendar, because there *is* a best time to buy a car: The last weekend of the month—either first thing Saturday morning or just before the dealership closes on Sunday.

"Buying at the end of each month can get you a better deal, because that's when everyone is scrambling to get cars off the lot in order to meet their quotas," says former salesman Michael Royce, who sold both new and used cars for eight years. "Weekends are best because it's the busiest time—there's more pressure to sell cars than during the weekdays."

Why early Saturday or late Sunday? "At the dealerships where I worked, there were often special bonuses given for the first sale on Saturday, to get salesmen motivated. On Sunday, there's another push to close deals before they close up."

But if you're shopping—wanting to take a test drive or do initial negotiations—weekends are the worst time to visit a dealership, Royce explains. "The sales staff is so busy on weekends that they may not give you the time you want. In fact, we used to be instructed to get the names and phone numbers of shoppers to schedule an appointment for a weeknight. On weekends, the motivation is to close deals, and priority is given to primed buyers."

PROTECTIVE DETECTIVE

Keep an Eye on F&I

More profit comes from financing a vehicle or selling extras for it than from the sale itself. Many a dealership's best salespeople therefore staff the "Financing and Insurance" office, or F&I. These "business managers" are in fact working on commission; they typically pocket 15 to 20 percent of the cost of all back-end products.

And what are these extras? An extended service warranty. Expensive paint and fabric protection. Rust-proofing. Window tinting. Life, health, or disability insurance. You can easily apply the fabric or paint protection yourself, using store-bought products. And that extended warranty is not needed for new cars; most carry their own multiyear factory warranties. Many warranties can be bought for less outside the dealership at websites such as www.warrantydirect.com.

Another prime source of dealer revenue—at your expense—is dealership financing. Unless a manufacturer offers unbeatable interest rates of 1 to 2 percent on select models through dealership financing, you can almost always get a lower-rate car loan through a bank, a credit union, or a money-lending website such as www.eloan.com. You can also check out a regional buying club, such as the United Buying Service that serves the D.C. suburbs, or a national buying club such as Costco (the latter has traditionally offered some of the most competitive rates available).

"It's not uncommon for dealerships to add a couple of percentage points to their financing," says *Car Buying Scams* author Peter Humleker. "They'll get a loan rate of 7 percent from the bank, for instance, then charge the customer 9 percent for that money."

Your protection: Before you sign any sales agreement, get preapproved for a car loan from an outside institution. This will arm you with a solid basis of comparison for whatever the dealer offers. But, adds former car salesman Michael Royce, "You don't necessarily want to mention that you've been preapproved to the salesman: You could get a better price if you make them think you'll be financing with them."

Before meeting with a dealer's F&I office, request your own credit-history report from Experian, Equifax, or Trans-Union. Knowing your FICO score (an acronym for Fair Issac Corp., which developed the credit-scoring method used today), you will be better able to parry a common dealership ploy: misrepresenting your credit score in order to sock you with a higher interest charge based on your purported "credit risk."

If you cannot qualify for outside financing, you will probably be stuck with an unfavorable dealership-offered interest rate. But if your FICO score is strong—especially if it's in the "excellent" range—the interest rate on dealership financing (like all else in a car sale) is negotiable.

Executive Breaks "Code of Silence." For instance, if you pay sticker price on a $30,000 car and assume that there's a $3,000 profit for the dealership, the salesperson's cut will be a commission of $750 to $900. But his paycheck dwindles by around $125 with every $500 reduction off the MSRP. If the car sells at the true invoice price—the manufacturer's initial charge to the dealer (not counting rebates, allowances, and other awards)—the salesman will be lucky to earn lunch money from the deal.

"There's really no way to make a good living selling cars unless you take advantage of people," says Humleker, who now advises car shoppers at www.carbuyingscams.com. With that sobering outlook in mind, here's what he and other experts recommend to protect yourself when buying a new car.

Preparation That Pays

Do the right research. Before you ever set foot on a car dealer's lot, do some research on car-pricing websites such as www.edmunds.com, www.kbb.com (the *Kelley Blue Book* site), www.autoweb.com, or www.invoicedealers.com. The most visible information offered on each site is often the MSRP "value" of cars, based on their model and options. But the information you really want may be buried deeper, requiring additional clicks: The approximate invoice price the manufacturer charges the dealer, as well as any rebates available to buyers. You may also be able to uncover manufacturer rebates being offered to customers or to dealers (the latter are usually listed as "Marketing Support"—code words for cash paid from manufacturers to dealerships).

Having the invoice price in hand lets you know your viable starting negotiating point—you want to haggle up from the dealer's cost invoice, not down from the MSRP. The rebate information, meanwhile, helps protect you against a common dealership tactic: playing one number against the other.

"When there's a customer rebate, which is often advertised

on television to move certain models, dealerships often twist it around to make you think the rebate is part of the discount," says Michael Royce, who sold new and used cars for eight years before writing a book about the experience called *Beat the Car Salesman.* "In reality, if there's a $1,000 customer rebate and the dealer says that gives you the car at invoice, you're really paying $1,000 above the invoice price." And that doesn't even take into account any "Marketing Support" rebates or other incentives offered by the manufacturer to the dealership.

Your protection: Although TV commercials advertise nationally available customer rebate programs—often on domestic cars—entering your zip code in an Internet rebate search may turn up additional offerings in your area. "One common myth," notes Royce, "is that rebates are the same everywhere. Yet some are regional. Manufacturers look at how many cars are sitting on lots in various parts of the country; if they don't like what they see, they may offer additional dealership rebates or other incentives to boost sales and give you a better chance of really getting the car at invoice." Edmunds.com is considered an excellent source for zip code–specific rebate information.

Check inventory in advance. The selling price of a car is often determined by supply and demand—the greater its supply at the dealership, the better deal you can demand there. "Pay careful attention to the number of cars sitting on the lot that are the same as the one you're interested in," Royce counsels. "That includes those in the same color. The more of them there are, the better your negotiating position is."

That's because the higher inventory usually means a longer "sit" time for that particular model. "Most people don't realize it, but dealerships don't actually own the cars they sell," says Royce, who operates the website www.beatthecarsales man.com. "Rather, they take out a loan from the bank and pay interest on each car. This is called a 'flooring' charge, and it must be paid for every day the car sits on the lot unsold. So the longer a car sits, the more money they pay."

Until you buy a car and the dealership gets your money, the dealer is in debt to the loan-carrying bank. To keep this flooring charge from flooring them, dealers are therefore anxious to move their products quickly. That's one reason why they often appear so eager for you to buy that very day.

Say you're shopping for a fully loaded red Ford Explorer. One dealership has 10 in stock; another has only two. Unless that model comes into sudden vogue, the dealership with 10 clones will have to work harder (that is, offer lower prices) to relieve its flooring charges than the lot with two models.

Your protection: Several weeks before you're ready to buy, visit dealerships—ideally, when they're closed—to get a rough idea of their inventory of your target model. If you notice an abundance of that model (or repeat visits reveal the model is not moving), casually mention this fact to dealership salespeople when you're ready to talk turkey. Sometimes, the bigger dealers with the greatest numbers of cars on the lot can offer the best prices, so turn their inventory liability to your advantage: Point out that a nice price equals a quick sell—and that means one less flooring charge.

Find the fleet manager. Who you deal with can play a big part in the deal you get. All things considered, you'll likely fare better by avoiding commissioned salesmen. One alternative is the dealership's fleet manager. "Traditionally," explains former car retailer Humleker, "these were salesmen who dealt in bulk sales to government agencies and private businesses. But the rules have relaxed. Most fleet managers now sell individual cars to individual buyers."

What makes fleet managers better contacts? They are paid according to the number of cars they sell each month—regardless of any vehicle's sales price. Many fleet managers earn a flat rate for each car they move off the lot; the more cars they sell, the more money they earn. Most also receive a com-

Nervous about negotiating? Credit unions and buying clubs such as Costco and Sam's Club sometimes agree to fixed-price discounts with select dealers. These can snag you low prices similar to those achieved by savvy hagglers.

mission—the amount varies from one dealership to the next.

Even without this fee, fleet managers are more likely to earn a cut from a "holdback" amount—an incentive that manufacturers offer to dealerships. "This holdback is usually about 3 percent of the invoice price," says Humleker, "and the check is sent to the dealership within 90 days after the car is sold." So if a car's MSRP is $25,000 and its invoice price is $22,000, the holdback amount awarded is typically about $650—20 to 25 percent of which goes to the fleet manager. "Because of this, fleet managers can earn a decent living selling cars at invoice. A commissioned salesman must sell the same car at a higher price to make money."

Fleet managers are not allowed to "compete" with the retail sales staff, so they can't pursue you—you have to contact them. "The best way to do that is to first call the dealership receptionist to find out the name of the fleet manager," advises Royce. "If you call and just ask for the fleet department or walk on the lot, chances are you'll get a regular salesman pretending to be the fleet manager." Once you make contact, fax or phone the fleet manager a price request with specifics on a car's make and model, options, and even its color. "Fleet managers take customers most seriously who request specific information on a car, rather than more generic 'give me a price' inquiries," says Humleker. After you make an appointment for a face-to-face meeting, get a business card; that will confirm you're dealing with the bona fide fleet manager.

Seek the geek. Another way to get a better price is through a dealership's Internet department, a newer spin-off of the fleet department. This staff handles customer inquiries conveyed by e-mail (and occasionally by phone) directly to the dealership via its own website or from car-pricing domains such as Edmunds.com, which publishes the inventory available at local dealerships paying for these listings.

Like fleet managers, Internet salesmen typically get a salary plus a bonus (for quantity) regardless of profit margin. This

"Special Sale" Ripoffs

A hyperactive salesman sticks his face in the television camera and promises you a hefty minimum trade-in amount for your clunker, whether it runs or not. Or he rips apart a price tag in front of the camera. Can those commercials for "special" sales be for real?

Not exactly, says former car salesman and dealership general manager Peter Humleker. Well versed in such sales, he reveals their fatal flaws below.

The Super Sale, sometimes called a tent sale, often involves the dealership hiring an outside company for a select number of days. In exchange for providing extra sales and financing staff, the outside company typically receives at least 20 percent of the gross profits from that sale. To recoup this outlay, the dealership may add several thousand dollars to the price of each vehicle. So even though you may indeed "drive away for only $99 down," the financing usually must be done through the dealership—which calculates monthly payments on the longest term possible, sticking you with a total debt that exceeds the car's trade-in value. Windshield placards trumpeting low monthly payments are designed to distract you from your eventual total outlay.

The Push, Pull, or Drag Sale promises an attractive set price for your trade-in—no matter what its condition. Sure, your clunker may fetch more than it's worth—but the price of the new car you're buying has probably been inflated (or discounted less than normal) to recoup the dealer's loss from acquiring your bomb.

The Slasher Sale, especially popular for TV ads, usually features a frenzied salesman tearing up price tags with his bare hands or recklessly re-marking windshields with sizable discounts. Never captured on film was the scene that likely occurred just before the camera started rolling, when all the vehicle prices were jacked up to justify the sale.

The Preapproved Sale is aimed at people with bad credit. Its opening salvo is often a letter sent to those with low credit scores; inside is a "preapproved" check for a certain amount, to be redeemed at the dealership. But the check is valid only for certain cars that are no bargain. Deepening the deception, the dealership may try to boost its profit by selling expensive back-end products—an extended warranty, for instance, tacked-on insurance, or other needless extras.

The Gift Sale involves the offer of a gift—often a certificate redeemable for electronics or other merchandise—in exchange for taking a test drive. The catch: The certificate must be redeemed at a specific website, or through a company that charges shipping rates so outrageous they may exceed the actual value of the merchandise.

▶ A BETTER WAY

Passing Gas Stations

How you drive can decide how much you save in fuel costs. Try these tips to improve your car's gas mileage:

Don't blow it in the wind. Because of increased air drag, traveling at highway speed with your car windows down can reduce your fuel efficiency by 10 percent.

Rabbits lose the savings race. Making jackrabbit starts and quick stops at intersections lowers gas mileage by 33 percent at highway speeds and by 5 percent around town.

Lighten up, leadfoot! As a general rule, expect to lose the equivalent of 21 cents per gallon of gas for each 5 miles per hour you travel above 60 mph.

Pump up tires, drive down costs. Keeping tires properly inflated will boost your gas mileage nearly 4 percent. You lose 0.5 percent in mileage for every 1 psi drop in proper pressure for all four tires.

means they, too, can usually sell for less than retail salesmen. "And because they know that people who ask for a price quote via a website have done their homework and are usually sending the same price request via e-mail to other dealerships in that area, they're more willing to work with you," says Philip Reed, who worked briefly as a car salesman before becoming the consumer advice editor at Edmunds.com. "At Edmunds, we maintain a fleet of cars—and I'm charged with buying them. I almost always get an incredibly low price with no hassles through the Internet department of a dealership. I can't say that when dealing with regular salesmen."

One possible explanation for the disparity, suggests Reed, is that Internet department personnel traditionally have backgrounds in computers, not in car sales. They are therefore simply (and refreshingly) less schooled in negotiating ploys and scams. Another advantage is that the Internet department is less likely to charge for extras offered by on-the-lot salesmen. "They know that Internet shoppers tend to be savvier buyers than walk-ins," adds Reed, author of *Strategies for Smart Car Buyers*. "Internet shoppers will not pay extra for items such as paint sealant or undercoating, which are traditionally pushed by retail salesmen."

At smaller dealerships, the fleet manager may double as the Internet designate; at larger dealerships, the two jobs are usually distinct.

Make their "goal price" your goal. The brass ring in car-buying is to buy at or below the invoice price. As noted above, lower-cost deals are easier to attain through a fleet manager or Internet salesman than they are through a commissioned salesman. You can get something else from these back-office personnel as well, says Mike Royce: straight talk on a vehicle's true "let-go" price.

"Every car on every lot has a 'goal price' set by the sales manager," he notes. "This is the true minimum amount that will be accepted to sell the car so the dealership still makes money." This goal price varies from one car to the next—it's a function of customer appeal, availability, and other factors—but the fleet and Internet departments have ready access to the figure. Commissioned salesmen, by contrast, may not. That's one reason for the oft-invoked "I need to speak to my sales manager" line from commissioned salespeople during purchase negotiations. (Another reason is simply to stall customers and wear them down, he adds.)

When you call the fleet manager for a quote on the car you want to buy, the goal price paperwork is right in front of him, says Royce. "You may be answered 'two over,' meaning the goal price is $200 above invoice, or 'five over,' meaning it's $500 above invoice. Then, when you come in to meet, he will gladly show you the invoice to prove it."

Knowing the goal price is a great way to sidestep a common negotiating pitfall: trying to "overhaggle" so the dealership can't make any money—in which case even the fleet manager will show you the door. "Occasionally," notes Royce, "fleet managers can sell you a car at or even below invoice if there are enough manufacturer incentives to make it worth their while, or if the car has been on the lot too long." More realistically, however, you should expect to pay $200 to $800 above the invoice price when buying from a fleet manager. However, a sought-after car would probably fetch thousands more when sold by a commissioned salesman.

Interestingly, lower-priced "economy" cars tend to have

higher relative goal prices. Why? "Often, the profit on economy cars is only a couple of hundred dollars," says Royce. "The reason that economy cars are sold at all is in hopes it will instill brand loyalty for future purchases of more expensive models by that manufacturer."

At the Dealership

Table that test-drive. Car salespeople like you to test-drive first, talk price second. The reason has to do with a saying popular among those in the business: "The feel of the wheel seals the deal."

Former car salesman Royce puts it a little less poetically: "An emotionally charged buyer is a less effective negotiator—and even tough buyers have a hard time resisting the feel and smell of a new car," he says. "They know that if you take a test-drive before discussing the cost of the vehicle, they have a better chance of selling you that car at full price. Even if you've been shopping at other car lots and have already test-driven that model, the salesman usually wants you to drive that car—to get you 'under the ether,' as they call it."

But there's another reason for the test-drive, especially if the salesman opts not to ride along: to make a photocopy of your driver's license. "They want your driver's license so they can pull your credit report and get the upper hand in negotiations," says former car salesman Duane Overholt, who now counsels consumer advocacy groups on dealership scams.

That maneuver is illegal. But at the dealerships where he worked, says Overholt, it was routinely practiced. "Armed with a computer, dealerships can use just your name and address, taken from your license, to pull a report within minutes; they don't need your Social Security number." If the dealership reviews your credit history but refrains from downloading it, you'll never be the wiser: The sneak peeks, Overholt reveals, are never reported as inquiries into the customer's

Where can you find cheap gas in your area?

Check out the AAA Fuel Price Finder (www.aaa.com/gasprices), which provides the cheapest local prices in your zip code. There's also www.gasbuddy.com, with gas-price information gleaned from 170 websites.

credit history. "Yet the dealership still pays the reporting agency for the look.

"By the time you return from the test-drive," says Overholt, "the dealer knows what you paid for your last car, what's on your credit cards, and what you pay on your mortgage. That information tells the dealer your spending habits—and we know that most people typically spend 10 to 15 percent more money on a new car purchase than the bottom-line price or monthly payments of their last vehicle."

Of course, with your Social Security number serving as the passkey, your credit history can be accessed in a flash. According to the American Association of Motor Vehicle Administrators, drivers in 17 states still have the option of using their Social Security number as the identification number on their driver's license.

You may even be unknowingly authorizing dealers to access your credit report yourself. If you sign "a demo-ride release" form, Overholt notes, "the fine print usually grants the dealership permission to run your credit." In their haste to get behind the wheel of a brand-new car, most customers typically don't pause long enough to read the document they are signing. (Obviously, they should.)

Your protection: Don't release your driver's license to a dealership—or sign any paperwork the sales staff offers—until you've agreed on a selling price. If you take a test-drive—and if you're a serious shopper, you will—ask the salesperson to ride along "to answer questions about the car." During initial negotiations and small talk, reveal only your first name; withhold your last name, address, or any other personal info the salesperson could relay to a colleague to access your credit history while you're test-driving the vehicle.

Be a binder finder. The dealer-cost invoice prices retrieved from a website search are accurate, but they represent ballpark amounts for a car model—not necessarily the specific car you're considering. To get the dealership's real cost on

Even the U.S. Department of Energy and the U.S. Environmental Protection Agency have joined the thrift craze with their own joint website, www.fuel economy.gov. It links to sites that give cheap-gas info, offers mileage-improvement tips, and publishes an annual Fuel Economy Guide.

that vehicle, ask to see the actual invoice. Be aware, however, that the first set of documents tendered in response to your request may not be the real deal.

"If they show you a computer printout," says Humleker, "they're jacking around numbers to make you think you're seeing the invoice. The real invoice is a paper document that's kept in a three-ring binder." The authentic document includes the manufacturer's name, logo, and corporate address; the factory where the car was built; the car's vehicle identification number, or VIN; the car's options; and the holdback amount. Fleet managers, he adds, are less likely to pull the printout ploy—another reason to deal directly with them.

PROTECTIVE DETECTIVE

Prevent Paperwork Ploys

Once you've made your deal on a new or used car, you'll probably have to sign a mountain of paperwork. Read each page carefully! Don't fall for the common request that you initial certain sections as the salesperson quickly "fans" the pile, showing you only the line where your John Hancock is needed.

Fanning suggests two dangers:

First, the contract terms may have been changed from those upon which you agreed.

Second, some dealers use the tactic to sneak in a binding mandatory arbitration (BMA) clause, which robs you of your right to sue the dealership.

"Many dealers know they overcharge, so they're worried about getting sued," says former car salesman Duane Over-

holt, who confesses he once specialized in this ploy. "By agreeing to binding mandatory arbitration, the customer relinquishes the right to take the dealer to court; instead, he or she must settle any dispute in arbitration." Legal costs are not recoverable under BMA, so you could wind up paying $800 or more out of your own pocket for an arbitration hearing.

Your protection: If you come across a BMA clause in your sales contract, write "No" in the space where it asks for your initials; that one simple act preserves your right to sue in court. "If a dealer balks at your refusal to agree to arbitration," says Overholt, "walk away; it's a sure sign that the dealer is ripping you off."

Beware of air. You may notice that some new cars have two window stickers: 1) the MSRP pasted in place by the manufacturer, and 2) a second "addendum," posted by the individual dealer, that may bump up the purchase price by as much as $1,000.

In some cases, the dealer sticker includes extra costs that are patently bogus. Because these costs appear on the MSRP as well, they represent nothing more than an effort to make you pay for the same item twice. In other cases, the extra costs may be for real—but outrageously overpriced—options.

"'Dealer prep' is one phony charge," says Royce. "You should never pay it. The dealers have to prep the cars for selling, and that's included in the MSRP price.

"Another scam to watch out for is any additional cost charged for 'market value.' When I sold Hondas, we used to add $2,000 to the sticker price of any car that was black or green, because those were hot colors. We'd tell customers it was because those cars had a higher market value. We would then discount them by $2,000 to still get full price—and customers thought they were getting a steal."

Other "air" charges you should be prepared to deflate:

- *Pinstriping.* A dealer-supplied accent stripe may add $200 to the sticker price. "But we paid a guy only $15 to pinstripe each car," says Royce. "That's what any customer would pay for pinstriping off the lot."

- *Undercoating.* This tarlike substance is sprayed on the car's chassis—in theory, to protect it from rust caused by road salt. The real cost for undercoating supplies and application is about $75, says Humleker. Yet many dealers charge $400 or more for this option. Topping things off, the treatment is pointless if you live in a snow-free climate.

- *Fabric protection.* A $6 can of Scotchgard, available at any hardware store, will protect cloth seats for hundreds of dollars less than the added fee some dealers charge.

- *An "etch."* This extra—selling for $200 to $1,000—involves the use of acid to inscribe the car's vehicle identification number (VIN) on the windshield, door frame, or under the hood. It is offered, the story goes, to prevent car thieves from altering the VIN—and thus could facilitate the car's recovery. However, alter-proof VINs are already displayed by the manufacturer elsewhere on the car—most visibly on the doorjamb sticker, but also on the engine block or in the trunk. The dealer's true cost for an etch, says Royce, is about $10.

- *Alarms and upgraded stereos.* Yes, these are bona fide upgrades. But do a little comparison shopping off the car lot and you'll find that you can pay a fraction of what the dealer charges. In fact, dealership alarms and stereos are often installed by vendors who are just as happy to sell directly to you.

Buying Used

Received wisdom says a new car depreciates 20 percent in value the instant you drive it off the lot. So buying a used car is often the better financial move. Yet it may generate higher buyer anxiety. Coupled with the risk of buying a lemon, the product pricing of used cars can be more muddled than that for new ones. How can you protect yourself?

Consider the source in making an offer. Check out car-pricing websites and you'll find three numbers for used cars:

- *The "trade-in price"* (sometimes called the "wholesale price"). This is what dealers typically pay for the car when it is traded in as part of a new car sale. It may reflect a below-value price or what the car might command when sold at an auction.

Lemon Aid: Clues to Spot a Clunker

When shopping for a used car, a few simple measures can help you separate the peaches from the lemons. Here are some safeguards endorsed by Austin Davis, the third-generation owner of a Houston car repair shop:

When meeting with a private seller, inspect the car first thing in the morning—after it has sat at that location overnight (as opposed to having been driven to a different location, such as a parking lot). This allows you to check under the chassis for leaked fluids.

Arrive at least 15 minutes before the designated meeting time to ensure the owner isn't "prepping" the car by taking special measures to hide problems.

When you start the car, have a friend stand off to one side to check the tailpipe for signs of smoke.

• *White smoke* often results from water or antifreeze entering the cylinders (the white smoke is steam). It could suggest the engine will overheat.

• *Blue smoke* is caused by engine oil entering the cylinders and may suggest failed gaskets or O-rings.

• *Black smoke,* typically the least problematic, usually means excess fuel is entering the engine's cylinders. It may signal problems with the carburetor, the fuel pump, the fuel injector, or the computer sensors.

When you take a test-drive, head for a highway with a solid side wall, jersey wall, or median barrier. This gives you a chance to roll down the window—with the stereo off—and listen for any untoward noises echoing off that hard surface. Ideally, you should hear nothing more than the sound of the car's tires on the road.

Check the car body for straight and even seams in the doors, hood, and trunk; deviations could betray a previous wreck. Place a magnet over a piece of cloth and gently drag it along each steel body panel; if it won't adhere in certain places, that indicates a putty "body" filler was used for a repair. Check the underside of both the hood and the trunk to make sure the paint color is consistent with the rest of the body.

Examine tires for even wear and uniform size and manufacturer. Is the spare tire properly inflated? If not, the seller may have been a neglectful owner.

Bounce each corner of the car; it should rock only once or twice before coming to a stop.

Check the interior carpeting for signs of water damage or excessive wear (and compare that to the mileage). Pay special attention to the carpeting just beneath the dashboard; stains there may indicate a leaky heater or air conditioner.

• *The "private party price."* This represents the typical selling price of a similar used vehicle by a private seller, which is typically less than what a dealer would charge.

• *The "retail price."* This is what a dealer would hope to get from selling the used car.

"Generally, most people get a better deal buying a used car from a private seller than from a dealer," says Edmunds.com's Reed. "It also tends to be a kinder, gentler transaction. The starting price and selling price tend to be lower, and you're usually not dealing with an expert negotiator. But here's the caveat: If you know the game, you can actually get a better price from a dealer, because they buy used cars at absolutely rock-bottom prices."

The first rule of the game is to ignore the retail price. It is

How Safe Is Your Ride?

In 2005, the Insurance Institute for Highway Safety published a study that singled out the cars with the lowest and highest rates of driver deaths in auto accidents. Here are the names it named:

Lowest rates of driver deaths
Mercedes E class
Toyota 4Runner 4WD SUV
Volkswagen Passat
Lexus RX 300 4WD SUV
Toyota RAV4 4WD SUV
Honda Odyssey minivan
Mercury Villager minivan
Mercedes S class
Nissan Pathfinder 4WD SUV
Cadillac DeVille
Nissan Quest minivan

Toyota Camry Solara
Cadillac Eldorado

Highest rates of driver deaths
Chevrolet Blazer 2-door 2WD SUV
Mitsubishi Mirage
Pontiac Firebird
Kia Rio
Kia Sportage 4-door 2WD SUV
Chevrolet Blazer 4-door 2WD SUV
Ford Explorer 2-door 2WD SUV
Chevrolet Camaro
Mazda B series 2WD pickup truck
Chevrolet Tracker 4WD SUV
Chevrolet S10 2WD pickup truck
Chevrolet Cavalier 2-door
Chevrolet Cavalier 4-door
Kia Sportage 4-door 4WD SUV

typically inflated several thousand dollars above the car's true value. (This could explain why dealerships make a bigger profit margin selling used cars than new ones.) Instead, do online research to ascertain the trade-in price; then, if you're buying from a dealer, focus on paying no more than about $500 above that trade-in amount.

How do you do that? The old-fashioned way: Start with a lowball offer. "For most foreign cars," advises Humleker, "start negotiating between $1,000 and $2,000 below the trade-in price. For domestic cars, start $2,500 below the trade-in price (domestics have a much lower resale value than most Japanese and German cars)."

Even though the salesman will try to talk down from the sticker price, raise your bid from that initial lowball price in increments of only $25 or $50—never by $100 or more. When dealing with private sellers, the goal is to pay the same as the trade-in value, which is probably more than a car dealer would have offered the seller. Walk your way up from the trade-in value by increments of $100.

Put time to work for you. Many of the same strategies to buy a new car for less can be employed when buying used. Do online research. Deal with the fleet manager or the Internet department rep. Visit or drive by the lot to determine the "sit time" of a choice used car.

Used cars do not incur the flooring charge that is levied on new cars, yet they face their own time constraints. "The general rule of thumb is that used cars stay on the lot for only 45 to 60 days before they're sold at auction," notes Humleker. "The reason is very simple: Used cars drop in value every month." No matter its condition or mileage, a used car that remains unsold drops in value a couple of hundred dollars every 30 days. Selling a used car at auction, dealers know, is almost always less profitable than selling that car to an on-site shopper. If you spy a certain car sitting for several weeks before your visit, it may be slated

Negotiating: Do It Like a Pro

YOU DON'T HAVE TO BE Donald Trump to practice and perfect the art of the deal—or steal—when shopping for a new car. Simply follow these proven tips and you'll be well on your way to becoming a savvy negotiator:

Never buy the day you shop. "The impulse purchase is probably the biggest mistake people make," says former car salesman Peter Humleker, author of *Car Buying Scams*. "There's nothing a car salesman likes to hear more than someone say, 'I was on my way to the grocery store, and now here I am about to drive off in a new car.'"

That's music to their ears—and gold to their wallets—because it is usually voiced by a buyer in the wake of an impromptu test-drive. "You're too excited to think straight right after you've been behind the wheel," says Humleker, "and that gives salesmen the advantage in any negotiation. That's how they usually get full MSRP."

Your protection: Take that test-drive on your way to buy bread if you must. Once you've talked price, however, say you need some time to consider the offered selling price. "Never buy a car the first time you visit a dealership," says Humleker. "The longer that vehicle sits on the lot, the stronger your bargaining power." If you walk away, chances are you'll get a follow-up phone call with a lower price.

Discuss only the bottom-line price. Salesmen often want to discuss monthly payments—not selling price. "The problem with quoting them a monthly payment you can afford is that you never really know what you're buying the car for," says Michael Royce, another former salesman who now counsels car buyers. "You may get an affordable monthly rate, but it will probably be at a longer loan term."

This "monthly maneuver" is also a ploy to hit you with a "packed payment"—a higher monthly payment stuffed with extras such as an extended warranty, insurance, or add-on items such as fabric or paint protection.

Although packed payments are illegal as a sales tactic in most states, says Humleker, some car salespeople routinely try the gambit anyway. "They may say that your monthly payment is $397, when it's really $357. If you accept that higher amount, the finance manager can load into your contract an additional $40 a month in products without increasing your payment. He'll say, 'I see they have you at $397 a month; that's great, because it includes the insurance that makes your car payments if you ever lose your job.'"

Your protection: When asked about monthly payments, reply politely but resolutely that you'd prefer to discuss the sale price before you discuss the financing. Then, when the time comes, make sure all extras are calculated only *after* the monthly amount has been determined—and that the monthly amount is based exclusively on the sale price you're financing.

It's always wise to shop—and get pre-approved—for car loans elsewhere before visiting the dealer; banks and credit unions often provide lower rates. They will also calculate your monthly payments and your down payment, giving you a specific (and affordable) bottom-line price.

Give yourself plenty of time. Car salesmen use various ploys to wear you down and weaken your defenses, warns Royce, so be prepared. "They want to get you 'in the box'—their well-chosen slang for the sales office—and keep you there. That makes you an impatient, ineffective negotiator."

Your protection: Prepare yourself for negotiations that could easily last several hours. "Always eat before you visit the lot," advises Royce, "and wear comfortable clothes. If you feel that the process is taking too long, say you'll come back at another time to resume the negotiations."

A good defense: Don't be offensive. "Some people think the way to get a better price is to act tough," says Royce.

"The truth is, dealers tend to give better deals to people they like. As part of human nature, they try to screw the people they don't like. A lot of the time, a salesman will go in the back and tell his sales manager 'There's a nice couple out there and I really think we should work with them.'"

Your protection: The sales manager customarily has the final say-so over the selling price. That makes it critical to show courtesy and respect toward this boss, who often plays "bad cop" to the salesman's "good cop." This is not to say that you should assume either player is working in your interest—their real goal is to maximize their profit. Acknowledge their position, but stick calmly to your guns.

for auction—and you may be better positioned to bargain.

The calendar plays an especially important role in certain specialty cars. "When buying a convertible," advises Reed, "it's always best to wait until the fall or winter. Four-wheel-drive cars, by contrast, have stronger value in the winter, so you'll get better deals buying them in spring and summer." How much better? A certain book author purchased a sweet, three-year-old convertible in the dead of winter for $4,200 less than what an identical model fetched at the same dealership when spring rolled around.

Seek security—and savings—with "certified pre-owned." You may notice the real creampuffs in used cars are tagged as "certified pre-owned" vehicles—and usually carry a higher price. That's because these late-model cars, often sold following a lease agreement, must meet specific mileage limits and have been carefully inspected according to the manufacturer's specifications—not necessarily the dealer's—"to be as close to perfect operating condition as can be determined," says Reed.

Even though "certified" used cars typically sell for $500 to $800 more than identical cars lacking that label, you can save money on them in the long run. "With a certified car," adds Reed, "they usually throw in an extended warranty that would normally cost $800 to $1,000 on a noncertified car. And if anything goes wrong with a certified car, it will be fixed for free."

Your protection: The key in buying "certified" is to make sure that no-cost fixes are included; unscrupulous dealers may try to charge you for a separate service contract or an extended warranty. A certified car may offer less wiggle room in price negotiations, but don't assume you have to pay its sticker price. After all, it's still a used car—and thereby subject to the same plunging-value gradient as any other unsold used vehicle. Again, use the trade-in value as your initial guide, but with certified pre-owned cars, start your negotiation at hundreds of dollars, not thousands, below the asking price.

Meanwhile, if you're interested in a car that isn't certified, some dealers will designate it as certified—and furnish the accompanying warranty—for a flat fee. Often this fee can be negotiated to cost less than the price of a separate extended warranty.

Get the facts from Carfax. Don't even consider purchasing a used car without first getting a Carfax report. This document, which you can purchase yourself or get through a dealership, traces the history of the vehicle in question via its VIN. The exercise turns up information from sources such as extended-service companies and state Department of Motor Vehicles. It's not flawless, but the system provides the best record of a car's often checkered past, including previous owners, reported accidents, and flood damage (sidebar, page 40).

A Carfax report may also contain information from state inspection records. "Every time you get an emissions test or an annual inspection on a car," says Reed, "the mechanic records the mileage and date and reports that information to the state DMV, along with any problems causing it to fail inspection." Many states then supply this information to Carfax. "That makes a Carfax report the best way to ensure that the odometer hasn't been rolled back, which happens all the time."

In other words, if the car you're considering displays fewer miles on its odometer than the mileage indicated in the Carfax report, you know it's been rolled back. On newer cars, rollback can occur by resetting the electronic chip that tallies miles; on older cars, the odometer can be manually altered by removing the instrument-panel cover and fiddling with dial indicators. However this chicanery is accomplished, tampering with a car's odometer is illegal. Penalties vary by state but typically include hefty fines—and possible jail time.

In addition to seeking out a Carfax report, be leery if the odometer shows low miles but the brake-pedal rubber or carpeting is excessively worn.

Has your car been declared a total loss? Ask your insurer to pay the sales tax and registration fee for its replacement.

Such restitution is mandatory in 29 states. The request may be honored elsewhere, too, because policies require insurers to "make you whole"—meaning you should recover all costs to where you were before the accident.

Don't Get Soaked with a Flood Car

What happens after a car is declared a total loss from water damage done by a hurricane or flood? If its engine, electrical system, or interior has been water-soaked for two days or longer, the insurer pays off the owner, then hauls the vehicle to a salvage auction—ostensibly to be sold there for spare parts.

But many flood-damaged cars are still drivable—in the short term. Every year, tens of thousands of these water-logged lemons are resold to unsuspecting buyers. "People called curbstoners buy them at auction, clean them up, and sell them privately," says Christopher Basso of Carfax, a vehicle-history tracking service. "Usually they're sold out of state, where it's easier to title them without disclosing the water damage." The trouble may not surface until months afterward: Wet wires dry and crack. Rust attacks the engine or body. Brakes, door locks, power windows, and heating and air-conditioning units fail.

Reselling a flood car is legal, but suppressing the extent and nature of a vehicle's damage is not. Subject any used car to a thorough mechanic's inspection; then, to avoid getting saddled with a sog story, follow these steps as well:

Examine engine crevices, the glove compartment, the wheel well for the spare tire, and beneath the seats for water lines or signs of mud, silt, or rust.

Check dashboard gauges for accuracy and water condensation.

Repeatedly test electrical equipment such as wipers, lights, turn signals, and the heater and air conditioner.

Make sure engine wires bend easily; if they're stiff, they will likely crack.

Be leery of new carpeting, which is typically replaced to hide water stains or remove musty smells. Existing carpet stains are likewise a red flag.

Get a "flood check" by entering the car's VIN at www.carfax.com/flood.

Your protection: Before you buy, write down the VIN from the doorjamb sticker. Then access www.carfax.com. A single report can be purchased for about $20; shell out $5 more and you get unlimited reports for a 30-day period, allowing you to track other vehicles as well. More dealers now provide a vehicle's Carfax history, at their cost, to customers who request it.

Hire a car inspector. Obviously, you should never buy any used car without first having it inspected—ideally by an "independent" expert not associated with the sale. But your friendly neighborhood mechanic may not necessarily be the best choice.

That's because mechanics who do used car inspections usually check only the "big stuff" to make sure the car runs right. They look for any leaks or cracks in the engine, for instance, or they assess the condition of the brakes and tires. A car inspector, by contrast, searches out every last defect, including the condition of the paint job, carpeting, and wiper blades—even the quality of the stereo. This inspection by fine-tooth comb is far more rigorous than a mechanic's cursory once-over. "Car inspectors do this every week," says Humleker, "so they know how to find the flaws that mechanics may not."

Another benefit from hiring a car inspector: Whereas a mechanic may give you a verbal report, car inspectors typically go through a checklist of 100 items or more—and provide a written summary of their findings. "Based on the problems they uncover," adds Humleker, "you can take that to the dealer and use it to negotiate a better price."

Expect to pay $50 to $100 for a car inspection this exhaustive (the fee may include a Carfax vehicle-history report). Some car inspectors work out of local garages; others will travel to your home or the dealership, schlepping their tools of the trade with them. To find a reputable car inspector near you, consult the Yellow Pages or a website such as www.carchex.com or www.automobileinspections.com.

Car Repairs

Get the right referral. Find an efficient, reliable, and honest mechanic—there are thousands of them out there—and you'll better protect both your car and your wallet. Most people attempt this by getting referrals from their friends and neighbors. Word-of-mouth is a workable approach, but it's certainly not the only way—nor even the best.

Instead, you may want to consider the recommendations of the die-hard car buffs who tune into the country's most popular weekly car-repair radio show, *Car Talk* on National Public Radio, which attracts 4.4 million listeners on nearly 600 stations. At www.cartalk.com/content/mechx, the *Car Talk* website offers a "Mechan-X Files" database listing more than 16,000 mechanics recommended by its audience. To find the best grease monkey near you, type in your zip code or the make of your car.

"We review each entry," says *Car Talk* producer Doug Mayer. "From time to time, there are ones that read as if they're from a mechanic about his own shop. But virtually all the postings that make it onto the website are legitimate reviews from fans. We've had hundreds of stories of people using the Mechan-X Files with great success."

Another option: Check with the Motorist Assurance Program (MAP), a nonprofit organization based in Bethesda, Maryland, that provides referrals by city, state, or zip code at its website, www.motorist.org. Repair shops must meet certain pricing and warranty criteria in order to win accreditation by MAP—and gain customer referrals through it.

Look at the lot. One way to predict the sort of service you and your car will receive inside a car-repair shop is to check what's outside it. "Drive by that shop and look at the parking lot," says Austin Davis, the third-generation owner of a large Houston car repair shop. "It's a bad sign if cars have been sitting there for a while. That usually means there's been some communication problem between the shop and the vehicle owner. Either the owner couldn't afford the charges, the mechanic did unauthorized repairs, or there's a lawsuit pending." At the very least, such "deadhead" cars signal a potential source of cannibalized auto parts—precisely the kind you don't want installed on your vehicle.

Another bad sign is a parking lot full of municipal-fleet vehicles, such as utility trucks or cars driven by city government workers. "Service contracts for local government fleets are usually awarded to the lowest bidder," notes Davis, author of the e-book *What Your Mechanic Doesn't Want You to Know.* "Because they're the lowest bidder, they may want to protect their profit margin; that gives them an attitude of 'What don't we have to do to fix this car?' Shops like that may be more likely to cut corners or not use the best parts for those repairs—and that extends to your car."

Your protection: What you want to see in the parking lot are cars like yours—preferably a new batch every day or so. Today's models are equipped with about 50 computers, making them technologically more advanced than the Apollo spacecraft that ferried American astronauts to the moon and back. "If you see mostly older cars awaiting repair," says Davis, "that could mean the shop is not outfitted for what's needed for newer cars. They might be able to service newer cars, but it will probably take them longer to do the job—and they'll pass that expense on to you. Even simple repairs are different on newer cars; a brake job for a 2000 Lexus requires different tools and know-how than one for a '68 Chevy."

But don't blame the mechanics for not keeping up. According to independent mechanics, certain auto manufacturers withhold the computer software needed to diagnose and repair newer, more high-tech cars. The intent—and the result—is to favor those service shops operated by the manufacturer's own dealerships. In a 2004 survey, 60 percent of independent mechanics reported being unable to access the instructions and computer updates provided to dealership mechanics. As a consequence, half of independents had to turn away business on later-model cars. So pervasive did this lockout become that in 2005, U.S. Representatives Joe Barton (R-Tex.) and 55 cosponsors introduced a bill in Congress—the so-called "Right to Repair Act"—that would forbid car manufacturers from withholding repair information they

Gas-saving products don't really deliver, the EPA reported after testing 100 such devices. The agency warns that they may even raise exhaust emissions or damage your engine.

now provide to their dealership-affiliated service departments.

Weigh expertise with expense. Ideally, you'll want a mechanic experienced in servicing cars from your vehicle's manufacturer—or at least cars from the same country. But this does not necessarily mean you must go to a dealership-affiliated service shop, where the hourly rate is typically 15 percent higher than at "independent" mechanics, according to research compiled by *Car Talk.* "There are independent German car specialists, Japanese car specialists, and even American car specialists," says Houston repair-shop owner Davis. "They may charge a higher hourly rate than other independent mechanics who service all types of cars, but it's still usually lower than the dealership rate. They specialize in these makes, so they take less time to diagnose problems and make repairs. That means a competitive or lower bill."

Even so, certain jobs—especially those involving computer systems that trigger warning lights—are often best left to a dealership service department, especially with high-end cars. "If you have a BMW, for instance, even changing the battery should be done by the dealership," advises Davis. "When you disconnect the battery, it wipes out all memory in the computer systems." That might mean a $75 charge to reprogram the stereo at an independent shop, whereas the dealership will probably include this service as part of its new-battery installation. Routine maintenance and "everyday" repairs, however, are likely to cost less at a good independent shop.

Your protection: For jobs that don't require immediate repair, call around to gauge price and experience. "In my opinion, the best long-term solution is to find a good independent with whom you can build a relationship," says Davis, who runs the website www.trustmymechanic.com. "Across the board, you'll pay more at a dealership. Also, from what I can tell, specialty brake and transmission franchises tend to have high employee turnover. But independent shops want to keep their loyal customers happy. When someone

Highway Robbery: Common Car-Repair Cons

Dishonest mechanics can attempt to scam anyone, but some cheats are especially skilled at fleecing out-of-state motorists who pull into service stations along busy highways. So whether you're navigating the interstates or simply in need of a neighborhood repair, watch out for these six common scams:

"Short-sticking" occurs when the station attendant pushes the oil dipstick only partway in, making it appear that your car is low on this vital fluid. Oil is then "added" from an empty container earmarked for the purpose.

Your defense: If informed you need oil, do your own dipstick check. If it's indeed low, add it yourself.

A smoking alternator is an easy-to-achieve effect: The mechanic simply pours a splash of antifreeze on the alternator. You are then warned that you need a new alternator. Doubling the deceit, what you may receive instead is your old one back—gussied up with quick-drying paint, but otherwise untouched and still in place.

Your defense: If your car wasn't smoking when you drove it in, assume you're being pegged as a pigeon. Problems shouldn't magically appear at a mechanic's touch.

Loosening spark plug cables, done by the mechanic, can make your engine run sluggishly—the perfect pretense for selling you a tune-up.

Your defense: A gentle tug on cables—as well as past "drivability"—can tip you to this possible ploy.

A leaking radiator or a leaking tire can result from a jab with a screwdriver.

Your defense: If a nail or other road hazard is causing a slow leak, it will be easy to locate imbedded in the tire; a small hole, by contrast, should raise suspicion. Radiators and hoses typically do not suffer punctures.

Don't tell your teenagers this, but **an exploding battery** can result if an Alka-Seltzer tablet is dropped into a battery cell during an inspection and the cap is replaced. This causes the cap to explode; upon your return to the inspection site, you're informed you "need" a new battery.

Your defense: Ask yourself—and the mechanic—why the battery would fail after an initial inspection (and whether he's got indigestion).

"Defective" shock absorbers can be the apparent result of a few strategic oil squirts while the car is raised on a lift.

Your defense: Do your own inspection while the car is on the lift: "If the oil is clean—free of the grime or dirt that customarily accumulates when driving—it was placed there by the mechanic to hit you with a $300 to $500 repair," says mechanic Mitchell Zelman.

gets all their service done at my shop—including oil changes that would be quicker at Jiffy Lube—they will be rewarded with top-notch service. I want to keep them coming back."

While you're at it, ask about an independent's experience with your car's computer system. Although some indies may be fully competent to make the repairs in question, they can't turn off the dashboard "warning lights" afterward because the manufacturer has withheld the instructions for doing so. In certain cases, these dashboard warnings can keep your car from passing its state inspection—even though the repair was made correctly. To prevent or remedy this result, you may have to visit a dealership service department. The sidebar on page 48 offers additional tips on finding expert mechanics.

Go by the books. When a mechanic quotes you a labor price for a given job, it's usually based on either the *Mechanical Labor Estimating Guide* by automotive publisher Mitchell or the *Labor Guide* by automotive publisher Chilton. If the guide says a job will take eight hours and the shop charges an hourly rate of $50, you will be charged $400 for labor. Parts are extra.

"This explains why you may drop off your car at 9 a.m. and be told it's ready at 1 p.m., only to discover you've been charged for 10 hours of labor on the bill," says Gillis. "If the job takes longer than the hours cited in the *Estimating Guide,* however, you don't get a break; you're charged for that extra time based on the shop's hourly labor rate."

If a time estimate for a job sounds high, you can double-check it by consulting either of the two estimating guides mentioned above in a public library. (Keep in mind that estimates vary by make and model.) Alternatively, advises Mitchell Zelman, owner of a car-repair shop in Brooklyn, New York, "You could ask your mechanic to show you that time estimate in the shop's own guidebook. The hourly rate is usually posted somewhere in the shop. Don't get your car serviced at a shop where it's not posted."

"If the repair time he estimates is considerably longer than what you find published in the guidebook," Zelman concludes, "either he's not a very efficient mechanic or he's trying to scam you."

Let the manual be your guide. Literally within arm's reach is another independent arbiter of the necessity of any given repair: It's the owner's manual in the glove compartment of your car.

Dealership service managers, as well as those at larger independent shops, are often paid a percentage of the jobs they "write." The more to-do items they can list on your service order, the larger their paycheck. This explains the frequency of the following question, especially from dealership service personnel: "How many miles on your car?"

Depending on your answer, you may be hit with a laundry list of recommended jobs. But remind yourself they are suggestions and nothing more. "A shop may recommend a 12,000-mile checkup that includes draining, flushing, and changing the transmission fluid," says Reed of Edmunds.com. "If you check the owner's manual, though, you may find that particular service is not needed until 60,000 miles. Meanwhile, you're out several hundred dollars for an unnecessary job."

Leave your mark. Several years ago, the California Bureau of Automotive Repair ran a sting operation that revealed nearly half of all the body-repair work charged to customers in the state was fraudulent. The bureau's investigative weapon of choice? A permanent marker.

"We discreetly marked auto parts before we took cars in for repairs," says investigator Warren Sam. "After the repair was made, we asked for our old part back. If it didn't have the marking we made, we knew the work had not been done."

Although that investigation focused only on bodywork, you can do the same thing before taking your car in for scheduled maintenance inspections or prescheduled repairs.

Inconspicuously mark filters, brake pads, alternator, or other visible or easily accessible parts. Then, when you pick up the car, ask for your old parts back. If they're missing your mark, you're probably receiving used components from another job—meaning the repair you needed has yet to be performed.

"I also recommend doing this before you take your car in for a tire rotation or a job that will require the removal of bolts," adds mechanic Zelman, author of *What the Experts May Not*

PROTECTIVE DETECTIVE

Where to Find an ASE Mechanic

A good gauge of any repair shop's expertise can often be found hanging on its walls. So look for posted certifications that the shop's mechanics have completed special training via accredited schools or programs. The gold standard in certification is awarded by the National Institute for Automotive Service Excellence, whose "diploma" is stamped with the blue and white ASE logo.

"Seeing ASE certification at a shop is a good barometer of the type of service you can expect," says Jack Gillis, author of *The Car Repair Book* and director of public affairs for the Consumer Federation of America. "The ASE certification requires an investment of time and money by that mechanic or shop. Using an ASE-certified mechanic won't necessarily guarantee you a better repair job, though; many good mechanics do not have ASE certification."

Not only that, but ASE certification comes in varying degrees. A mechanic receives an ASE certificate for complet-

ing specialized courses and then passing a test in any one of eight specialties:

- Engine Repair
- Suspension and Steering
- Brakes
- Engine Performance
- Automatic Transmission/Transaxle
- Electrical Systems
- Manual Drive Train
- Heating and Air Conditioning

"If your car needs a brake job and the guy's certification is in air-conditioning and heating systems, that won't help you very much," Gillis adds. "You want to see ASE certification in the area for the specific repair you're getting."

ASE certificates, as well as others, usually note which type of training has been completed. A mechanic who is certified in all eight areas is called an ASE-Certified Master Automobile Technician.

Tell You About Car Repair. "For instance, if you put a small dot of Wite-Out somewhere on both rear tires before bringing in your car for a tire rotation, and you see that mark on the rear tires when you pick up your car, the job wasn't done."

Of course, notes Zelman, it's often easy to spot new replaced parts: The lettering will be clear on newly purchased belts, for example, while other components will appear shiny and free of grime and other signs of wear. If you ever doubt that an old part was really replaced with a new one, he suggests you just ask for paper proof: Most independent mechanics don't stock replacement parts, so they should be able to produce a purchase receipt from an auto supply house.

Items such as fenders or hoods may not come with a receipt, but they usually bear a factory stamp or a sticker guaranteeing they come from the manufacturer. Look for this seal of freshness on the underside of replacement hoods, truck lids, and other parts.

Prevent & Fight Traffic Tickets

Shun the left lane (usually). Have a need for speed? According to the National Motorists Association—a membership-funded advocacy group that prompted the federal legislation to eliminate the national 55 mile-per-hour speed limit in 1995 and now helps motorists fight traffic tickets—you're more likely to be ticketed when traveling in the far left lane of an interstate highway.

"Officers watching for speeders can be anywhere," notes NMA spokesman Eric Skrum, "but they're more likely to be sitting in the median—and focusing their radar on the lane that's closest to them." Because police get the most accurate readings when cars are traveling toward them, they often face traffic and point their radar guns at the extreme left lane.

Avoid the Sunday morning "non-rush." Paradoxically, taking the road less traveled may not spare you a speeding ticket.

Shopping for tires? Maybe you should be.

Ford recently became the first U.S. automaker to recommend that tires be replaced after six years—even if treads are not worn. "Tires degrade over time, even when they are not being used," the company warns.

"All things considered," says Mel Leiding, a California attorney who specializes in representing traffic violators, "more tickets seem to be issued on Sunday mornings than at any other time. Highways tend to be less congested then. It's easier for cops to pull you over when they don't have to fight traffic to do it."

You can get nailed at any time, of course. But statistically, says Leiding, rush-hour speeders are less likely to be pulled over—unless they are weaving in and out of traffic or otherwise calling attention to themselves. "Then the officer will have to fight the traffic—and, as a result, he or she will most likely issue you a ticket."

Newly licensed teens with a B average or better are usually entitled to "good-student discounts" of 10 to 15 percent on their car insurance. Taking driver's education classes at school warrants a separate, similar discount.

Be prepared to show report cards and driver's ed certificates.

Make your first impression count. Knowing how to handle yourself in the first few minutes after you are pulled over can dictate whether you drive away with a warning or a hefty fine. "Issuing a traffic citation is up to the individual officer's discretion," says Tom Marshall of the California Highway Patrol, which issues 2.5 million traffic tickets a year. "As a rule, however, you'll fare better in not flunking the 'attitude test.'"

To pass that test, use short, respectful answers ("Yes, officer," "No, officer"). Avoid small talk or jokes; traffic violations are serious business to those handling accidents. Above all, refrain from editorializing ("I see you're trying to meet your quota" or "Why aren't you out catching *real* criminals?") Some officers have been known to flag copies of tickets issued to tart-tongued drivers with the notation "ND"—a shorthand the prosecutor readily understands means "No Deal in court." The sidebar on page 52 cites some additional, nonverbal clues that can keep your driving record ticket-free.

Don't admit guilt—or anything else. If you're asked, "Do you know why I stopped you?" and you respond, "Yes, because I ran a red light," then you've just admitted guilt—and you will get a ticket. (Another common "set-up" question: "Do you know how fast you were going?")

▶ A BETTER WAY

The Donor Defense

Showing that you subscribe to the credo "To protect and serve" may be of value in a traffic stop.

On the record, police officers maintain they do not play favorites in deciding who gets a ticket and who escapes with a warning. Unofficially, however, some law-enforcement officers concede that another factor—the designation "organ donor" on a driver's license—occasionally sways them not to issue a citation.

That distinction alone will not protect you, of course; you'll want to stack the deck in your favor by displaying a polite demeanor and a clean driving record. But to some cops, being an organ donor suggests you possess a "good citizen" attitude—and the desire to help others, after all, is what motivated many men and women in blue to enter law enforcement in the first place.

Some police agencies encourage drivers to designate themselves as organ donors. In the event you are involved in a deadly car accident, this authorizes medical personnel to use your vital organs as transplants. The "organ donor" designation on your driver's license may therefore single you out as a citizen who has heeded—and responded to—this important message. Traffic tickets aside, organ donation is a noble deed; you can sign up (and have your license duly noted) at any Driver's License Bureau.

"Never admit you know the reason why you've been stopped," advises Leiding. "The less you say, the better, because the officer will write down any incriminating statements that could be used against you."

Your protection: Answer questions like the ones above as neutrally as possible: "No, officer, I'm really not sure why you stopped me..." or, "I believe I was traveling a safe speed for the conditions." Replying, "No, I don't know how fast I was driving" is inadvisable; it suggests carelessness, arrogance, or outright lying.

As you hand over your license and documents, if your driving record is clean, it may not hurt to add: "When you run my license, you'll see that I have no previous infractions, so I hope you can excuse me this time with only a warning."

But before doing that, make sure your driving record *is* clean; you can get a copy of it from your state Department of Motor Vehicles for a few dollars.

Talk the talk. What *shouldn't* you say to schmooze your way out of a ticket? Apologizing, for one, may or may not work. "If you offer a valid reason and really seem sincere," says Marshall of the CHP, "that may sway the officer in your favor. But they know that everyone is sorry when they're caught."

Don't offer excuses, blame other drivers, or use the classic line, "I was just going with the flow of traffic." Each of those reactions is viewed—and reported—as a bid to justify guilty behavior, says Leiding, who has handled hundreds of traffic violation cases. Nor should you resort to begging or pleading, which may be seen as weakness. And never try to intimidate

---

PROTECTIVE DETECTIVE

Body-Language Basics

Body language can be key in dodging a ticket. "Probably the most important thing to do when you're pulled over," says Mel Leiding, author of *How to Fight Your Traffic Ticket and Win,* "is to let the officer know you are not a threat." His advice:

Stay in the car and open the window completely; if it's nighttime, switch on the dome light.

If you're wearing a hat or sunglasses, remove them. When the officer approaches you, maintain eye contact.

Keep both hands on the steering wheel. Don't unlatch your seat belt until after the officer has approached your car. "Many people automatically release their seat belt to get out their license or other documents, but that can bring you a second citation (for driving unbuckled)."

Don't reach for your driver's license or registration until you've been asked to do so. "Tell the officer it's in your wallet, purse, or glove compartment, so he knows you're not making a sudden move"; this also shows you're aware who is in authority. If you have a purse, open it wide on your lap to give the officer a good view of what's not inside—namely, a weapon.

---

an officer by naming your buddies on the force; that pad-holding officer is the authority of the moment. Conversely, although politeness counts, avoid overusing "Sir" or "Ma'am" as forms of direct address; they tend to sound insincere with repeated use. Better: Use "Officer" for all law enforcement personnel, "Trooper" for highway patrol, and "Deputy" for rank-and-file Sheriff's Department personnel.

If issued a ticket, contest it. Never retort, "I'll see you in court!" when issued a ticket. Instead, suggests Skrum of the National Motorists Association, you want to leave the scene as inconspicuously as possible. "You don't want to be remembered, because if you choose to fight the ticket—and we recommend that you do—the officer is less likely to recall the particulars of why you were pulled over."

Although fewer than 5 percent of issued tickets are contested—most drivers simply pay the fine—having your day in court can yield dividends. Depending on where the ticket was issued, contesting a ticket may involve a potentially multi-date process, including an initial arraignment in which you enter your plea and then another court appearance for your trial. (It's an urban myth that the ticket-issuing officer must be present at the arraignment.)

But it's worth your while, because attorneys or judges will often reduce or dismiss a fine merely to avoid court expenses. "If you fight a ticket and they think it will go to trial," says Skrum, whose group sells defense kits on how to dispute a traffic ticket, "you're cutting into their profit margin. The jurisdiction that benefits from your traffic fine has to pay the judge, the prosecuting attorney, and the officer for appearing in court."

Your protection: Prepare for your court appearance as you would approach a school presentation. First, dress respectfully—leave the bling and shorts at home. Second, do your homework. If the officer used radar to catch you speeding, call that police agency to determine when the equipment was last calibrated. (Call well in advance, because if the equipment isn't up-to-date, it works in your favor come trial time; if it is, expect that fact to be used against you.)

Inquiries made through manufacturer websites may also turn up data on the radar's accuracy. According to attorney Leiding, a good strategy is to question whether the radar beam used to "paint" your car might not have been focused instead on the car in the next lane. (Granted, this strategy will backfire unless another car was indeed speeding alongside you.) You may also want to challenge the radar's efficacy if it was deployed from behind trees, bushes, or other places of concealment. "If you can't see the officer because he was hiding," says Skrum, "mention that in court. Obstacles in the beam directed at you could affect the accuracy of its reading."

It also pays to check the vehicle code or traffic laws for the jurisdiction in which you were cited; these are often available online, or at your local library. "The officer has to prove that you were pulled over because you violated sections of the vehicle laws," says Leiding. "You want to pick away at those laws, offering valid explanations."

Another thing to pick, of course, is your battles. "If you're caught speeding in a school zone, especially when kids are coming or going," says Marshall, "that's taken far more seriously than speeding on an interstate highway on a sunny, dry day when traffic isn't too heavy."

In other words, the best defense may be the least offense. You'll fare better fighting infractions not believed to be clearly dangerous.

HOMES

2

Defend Your Dream

HOME IS WHERE the heart is—but paying for the place can be downright disheartening.

First there's the purchase price, which—according to real-estate canon—should not exceed 2.5 times your annual household income. But consider reality: In mid-2005, the median selling price of an American home was about $218,000—roughly 3.3 times higher than the median annual household income of nearly $66,000 for a family of four.

So it's easy to understand why, after comparing the regional salaries of 60 professions against home prices in nearly 200 metropolitan areas, the Center for Housing Policy reported a distressing trend in 2005: Members of certain of the country's most admired professions—teachers, nurses, firefighters, police officers—can overwhelmingly no longer afford to own a home in many of the very same communities they serve.

Financing a home is no easier. As part of the loan process, lenders and mortgage brokers are allowed to charge you for some 50 line items that constitute "closing costs"—everything from $50 to send e-mails to their co-workers to thousands of dollars for a public-records search that takes all of five minutes to complete. And once you get that mortgage, the interest payments alone will likely exceed the amount you actually borrow. Case in point: Finance $200,000 with a 30-year, 6 percent "fixed" mortgage and you will pay $231,676 in interest over the life of that loan.

Even if you already own a home, chances are you possess less of it than did previous generations. Today, on average, the equity stake for an established homeowner is only about 56 percent, according to Demos, a New York-based public-interest group that researches housing and other consumer issues. In the 1950s, by contrast, the average equity stake topped 80 percent. The reason for the difference: Fewer than half of borrowers can now afford the traditional down payment—20 percent of the total purchase price—and record numbers are using their homes as collateral for loans to pay off other debts.

There are also ever-soaring utility bills and property taxes. Planned and emergency home repairs and renovations. Door-to-door and telemarketing scamsters trying to get their slice of your shekels (see Chapter 12). No wonder it costs an arm and a leg to keep a roof over your head. Here's how to keep more of your money:

Mortgages

Check your credit score before mortgage rates. These days, more would-be buyers wisely shop for a mortgage before they start scouting out available homes. After all, their maximum buying price is frequently dictated by what they can afford in monthly payments once the purchase has been finalized. Unfortunately, most buyers start calling around for mortgage-rate quotes before they possess a vital piece of information: their FICO credit score. (The acronym refers to the Fair Isaac Corporation, the company that calculates scores for creditors.)

This number—usually between 300 and 850—is crucial for snagging a better rate: The higher your number, the lower the interest rate you can get on a mortgage or other loans. "If your credit score is over 750, you're considered a grade-A borrower, and qualify for the best mortgage rates," says M. Thomas Martin, whose National Mortgage Complaint Center reviews mortgages, upon the applicant's request and for a fee, for overcharges. "If you're over 800, you glow in the dark."

These high-score applicants are deemed the best mortgage customers because they pay their bills on time and usually carry less credit-card and other debt. They stand the best chance of securing the low "teaser" rates often advertised—those that mysteriously elude the masses when they call that company for a mortgage quote.

"There is enormous abuse of people with credit scores in the 600 to 700 range—which many people fall within," says Martin, whose website is www.nationalmortgagecomplaint center.com. "That's still considered the acceptable range to borrow, but frequently banks will tell consumers that a score in the 600s is horrible, and then the consumers wind up paying more."

How much more? An applicant with a score over 720 looking for a fixed-rate $150,000 mortgage may get a 5.55 percent rate, according to June 2005 research by *Consumer Reports*. Those with a FICO score between 620 and 674, by contrast, would be charged around 7.36 percent to borrow the same amount. Over the life of that $150,000 loan, lowest-scoring applicants would pay about $138,000 more in interest than highest-scoring customers.

Your protection: By knowing your FICO score, you can better defend against duplicitous mortgage providers—and avoid overpaying on interest rates. FICO scores—the type that mortgage providers check to determine your interest rate—must be purchased; they are not part of the free credit reports available to all Americans at www.annualcredit report.com.

FICO scores start at about $15, says Barry Paperno, manager of consumer operations at Fair Isaac Corporation, and they can be ordered from www.myfico.com, www.equifax.

"Preapproved" for a mortgage signals that you have submitted the tax returns and pay stubs needed to apply for a mortgage, and that your credit history has been verified.

"Prequalified" for a mortgage carries less heft. It means only that a lender has told you how much money you can probably *borrow*, based on your reported income, debt, and projected down payment.

Which Mortgage Is Right for You?

SHOULD YOU PAY points to get a lower interest rate on a mortgage? Should you choose an adjustable-rate mortgage (ARM) or one whose rate is fixed? And what about the length of the repayment period: Should you opt for a 30-year mortgage? Or for one that you can pay off in just 15 years?

The answers to these and many other mortgage questions often hinge on the specifics of your situation: What can you afford to pay each month, and how long do you plan to live in the house? Yet some general advice pertains as well. Consider the following pointers from Jack Guttentag, Ph.D., professor of finance emeritus at the University of Pennsylvania's Wharton School:

Points well taken?
Points are fees that the borrower pays the lender in order to lower the mortgage interest rate. One point equals 1 percent of the total loan amount, so one point on a $150,000 loan would equal $1,500. Each point paid by the borrower typically drives down an offered interest rate by about 1/4 percent. Pay two points on the sample loan amount above, therefore, and you'll shell out $3,000 more at closing; at the same time, however, you'll likely get an interest rate about 1/2 percent lower than the rate you could secure with zero points.

Does paying points pay off? "If you expect to be in your house and hold that mortgage more than six years," says Dr. Guttentag, author of *The Mortgage Encyclopedia* and *The Pocket Mortgage Guide,* "it generally pays to pay the points to lower your rate; over the long run, you'll usually pay less that way. But if you plan to leave that home earlier, you'll probably want to minimize up-front costs. In that case you should not pay any points, and take the higher interest rate instead." To calculate your break-even point—that is, the point at which the money you have saved over time on the lower interest rate exceeds the lump sum you paid in points at closing—visit www.decisionaide.com/mpcalculators/frmbreakevencalculator/frmbreakeven.asp.

The fix is in. Fixed-rate mortgages are

normally the better choice for home-owners who plan to live at least six years in the house they are financing. Adjustable-rate mortgages (ARMs), whose rates are likely to rise after an initial grace period of one to seven years, are typically better suited for short-timers.

Beware of super-low "option" ARMs: Their rates may change as often as every month, and the rate increase can be significant. "Some of the newer ARMs initially charge only a 1 percent rate," Dr. Guttentag points out, "but the rate can rise substantially in the second month. Payments are low initially because they are calculated at the introductory rate, but they rise by 7.5 percent a year—and the increase can escalate if rates go up."

Coming to terms. When debating the merits of a 15-year fixed-rate loan versus one that lasts 30 years, Dr. Guttentag suggests that you ask yourself the following question: Do you want to minimize your monthly payments or maximize your future wealth? If you choose the latter, Guttentag says, there are a couple of distinct advantages to 15-year loans:

First, these shorter-term loans typically have lower interest rates—about 1/2 percent less than a 30-year fixed loan for the same amount.

Second, despite the hardship of a higher monthly payment, 15-year notes build equity at a much faster rate, meaning more in your pocket when you sell the property. And the savings in interest payments—money that otherwise would have gone into the lender's pocket—is substantial. For example, the monthly principal-and-interest payment on a 30-year, $100,000 loan at 7 percent is $665; the monthly payment on a 15-year loan for the same amount at 6.5 percent is $871. Though the difference is a sizable $206, after five years the 30-year borrower will have repaid only $5,868 in principal on that loan, whereas the 15-year borrower will have repaid a far more impressive principal amount of $23,283. And the interest paid over the life of each loan? It's a whopping $139,509 for that 30-year loan, but just $56,799 on the 15-year note.

Even if you choose a 30-year loan, you can usually add a little extra to each monthly payment to build equity faster and pay down your mortgage more quickly. Don't fall for biweekly payment programs: In exchange for a fee that enriches the lender by $300 or more, these "allow" you to make one additional payment every year. Instead, if you can afford it, divide your regular monthly payment by 12, then add that amount—or even more—to your mortgage check each time. This allows you to pay off that loan as early as a biweekly program would.

com, or www.transunioncs.com. "You get another credit score, but not a FICO, when you purchase a credit report through Experian (www.experian.com)," he says. "But it's the FICO that lenders look at."

With your FICO in hand, you can determine the rates for which you qualify by visiting a website such as www.eloan.com or www.indymac.com. "At these websites, you can price your deal because they ask for your credit score, and offer qualifying rates based on that and other data," advises Jack Guttentag, Ph.D., professor of finance emeritus at the University of Pennsylvania and author of "The Mortgage Professor," a syndicated newspaper column. "Then you can compare those rates to the ones you've been offered by phone." He adds that those two websites also usually offer the best rates.

Other websites, however—including those where multiple lenders allegedly "compete" for your business—may not be as competitive: They usually require lenders to pay a hefty fee for applicant referrals. The lenders, in turn, are likely to pass that expense along to would-be borrowers.

Wise up to the YSP. The reason you may be quoted a higher interest rate than the one you in fact qualify for is so mortgage providers and brokers can pocket the difference. Blame it on a little-known but nefarious trade secret: the Yield Spread Premium, or YSP. The YSP is a kickback often paid by lenders to mortgage brokers for bringing in borrowers at an interest rate higher than the lowest one the borrower in fact qualifies for. (Mortgage brokers—independent agents who now handle 2 of every 3 mortgage transactions—offer loan programs from many different sources. They should not be confused with mortgage lenders—typically banks or mortgage companies that offer only their own loans. See sidebar, page 62.)

"For instance, if you qualify for a 6 percent loan, the mortgage broker may raise it to 6.25 percent without telling you, and make an extra $5,000 on a mortgage for a $500,000 house,"

says Martin, a former construction manager who started his Northwest-based mortgage-review business after getting burned on his own mortgage loan. At the higher rate, you could pay at least $100 more each month.

Of course, knowing your FICO score—and, by extension from that, knowing what rate you qualify for—is a good way to deflect this sort of shabby treatment. But that knowledge is no guarantee you won't be quoted a higher rate—the reason why it's wise to shop around. "Had the borrower in the example above known he was serving as a profit vehicle for the broker," says Martin, "he never would have closed on the loan."

Mortgage lenders, too, may inflate your interest rate in order to pay the YSP kickback to themselves, but federal law does not compel them to disclose the YSP. Mortgage brokers, by contrast, are required to reveal the kickback transaction. Yet when Martin surveyed 1,000 homeowners, he discovered that 97 percent of them had no idea the broker received extra compensation.

Your protection: The first step in preventing a YSP—think of it as an abbreviation for "You Silly Patsy"—is to request and secure assurances that it is not being charged. As a condition of landing your business, Martin suggests, ask brokers to sign a document revealing whether or not they are getting this kickback. If they refuse to sign, assume they're trying to fleece you. If they do sign, check the 800 section of your

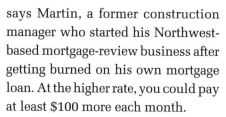

▶A BETTER WAY
Flex Your FICO

To lower your mortgage interest rate, boost your credit score. To do that, pay down your credit-card balances as far as possible at least two months before you apply for the mortgage. "If you can't pay them off," advises Barry Paperno of credit scorer Fair Isaac Corporation, "try to lower the amounts owed so that the outstanding balance is no more than half the credit limit on each account before applying."

Additionally, make sure you have no overdue library books, unpaid parking tickets, or bills past due from your doctor, car mechanic, or other service provider. "These and other bills are often reported to a collection agency," explains Paperno, "which in turn reports them to a credit bureau."

An unresolved collection account could produce a negative effect similar to being late for two months or more on a credit-card bill or car loan. "Even if you have a perfect credit record," says Paperno, "a collection account for a $5 parking ticket can drop your score."

Who's Who in Mortgage Lending

O, the lingo of lending! Here are some definitions to distinguish the players processing your mortgage:

Mortgage lender: A representative of a bank or other financial-services company who offers loans directly to consumers. This makes the mortgage lender the one providing loan funds to the borrower at the closing table. *Retail lenders* usually handle all loan-origination tasks; *wholesale lenders* may perform some functions in house but out-source others—taking loan applications, for example—to a mortgage broker.

Mortgage broker: An independent shopper who finds, compares, and offers loans to home buyers from a variety of lenders—ideally, to give the buyer the best rates. Though mortgage brokers do not actually make home loans, they now handle 2 of every 3 mortgages.

Loan officer: An employee of a lending institution or large mortgage brokerage who does the paperwork needed to process your loan application. In return for serving as your day-to-day contact, the loan officer usually earns a commission of 0.5 to 1 percent of the loan amount. (In a one-person mortgage broker firm, the broker doubles as the loan officer.)

Which of these creatures is easiest to subdue? There's no clear answer. The main advantage of mortgage brokers is that they can get "wholesale" rates from multiple lenders. Yet there are disadvantages, too: Most mortgage brokers dictate their own markup—routinely the maximum amount they believe they can persuade you is the best available loan.

Mortgage lenders may have the edge when it comes to after-the-sale customer service—assuming they don't sell your loan to another lender, that is. Until then, however, they may not be able to offer a wealth of mortgage choices, given that they have only their own institution's loans to choose from. Mortgage lenders also tend to charge more in processing costs, raising your costs at closing.

Still, if you're a savvy consumer who has shopped around (after getting your current credit score), you may fare better with a mortgage broker, suggests Jack Guttentag, Ph.D., author of *The Pocket Mortgage Guide.* His advice: "Try to find an *up-front mortgage broker*—industry argot for one who works as an agent for the buyer for a predetermined, set fee for his or her services." This fee can be a fixed dollar amount ($1,500 for the entire mortgage-securing process, say), an hourly rate, or even up to 1 percent of the loan amount—a bargain when compared with the 2 percent or more that other mortgage brokers habitually charge. Up-front mortgage brokers pass wholesale prices along to their clients—without skimming off additional fees for themselves. To get a state-by-state listing of up-front mortgage brokers, visit the website run by Dr. Guttentag: www.mtgprofessor.com.

HUD-1 form (Housing and Urban Development settlement statement); this charge is usually listed as a "YSP" or "POC" (Paid Outside of Closing). The appearance of a YSP or POC charge on your HUD-1 form is a good reason to suspect that you qualified for a lower mortgage rate but did not get it—in which case you can sue the broker for fraud.

"The closing agent may claim it's not a cost to you," says Martin, "but when you're paying one-quarter point more in interest over the life of a loan, it is a cost to you."

Get, don't give, information. When calling brokers or lenders for mortgage-rate quotes, you'll likely be asked for your Social Security number—along with other personal data. That's so banks and mortgage brokers can run their own credit check on you before quoting you a set-in-stone interest rate (another good reason to know your FICO).

If you reveal that information, you're likely making two mistakes.

The first is that you may inadvertently depress your own credit score. "Every time a lender, mortgage broker, or anyone else runs your credit history, it has the potential to lower your credit score," says Martin. "Frequent inquiries in a short period of time have the potential to drop your score as much as 50 to 100 points."

The second false step is that revealing your personal data for a credit check is seen as a green light to be charged for that service—along with an application fee and an appraisal fee. "Once applicants pay hundreds of dollars to get the mortgage process going," Martin observes, "many are hesitant to walk away from that company because they've already invested so much money. But it's a drop in the bucket if that lender or broker comes back with a rate that's not the best they can get."

Your protection: Have your current credit score on hand. That way, when you call for loan-rate quotes, you can inform the lender or broker that you have just retrieved your FICO score. Then, before you officially "apply" for a mortgage with that company or broker, request your qualifying interest rate based on that number—without revealing your Social Security number. "Understand that even by having your credit score, banks and mortgage brokers will still run their own credit check—and calculate their own score—on you," says Martin. "But that should be done only by companies you're really serious about. During this rate-gathering phase, do not complete an application. Do not let anyone do a credit check on you. And ask for—and secure—their best rate in writing before divulging any vital personal data or forking over any processing fees."

Shop around—really. It may seem obvious: The more research you do, the better your chances of improving your deal. But guess what? About 1 in 3 home buyers never compare quoted rates. Instead, they choose their eventual mortgage provider based on a single referral—a referral made by the realtor who is selling them their house, says Douglas Duncan, Ph.D., chief economist for the Mortgage Bankers Association. "When you're getting referrals from a Realtor," he notes, "you're dealing with someone who is interested in closing the deal quickly. Getting you the best rate is a lower priority." Besides, if you talk to only one lender, what are your chances of snagging a better deal via the perfectly kosher practice of playing one offer against another?

Dr. Duncan's recommendation: Talk to no fewer than three lenders, whether you're seeking a new mortgage or refinancing an existing one. On his own home, he has refinanced his mortgage three times. "Each time I ended up with a better deal than the first lender I called—in both interest rates and fees," he notes. "When one lender offers to waive a certain item in closing costs—the initial application fee, say, or any of umpteen other 'processing' charges—call another lender and ask if he'll waive it as well. This becomes part of the negotiating process. After all, lending officers and mortgage brokers

Save Yourself From "Rescue" Lenders

Predatory "rescue" lenders victimize tens of thousands of American homeowners each year. The bait: They promise to help "save" the 1 of every 25 homeowners who face foreclosure of their mortgages in any given year. The hook: Instead of rescuing householders, they leave them high and dry by tricking their way into taking possession of the property.

In addition to those facing foreclosure, says Steve Tripoli of the National Consumer Law Center (NCLC), a consumer advocacy group, other likely victims include those with substantial equity in their homes, notably older people. For them, an offer is made to refinance their homes—to pay for medical expenses, for example—but the scammers then doctor paperwork to seize ownership of the property under the guise of providing a loan.

How do the scammers learn of impending foreclosures? You can thank an obliging lending industry, which broadcasts the bad news of impending foreclosures in newspapers and professional journals as part of its duty to update the public record. Once a so-called rescue lender gets a whiff of ruination in the wind, he mails to the victim's home an offer to "save your house" or "pay off your loans." Next, the rogue takes one or more of these destructive steps instead:

Tricks homeowners into unknowingly signing "sale" documents by rushing the owner through the loan closing, or by burying crucial documents in a mountain of paperwork.

Falsifies signed documents, or forges documents and keeps their existence a secret from the homeowner.

Buys the home for a fraction of its value from the desperate owner, who may knowingly surrender title—sometimes in exchange for a "rent-to-own" or other buy-back arrangement during a time of financial need.

Strings along the time-pressed victim, levying outrageous "processing" fees for a loan that is never delivered.

If you are facing foreclosure, first ask your mortgage lender to grant you more flexible payment terms; many will. If you have no option but to refinance your mortgage or take out another loan on your home, contact your state attorney general, state housing department, or state banking commission. Any of these agencies can help you distinguish legitimate lenders from unscrupulous "rescuers," says Julie Ralston Aoki of the Minnesota Attorney General's Office. Housing agencies, including the local offices of Habitat for Humanity and ACORN (the Association of Community Organizations for Reform Now; www.acorn.org), also offer counseling on preventing foreclosure. So do local Legal Aid offices, which should be listed in your Yellow Pages.

get paid on commission; they make nothing if you don't take their loans." To effectively compare the offerings from various companies, Dr. Duncan suggests that you make a line-item list of the rates and fees charged by each one.

Get paper proof. Federal laws require that you be provided with a Good Faith Estimate (GFE) within three business days of first applying for a mortgage from a particular lender or broker. According to consumer watchdog Martin, however, 70 percent of mortgage applicants do not receive this crucial document until just before they're ready to sign the settlement papers. "Without getting this estimate in the mandated time period," he says, "you have no real way of knowing what interest rate or mortgage fees you're being charged. And if you walk into the closing without having reviewed it, you could be overcharged."

Even if you receive the Good Faith Estimate within the mandated three days of starting the mortgage-application process, review it carefully. Lenders and mortgage brokers are quick to note that the document is, as its title states, only an "estimate." Certain charges (notably the payoff amount of any previous mortgage) will change depending on exactly when you close, but fixed fees should not. Fixed costs include the appraisal fee, processing fees for the mortgage paperwork, and the "locked-in" interest rate and mortgage term.

Your protection: If you don't receive your GFE within days of initially filing a mortgage application, notify your lender or broker in writing that it is liable for a $2,000 fine. Even if you do receive the GFE on time, respond with a letter or fax informing the lender or mortgage broker that you expect a copy of your final settlement costs—called the HUD-1 form or the Truth-in-Lending statement—to be sent to you within one day before closing so you can compare mortgage terms and costs with those on the "final" closing papers.

"I recommend you announce early in the process—well

New-home buyers have less price-negotiating leverage than those purchasing an existing home.

But they can cut costs another way: Builders buy title insurance policies in bulk, so they may pay as little as $25 for a policy that would cost an individual homeowner $1,000. Builders rarely volunteer these discounts, so ask—before you make a deposit on that new home.

before closing—that you expect these papers in time to carefully review them without the pressure that comes at closing, when you are quickly signing many documents," says Dr. Duncan of the Mortgage Bankers Association.

Closing Costs

The industry calls them "closing costs." Consumers brand them as "junk fees." Regardless of nomenclature, settlement charges—the bane and boon of every mortgage that is issued—extract thousands of dollars from the pockets of borrowers.

"The typical borrower overpays about $1,250 in closing costs," says mortgage maven Martin. Each month, hundreds of borrowers contact Martin's National Mortgage Complaint Center for the main service it provides: reviewing mortgage closing statements to weed out overcharges. The $45 they pay for this analysis can be money well spent: Lenders and mortgage brokers can charge borrowers for about 50 different services—much of it mundane paperwork that in a just world would be covered by their four-figure commissions. Martin then informs his clients which costs can legally be disputed or negotiated before signing, including third-party charges such as conducting property-title searches.

But how do you separate bona fide charges from blatant ripoffs? The initial Good Faith Estimate should give you a heads-up of expected lender or broker closing charges—with plenty of time to protest those that are unreasonable, such as Yield Spread Premiums and duplicate processing fees. The savvy borrower will also contact title companies and escrow services for a pre-closing list of their fees. Although you have three days after closing to rescind your mortgage (a consumer privilege known as the "right of rescission") and recoup all the money you paid in up-front fees, moving hassles make many home buyers reluctant or unable to do that.

"I always recommend that people get a list of their closing

costs a couple of days before the actual closing," says Martin. "By then, all the paperwork has been completed and you're seeing the actual costs you will pay."

If you detect blatant or duplicate overcharges, take issue with the charges—before closing. "Say you will not pay these charges for this or that reason," advises Martin. "In my experience, some will be dropped or reduced about half the time because they don't want you to walk away from the loan that near closing."

Below are some charges you'll likely encounter. The list spells out two very different sets of figures: what you will be charged for each item, and how much you should agree to pay for it.

- *Application fee.* Many lenders charge an origination fee—typically 1 to 2 percent of the loan amount—yet half of borrowers are charged an additional fee just to complete an application form, says Martin. Although this application fee averages about $175, some lenders have been so brazen as to charge $650 for it. If you are required to pay an application fee and it is not later applied to paying down the origination fee, you're being fleeced.

- *Administrative fee.* This should also be part of the origination or application fee, yet it is charged separately in roughly half the closing statements that Martin reviews—at an average cost of $400. Make sure it's not being charged when you get your Good Faith Estimate early in the process, if you're paying either of those two other charges.

- *Appraisal fee.* Most large lenders have their own stable of approved appraisers, whom they pay to assess your home's value to make sure it's a good lending risk for them. "The lender pays the appraiser an average of $200 for each assessment," says Martin, "but it usually charges the borrower $400 to $500. Before closing, tell the lender you will pay the appraiser himself at the door—and that this cost should not be part of closing." Some lenders permit you to find your own appraiser; others do not. Select your own when you can.

- *Courier fees.* Sending documents is a legitimate charge, but to what degree? "I've contacted UPS, Federal Express, and the U.S. Postal Service," says Martin, "and their charge for sending documents from New York to Los Angeles ranges from $22 to $25. Yet most borrowers are charged in the neighborhood of $75 for this." The likely explanation isn't multiple deliveries, but rather a tack-on charge that can be disputed.

- *Credit-reporting fee.* Lenders and mortgage brokers customarily examine your credit history as part of the application process. Some charge additionally for this service, and that's fine—so long as you're charged only their cost (about $20 for a couple, $10 for an individual borrower). "But borrowers are routinely charged $50 to $75 to run their credit," says Martin.

- *Document-preparation fee.* This charge is for drawing up the mortgage note, deed, and other legal papers. Sometimes, though, the task is performed not by the lender but by the escrow agent or closing agent— a state-licensed notary who ensures that all paperwork is properly signed and stamped. If that's the case— and you should ask whether or not it is—don't pay twice for this service. It averages $250 but can cost as much as $500.

- *Document-review fee.* Although there's not much you can do about it, this fee of $100 to $200 is to cover the cost of what often amounts to a five-minute review of paperwork that has just been prepared by the company. Often it's done by a low-level clerk, says Martin.

Replacing a 1990s-era refrigerator with a newer, energy-efficient model can save the typical household $85 in annual energy costs. Newer washing machines use half the energy of their older counterparts; they can slice $110 from that yearly bill.

- *E-mail fee.* This newer charge of up to $100 is supposedly to defray the cost of sending electronic messages between same-company employees, or between the lender and various third-party firms. Your lender, broker, or title insurer may invoke "corporate policy" as the authorization for this bogus charge. If he or she does that, dispute it: E-mail fees have sparked a number of class-action lawsuits.

- *Funding fee.* Ranging from $50 to $275, this charge is levied purely to give you the money you're borrowing. It's a red-flag ripoff, says Martin. If you see it, fight it—then immediately start scrutinizing the HUD-1 form for other overcharges as well.

- *Processing fee:* Here's another cost that should be part of the origination fee. If you allow this fee to be assessed as a separate HUD-1 line item—which you should not—it will typically set you back $395. Be aware, however, that unscrupulous lenders have succeeded in charging naïve borrowers nearly $2,000 for this single bogus fee.

- *Title-insurance fee.* This charge can be inflated as high as $6,000. It funds a review of court records to examine the history of a property's title—a crucial step for establishing that the title is not part of a pending lawsuit. It also clarifies whether the title has tax or other liens against it, such as those issued by contractors unpaid for work they performed on the property. Buyers who purchase costly properties tend to pay more for this fee. Still, basic title insurance should cost the same amount ($300 to $400) regardless of a home's value. Anything above that, Martin warns, is typically pocket-padding.

- *Underwriting fee.* Another unnecessary charge, according to Martin, for isn't this the purpose of the mortgage itself? Anticipate—but do not allow—a range of $225 to $1,100, with an average of $286.

Strategies for Buying & Selling

Love those locals. Everyone's sick of this old canard: "Only three things matter when you're buying or selling real estate: location, location, and location." But did you know that adage applies to agents too? "Real estate is a neighborhood niche," says real estate columnist Alan J. Heavens of *The Philadelphia Inquirer.* "You want someone who knows and has experience in the neighborhood where you want to buy or sell."

Here's how to uncover that knowledge and seasoning: Ask potential agents to document their experience in that specific area. They should be familiar with local amenities and happenings: shopping, parks, and—if your state allows such a query—the quality of local schools. (Real estate agents are forbidden from commenting on schools in some states, but a savvy agent can steer you to robust sources of that information.) Before you sign a contract committing you to deal exclusively with any real estate agent, walk around your target neighborhood and ask residents for recommendations of their own. You can also do an informal count of which agent seems to have the most "For Sale" signs in that area.

Nix the six. If you're trying to sell a home, real estate commissions can gobble up to 10 percent of its selling price. (To get a sense of their collective impact, consider that Americans paid out $70 billion in these commissions in 2005.) Since roughly 1995, the standard commission on the sale of a home has been 6 percent, depending on the market conditions of supply and demand. The sale of a $200,000 house would therefore generate a commission of $12,000, which would be divvied up among the buyer's agent, the seller's agent, and their respective companies.

Many agents still quote 6 percent as standard. It is not. Thanks largely to the real estate boom (some say bubble) that swept the U.S. beginning in the late 1990s, the average commission nationwide had dropped to 5.1 percent by 2005. So before you sign an agreement to work with a certain agent to sell your property, try to negotiate a lower commission. If the agent balks at your suggestion, try one of the four alternative tacks spelled out below. Any arrangements that you agree to must be written into the contract.

- *Offer to handle some standard services yourself,* such as hiring a lawyer to handle the paperwork or purchasing newspaper classified ads. Or specify that you'll be satisfied with X number of ads rather than the usual Y. When you sign with an agent, the contract should specify a set amount of advertising and list its channels.

- *Do some negotiating* after a prospective buyer makes an offer. Explain to the agent that you may be willing to accept a lower selling price (and a faster sale on his or her part) in exchange for a lower commission. For example, with a 6 percent commission, the seller's net on a $265,000 home is $249,100. In order for the seller to clear the same amount at a sale price of $260,000, the agent's commission would have to drop to 4.2 percent. Many agents will resist this, of course; in the example above, it flattens their take from $15,900 to $10,920. Still, it's a worth a try—especially if you live in an area where homes sell quickly.

- *Set a time limit for a sale.* Stipulate that if a sale is made within 30 days, the agent will get the full 6 percent commission; if it takes longer than that, the commission will drop to 5 percent.

- *Consider your home's desirability.* If you list your home at $400,000, does the agent who sells it truly invest twice as much time and money as in moving a $200,000 home? If your home has soared in value in recent years or happens to be sited in a hot market, it may "sell itself"—another strong argument for a quick sale that justifies a lower commission.

Who's Who in Real Estate

O, the rhetoric of real estate! If you're unsure who represents you—and who is watching the back of those on the other side of the transaction—here's some help:

Real estate agent: An individual licensed by a state to represent the buyer or seller in a real estate transaction in exchange for a commission.

Real estate broker: A person, corporation, or partnership that handles real estate transactions, often supervising licensed sales agents.

Listing agent: A broker or agent who signs a contract with a seller to handle the marketing and sale of a piece of property.

Selling agent: A broker or agent who writes the purchase offer for a buyer, whether he or she represents the buyer or not.

Buyer's agent (also called "Buyer agent"): An individual contracted by a buyer to protect the buyer's interest. The agent searches homes on the market, negotiates purchase terms, and handles the transaction from the buyer's point of view.

Realtor™: An agent or broker who belongs to the National Association of Realtors and who has completed training in professional business ethics mandated by the association. Only about 1 real estate agent in 3 is a Realtor™.

Shut your mouth at open houses. Home buyers usually check out possible purchases in one of three ways: 1) spotting "For Sale" signs and arranging a walk-through, 2) answering real estate ads in newspapers or "shopper" magazines, or 3) attending "open houses" at new developments or in established neighborhoods. In all three cases, the smiling people on hand to answer your questions about the home's many attributes are there for one reason: to sell the property for the owner or builder.

Not coincidentally, they also work in a few questions of their own—usually about your "situation."

"The biggest mistake potential buyers make is being overly open with the realtor or other agent of the seller," says Leo Berard, the founding president of the National Association of Exclusive Buyer Agents, which represents agents who work solely for buyers. "Too often, shoppers reveal personal information or emotions that put them at a negotiating disadvantage."

Mentioning your occupation, for example, permits a quick gauge of your income—crucial data for sifting serious buyers from those seeking decorating ideas or a bathroom break. Saying you've been preapproved to borrow a certain amount may satisfy the realtor's immediate curiosity of whether you're in the price-range ballpark. But in the long run, warns Berard, it may also cause you to overpay. Statements such as "I have a buyer for my house" or "I'm being transferred here" lets him or her know you're pressed for time—and may lack the luxury of shopping around.

"Never gush over a home you're visiting—even if you love it," cautions Berard, who works on Cape Cod, Massachusetts. "It gives the seller the upper hand." Instead, focus the conversation on your questions—not theirs. When a fact-finding query is directed at you, give a noncommittal reply: "If I'm interested, I'll have my representative get in touch with you."

Don't be upstaged. Only about 2 in 100 buyers, says Berard, visit a home that they are interested in purchasing with the most important item they should bring: a tape measure. "Listing sheets typically have room dimensions," he explains, "but they are often rounded off generously and therefore can't really be trusted. Always measure the rooms yourself."

Long before cable television showed viewers how to "stage" a home for sale by making its rooms appear larger and less cluttered, professional designers had hatched a far more clever ploy: They made the rooms in model homes appear larger than they were by populating them with smaller furniture. Rather than installing a sofa in the living room, for example, they might outfit that room with a loveseat; instead of furnishing a bedroom with a queen or king bed, they might put a full bed in place.

Those tactics still succeed today, when smart sellers routinely remove clutter and excess furniture to create the illusion of space. "Having a tape measure on hand allows you to really determine whether the rooms in a home you're considering will accommodate your current furniture," says Berard.

Make the calendar your calculator. It's common sense that the longer a home sits for sale, the less likely it is to fetch its initial asking price. But is there a specific "shelf life" for new offerings? As a general rule, says Berard, "Once a home has been on the market for at least 90 days with little activity, buyers are in a much stronger position to buy it at a lower offer." Although the eventual selling price will hinge on a number of factors—including the health of the market and the condition of the home—Berard recommends offering 10 percent less than the asking price once a listing hits that 90-day threshold.

You can tell when it first came on the market by asking your real estate agent to provide printouts from the Multiple Listing Service, the database that tracks homes for sale in the area. The full listing—replete with the number of days a house has been on the market—is accessible only to realtors, but an abridged version is available from www.realtors.com. Your realtor can also send you MLS listings via e-mail.

Home Repairs & Renovations

Renovate to stay, not to sell. Certain renovations—notably an updated kitchen or bathrooms, new siding, or the addition of a deck—enhance a home's salability and increase its value. Do not assume, however, that you will be able to recoup your renovation expenditures dollar for dollar with a higher selling price. "Never renovate to sell—renovate to live there," advises real estate writer Heavens, author of *What No One Ever Tells You About Renovating Your Home.* "Putting in a

$60,000 state-of-the-art kitchen most likely won't add $60,000 in value to your home. In fact, it will add very little, if anything, if you have the only $60,000 kitchen in your neighborhood."

Although you'll want to modernize outdated wiring, replace a deteriorating roof, or fix other "usability" essentials that play a key role in a home's passing inspection for sale, don't undertake major esthetic renovations just before you put your home on the market—unless it's to keep up with the Joneses. "Never overimprove for your neighborhood," advises Heavens. "If your neighbors are all redoing their siding, of course, you won't want your house to be the only one with old, faded siding. But adding an addition to make your home a five-bedroom when the others on your street have three bedrooms won't get you two bedrooms more in price when you sell, and your home will probably sit longer on the market."

So instead of healing eyesores—replacing threadbare carpet, for example, or finishing a dungeon-like basement—cut something off the selling price as an "allowance" for the homeowners to pick their own products. "You may go to the expense of replacing your worn white carpet with new white carpet when they want to rip it up for hardwood floors," says Heavens. "You can't anticipate buyers' taste—and virtually all homeowners change something about a home's appearance after they move in."

What should you do to improve the interior look of your house and maximize its curb appeal? "When you're trying to sell a home," adds Heavens, "it's the little things that work. Most sellers can do these easily: Applying new paint; fixing the lawn and planting shrubs or flowers; cleaning windows, replacing lightbulbs, and repairing leaky faucets."

Get the right recommendations. Home-improvement contractors historically rival car salesmen and mechanics as rich sources of consumer complaints. The most common objections cite hired handymen who take the money and run without finishing a job; contractors who work at a snail's pace while juggling other projects; or that universal bane, shoddy work. Although pickup-driving shysters abound, there are also plenty of hardworking, talented craftsmen out there, eager to devote an honest day's work to completing your much-needed home repairs or improvements.

How do you find them? "Good contractors are usually found by word of mouth," says shelter guru Heavens. "That means referrals made by your friends, neighbors, and people in your church." However, those who find you—knocking on your front door with an offer to make a much-needed repair they "just happened to notice while driving by"—should be avoided.

That's not to say you can't find a quality contractor by looking in the Yellow Pages or other media. "But many good contractors don't have to advertise," notes longtime contractor Tom Silva of *This Old House*, the popular home-improvement show on public television. "They build a business—and their clientele—by word of mouth."

In addition to getting recommendations from people you know and trust, Silva suggests you check with city hall. "Probably the best source for the real story of the quality of their work is your local building department," says Silva. "Building inspectors see the 'bones' of buildings, so they know who does quality work—and who doesn't." Additionally, many bigger jobs require construction or improvement permits issued by this department. (These permits, by the way, should always be secured by the contractor—never by you!)

Inspectors will readily recommend praiseworthy contractors. But if an inspector cites "policy" for not making a recommendation, that's often his or her coded way of saying "Pass on this bum." It's equally informative to be able to read the civil servant's body language. "If you ask about a contractor's reputation and the inspector rolls his eyes," says Silva, "you just got your answer—with no words said."

▶ **A BETTER WAY**

Calculate Appliance Costs

To estimate the cost of running a certain electric appliance, try this formula: Multiply the item's wattage (posted on the back or on its "nameplate") by the number of hours you use it per day, then multiply the result by the number of days you use it per year. Finally, divide by 1,000 and multiply that number by your utility company's kilowatt-hour (kWh) charge.

For instance, if you pay 8.5 cents per kWh and use a 200-watt fan for four hours a day approximately 120 days a year, it's:

200 watts x 4 hours/day
x 120 days/year ÷ 1000
= 96 kWh
x 8.5 Cents/kWh
―――――――――――――
= **$8.16 a year.**

Typical wattage by appliance, according to the U.S. Department of Energy:

Aquarium:	50-1,210 watts	Personal computer	
Clock radio:	10	*CPU:*	120
Coffee maker:	900-1,200	*Monitor:*	150
Clothes washer:	350-500	*Laptop:*	50
Clothes dryer:	1,800-5,000	Stereo:	70-400
Dishwasher:	1,200-2,400	Refrigerator:	725
Dehumidifier:	785	Televisions	
Fans		*19- to 27-inch:* 65-113	
Ceiling:	65-175	*53- to 61-inch:* 170	
Window:	55-250	*Flat Screen:*	120
Hair dryer:	1,200-1,875	Toaster oven:	1,225
Iron:	1,000-1,800	VCR/DVD:	17-25
Microwave oven:	750-1,100	Vacuum:	1,000-1,440

Another good source for references is specialty stores that cater primarily to contractors. These stores include lumberyards, mill shops, and electrical and plumbing supply stores. Although quality contractors may sometimes shop at the neighborhood hardware store or a home-improvement chain store, chances are they don't patronize these "weekend-warrior haunts" frequently enough to become well-known to the staffers there.

As a final check, you can scan county court dockets, including that of small-claims court, to discover if any suits have been filed against a contractor you are considering hiring. Your state attorney general's office or state office of consumer protection (or your local Better Business Bureau) may also be able to help you perform this due diligence.

Consider the source of references. Most contractors eager for work—or your money—are happy to provide you with references from past customers. But what's to prevent a contractor from handing you the name and phone number of his brother-in-law?

That's why you should never accept anything less than contractor-provided references listing local people—ideally, those you know and trust. "If you get references from a contractor," advises Silva, "don't just call, as many people do. Instead, go to the client's house and inspect the job done." Ask to examine "before" photos, if any are available, to see exactly how well the job was done. (Many enthusiastic references, you'll find, are more than willing to share these.)

Additionally, Silva recommends, check up on jobs that are in progress, not just those that have already been completed. And finally, to make sure you see both sides of the coin, ask to interview the homeowners themselves.

Hold out for show & tell. After you've found three or four contractors backed by credible references, you'll need more than mere estimates to decide which contractor is the right one to hire. "In your initial meeting," says Heavens, "present the contractor with the project and tell him what you want—and what you want is for him to tell you how he's going to do it. You're looking for someone who is willing to listen to you, someone with whom you can get along. If the contractor responds 'I don't do that' when you mention a particular

It's not worth getting professional service for household appliances that cost $150 or less to replace, advises Consumer Reports.

That buyers' bible likewise suggests that you nix any repair that costs more than half an appliance's replacement cost. Indeed, many cordless phones, countertop microwaves, inkjet printers, CD players, and TVs under 30 inches are simply not serviceable.

product or feature you want in the job, ask why. If the explanation sounds reasonable, you can go on from there. But if he dismisses your ideas, that's a sign of trouble ahead, and you should move on."

Often, hiring a contractor comes down to price—not always the price you want to hear. "You may pay a little more than what you expected for good contractors," says Silva, "and you may have to wait for the good ones."

Meanwhile, less-qualified workmen are more likely to give you lowball estimates: Either that's how they get business, or they don't know how to estimate correctly. "You may have to pay more to get a job done right than you think you should," Silva points out, "but down the road you'll forget the extra money you spent. On the other hand, you'll never forget the crappy job you got in exchange for a bargain price."

This is not to say you should always hire the highest bidder. Indeed, to avoid overpaying, get several estimates; most should be reasonably similar. Although you may notice one lowball estimate (a possible clue to a contractor overeager for your business), the highest estimate should not exceed the others by more than 20 percent or so.

Here are two final ways of backstopping your due diligence in the contractor arena:

- *Visit* www.remodelingmagazine.com or www.contractor. com, which ballpark various projects—sometimes by zip code.

- *If you're using* a certain product for a renovation, suggests Heavens, feel free to call that product's manufacturer and request an approximate cost for the project. At the very least, you can better determine if the contractor is charging you a hefty mark-up in materials used. (He shouldn't be.)

Sign a contract, not a check. When interviewing contractors, it's imperative that you get written estimates

Inside Tips from a Cat Burglar

In 20 years as a cat burglar, Bill Mason stole some $35 million in cash, diamonds, and other valuables. His targets included Johnny Weissmuller, Truman Capote, Armand Hammer, Phyllis Diller (twice), and a Cleveland mob boss. Retired from a life of crime after doing time, Mason wrote *Confessions of a Master Jewel Thief.* He suggests taking these steps to keep your home safe:

Use the laundry room to avoid getting cleaned out. Accomplished crooks are well aware that most homeowners keep easy-to-steal valuables in their bedrooms. "The bureau and the bedroom closet are the first places that burglars look," he says. The laundry room, by contrast, is probably the safest place to hide your valuables. "Thieves want to get in and out of a home as quickly as possible; most of them would never take the time to look there."

Be on high alert if you live sky-high. Mason specialized in high-rise heists—tall apartment buildings and hotels—for a reason. "People become complacent when they live on upper floors," he says. "It was easy to get to the roof, then scale down a rope onto their patio." Most times, patio doors and windows on these upper floors had been left unlocked; when they were secured, Mason used a glass cutter and suction cups to gain entrance, à la James Bond.

Create phantom listeners. Barking dogs were no deterrent, Mason says. Unafraid of dogs, he calmed growling canines with a calm hand-sniff, or led yapping pups into a bathroom and locked them in. "The smartest thing people can do to prevent being burglarized at home or in a hotel is to leave the TV or radio on while they're not there; this creates the illusion that someone is inside."

Buy the right lock. Mason recommends fortifying your house with a high-end Medeco lock. They are the hardest to break, he says, and that lock manufacturer, in his experience, is less likely than others to issue replacement pass keys on request.

Keep a low profile. Until he was nabbed, Mason frequently hit the homes of Palm Beach, Florida. He would identify targets by reading the society page of the local newspaper, then strike the afternoon of that evening's society ball—"when you know their jewels and clothing are laid out on the bed while they're at the hairdresser." His advice: Don't advertise when you won't be home.

Diversify. "Don't hide all your valuables in one place," counsels Mason. "Instead, scatter the goods, so when the thief finds a little stash, he'll think that's all there is and get out."

(and then a written contract from the one you hire) for each project to be undertaken—especially those that require longer than one day to complete. But don't fall for a common request made by many contractors: an up-front payment equaling one-third (or even one-half) of the contracted amount to "buy materials."

The R-value of a material such as insulation denotes how well that substance resists the passage of heat through it. The higher the R-value, the more energy-efficient the material.

"As a homeowner," says Silva, a second-generation contractor himself, "you never want to pay a contractor even a single dollar until all materials have been delivered to your home and have been inspected to be correct, and the work has begun. Any contractor who asks for money to 'buy materials' before starting the job should be seen as a red flag—good contractors have a credit line to buy those materials." His advice: Never pay more than one-third of the estimate until after the first day of work has been completed; do not pay the balance until the job's successful completion.

Cold-shoulder the contract shuffle. What happens when the job costs more or takes longer than what's spelled out on paper? With few exceptions, that's the contractor's fault. "You're hiring a contractor based partially on his expertise to make an accurate assessment of the job," notes Silva. "If he's underestimated his price or time to complete the job, you shouldn't be the one to pay for it."

This especially applies to new installations, repairs, and other jobs that harbor no hidden surprises—literally. This does not apply to behind-the-wall jobs, where unexpected damage may necessitate additional work, nor to excavation jobs, where unanticipated obstacles may be encountered at any time. (If you hit such a snag, discuss any additional payment or time with the contractor before the "new" work is undertaken).

If it's a straightforward job, on the other hand—a toilet installation or a simple addition, say—refuse to pay if the contractor ups the amount without citing reasons why. "Unless there are extreme circumstances," says Silva, "the contractor probably doesn't have a legal leg to stand on."

Your protection: To deflect a common contractor headache—jobs that take longer than expected—write a penalty clause into the contract. "Contractors are usually juggling several jobs at a time," says Silva, "so if he says it will take two weeks, I recommend this reply: 'I'll give you three weeks—but at the end of that time, if the job has not been completed to my satisfaction, I will deduct 20 percent from your final payment.'" Then formalize this agreement by writing that language into the contract. Any contractor who balks at this clause—a provision commonly invoked by savvy homeowners—has no intention of finishing on time and should be avoided.

Seek a written guarantee. It sounds like such a simple request: Will you guarantee your work? But most home repair or improvement jobs don't come with a warranty, so ask for one in writing. "Some guys will agree to that," says Silva, "but others won't." Contractors in the latter category, he notes, are only too happy to give you vague reassurances that they will take care of any problems related to the finished job. "This is why I advise homeowners to ask that a warranty be written into the contract."

What's reasonable? For minor jobs such as plumbing repairs or the installation of new parts, one year is customary. Major electrical, plumbing, and carpentry work, by contrast, should be guaranteed for at least three years on the workmanship; any appliances should be covered by their manufacturers.

Check insurance certificates. Most contractors will inform you they're covered out the wazoo, but to protect yourself you should ask them to furnish the proof. "Unless they can show you their workman's compensation certificate," Silva explains, "you could be socked with medical bills if someone gets

U-values rate the energy efficiency of combined materials, such as the glass, frame, and weatherstripping of a window. The lower the U-value, the more energy-efficient the composite material.

When shopping for windows, look for a U-rating of 0.35 or less in northern climes, 0.40 or less in a moderate climate, and 0.65 or less in Gulf Coast areas.

Avoid Pet Regrets

When good pets go bad, they may chew furniture, stain the carpet, or endanger your family. The following tips will help you keep your dog or cat from wreaking havoc on the household:

Flag the wag. When selecting a dog for possible adoption, a wagging tail does not necessarily denote a happy, loving pooch. "A wagging tail displays strong emotions of some kind," says Liz Palika, a dog trainer in Vista, California, who has written 50 pet books. "It could be the dog's way of displaying dominance or anger." *Hint:* Happy dogs are apt to wag their tails quickly, with the tail in a horizontal position; angry or less trainable dogs wag more slowly (but still consistently), with the tail held more vertical.

The fetch test. To gauge "trainability" when choosing a new pup, try this maneuver favored by guide-dog schools. "Toss a small toy or a crumpled piece of paper in front of a puppy about eight weeks old," advises Palika. "If he runs out and grabs it and brings back to you—or tries to—that's a good sign he wants to cooperate. Those who chase it and keep going are a bit too independent and may be harder to train. A dog who attacks the item is too intense."

Ease chewing anxiety. Older dogs, in particular, may chew furniture and other items to relieve stress, says Myrna Milani, D.V.M., a New Hampshire veterinarian who has written seven books on animal behavior. But what causes those frazzled nerves? "Just like with a stressed child," explains Dr. Milani, "you need to stay one step ahead." Distract the dog with toys or other acceptable outlets before the bad behavior surfaces. Dog-Appeasing Pheromone (DAP), a synthetic hormone, may also ease canine anxiety. Available at pet shops, DAP can be sprayed on furniture or used as a whole-room diffuser.

Tailor scratching posts. Cats claw furniture, says Dr. Milani, to keep their nails healthy or to mark their territory. Commercially sold scratching posts, with their thick carpet, may not satisfy the first need; the surface is too dense. If your pet cat is shredding your door or chair legs, provide a piece of bare wood or a split log as a scratching post; if it attacks the upholstery, buy a piece of similarly textured fabric to serve as a substitute victim. For added incentive, rub some catnip on the "new" post.

Spray away spraying problems. Many cats spray indoors at the mere sight or sound of other cats outside—especially during mating season. (The telltale signs appear near windows or doors.) Restricting your cat's exposure to the outdoor commotion (and potential competition) may help. Feliway, a product that mimics "friendly" feline pheromones, can be applied on problem areas.

injured on the job. The same goes for their proof of liability insurance: Make sure it covers the entire value of your home—not just the cost of the job or the room itself."

Contractors should carry these documents with them; you can run off copies if you have a home printer. If a handyman is able to produce this paperwork on the spot, make sure you check the expiration date on any certificate, bond, or license he submits for your inspection. If he cannot produce the requested paperwork, inform him you must have copies in hand before you will allow any work to begin.

Holding your ground now is a smart way to avoid holding the bag later, when you look up from your morning coffee to discover that the foreman's 17-year-old son has just driven a backhoe through your living-room wall.

Scrutinize license plates. Mirror, mirror, on the wall, who's the most fraudulent scamster of all? The crown goes to those ripoff repairmen who knock on your front door, offering their services for some urgently needed repair they just happened to spot while driving by.

Ripoff tip-off: Check their truck's license plate. If it's out of state or even from a distant county (assuming you live in a state where tags indicate the county of residence), the smart money says you're talking to a fly-by-night operator, warns New Jersey home inspector Tom Kraeutler. "Good repairmen don't need to drive several hours for your home repair. And they don't go door to door."

Of course, even repairmen that you contact on your own initiative may try to talk you into unnecessary repairs. A chimney sweep, for instance, might tell you that your fireplace is unsafe, or that it needs a new liner. But unless you have clear-cut problems—large, visible cracks, for example, or loose or missing masonry—it's probably a scam, says Kraeutler, who hosts a nationally syndicated radio home fix-it program, *The Money Pit.*

Although any contractor can try to push your panic button

for a quick repair, be especially wary of high-end projects. Before you agree to "waterproof" your basement—it can cost $25,000—check to make sure that your gutters are long enough to drain at least five feet from your home, and that the sump pump is working. Before you accept the "need" to replace a nonleaking roof, get multiple bids to ensure it truly merits repair. Finally, never okay tree-trimming bids until you have clarified that the quoted price is for the entire tree; one common scam among shady tree trimmers is to offer a bargain rate—only to inform homeowners after job completion that it was on a per-limb basis.

CREDIT CARDS
Save Paper on Your Plastic

3

IN THE BAD OLD DAYS, charging interest rates as high as 30 percent on "fronted" money was the exclusive preserve of thumb-breaking loan sharks. Today it is done by credit-card companies that leave your digits intact but employ hands-on tactics to break something else of vital interest: your bank account.

As the credit-card industry enjoys $30 billion in annual gross revenues, the average debt per U.S. household from using plastic rather than paper nears $10,000—more than triple its average during the early 1990s. In addition to the double-digit interest rates that cardholders must pay when they commit the sin of carrying a balance (as 60 percent of American cardholders do), plastic users get hit with $24 billion a year in credit-card fees. These include nearly $15 billion a year in late and over-limit penalties, $6 billion a year in cash-advance charges, and $3.5 billion in annual fees for the "privilege" of using the cards.

Nor does the gouging end there. You may be charged additional penalties for not using your card. You may fall victim to legally sanctioned bait-and-switch offers. And, in a twist that drops Ebenezer Scrooge straight into *Brave New World,* you may incur penalties that raise your card interest rate even if you pay your bill on time but are late with a payment to an entirely different company. By the same tortured token, paying your credit card late can increase the fees you are assessed on those other, seemingly unrelated accounts.

Yet the American love affair with debt and debit spending rages unabated. With nearly 1.3 billion of the 2-by-3.5-inch plastic rectangles in circulation, credit cards now outnumber U.S. adults 6 to 1. Indeed, they have surpassed checks as the preferred method of noncash payments: In 2003, credit cards, debit cards that deduct charges instantaneously from your savings or checking account, and other electronic payments constituted 54 percent of all noncash payments; checks accounted for only 45 percent.

So how can you save money while enjoying the convenience—and, all too often, the necessity—of using plastic? To find out, read on.

Tricks of the Credit-Card Trade

The "preapproved" bait-and-switch. The typical American household receives eight credit-card offers each month. Typically these tout low, "preapproved" interest rates; rewards in the form of frequent-flier miles, store discounts, or cash back; or a credit line fit for a Saudi prince.

But what does "preapproved" really mean? "That you have been preapproved to have your credit history *reviewed for consideration* of that offer," says consumer watchdog Ed Mierzwinski of the U.S. Public Interest Research Group (U.S. PIRG), a national advocacy organization in Washington, D.C. "And based on that review, more often than not, the card you get will probably differ from the offer you got in the mail."

Read the fine print: "The big print may advertise an interest rate of 8.9 percent," says Robert McKinley, founder and CEO of CardWeb.com, a leading payment card research firm. "But in the small print, it says the card you get may in fact be anywhere from 8.9 to 22.9 percent—depending on an evaluation of your credit history." The determination of who lands that great rate is frequently subjective. People with

---

Why do so many credit-card bills seem to originate in Delaware, South Dakota, or Utah?

All three states have weak or nonexistent usury laws. That means there's no cap on the interest rate that can be charged by companies operating within their borders. Other states that are home to the 10 largest card issuers include Arizona, New Hampshire, and Virginia.

"excellent" credit scores are still sometimes issued cards at higher-than-advertised rates.

What happens? "People get enticed by an offer for a 0 percent card or a $50,000 credit line, and they mail off the application," says Mierzwinski. "They're approved, they receive a new card, and they activate it. What they don't realize until they start carrying a balance is that the terms of the card they received differ from those of the preapproved offer they first got in the mail."

Your protection: Do the obvious: Before submitting any

PROTECTIVE DETECTIVE

Credit-Card Insurance? Not So Sure!

There are two types of credit-card "insurance." According to consumer experts, one is useless and the other may have limited value.

Many credit-card companies sell credit-card theft insurance as protection against fraudulent purchases if your card is lost or stolen. But that insurance is essentially redundant: Federal law holds you liable for only $50 in bogus buys if your card falls into the wrong hands. Not only that, but most credit-card companies waive that fee if a card is reported missing within two days.

The other type of credit insurance ensures that some or all of your outstanding balance will be paid if you lose your job, become disabled, or die. But this credit life insurance, as it is called, has a sumptuous price. The average rate is 75 cents for each $100 of loan coverage, meaning that if you carry a balance of $3,000, your monthly premium will run about $22, or $264 a year. A 2000 study by the Consumer Federation of America found that for each dollar customers paid in credit-insurance premiums, they received only 34 cents in benefits. That's barely half the minimum 60 percent benefits-to-premium ratio recommended by the National Association of Insurance Commissioners.

Although credit life insurance pays the balance remaining if the borrower dies, credit disability insurance and credit unemployment insurance pay only the minimum monthly amount (typically 4 percent of your balance) for a specified number of months. A fourth variety—credit property insurance—pays to repair or replace items bought on that card. Many consumer advocates advise against buying credit insurance of any type.

▶ A BETTER WAY

Low Profile = High Score

Your credit-card interest rate, like that of other loans you secure, is dictated largely by your FICO (Fair Isaac Corporation) credit score, usually between 300 and 850 (the higher the better).

But what determines that score? Roughly one-third of it is based on your past payment history, another third on the amount you owe, and the remaining third on your length of credit history, new credit, and types of credit used.

To maintain or improve your score, take these steps:

• *Pay all your bills* on time, or even early.

• *Regularly pay* at least half your outstanding credit-card balances.

• *Don't open* too many new charge accounts.

• *Prevent collection-agency* accounts that can result from overdue library books, unpaid parking tickets, or other seemingly trivial bills.

application, says McKinley, read the fine print. "Use a magnifying glass if you have to," he says. "And you may have to do just that, because credit issuers don't make it easy for you." (Some card applications, in fact, "hide" these terms using type sizes as tiny as 7 points—about this small.) "Avoid any offer," McKinley suggests, "with a fuzzy or broad range in advertised interest rates; it should be a firm number or a relatively small range, and its high range should be within just a few percentage points of what's mentioned in the big print."

Also take note of any "introductory periods." Attractive offers may expire after a few short months, at which point the card issuer can play catchup with a higher-than-average interest rate and additional fees. Before you submit your application, make a copy of its terms and conditions. Then, once you receive the card you applied for, compare its terms to those in the original offer; if the two don't match, urges McKinley, do not activate the card—and let the company know you'll drop their card unless you are granted the advertised terms.

The fixed-rate follies. Despite the promise inherent in its name, a "fixed" interest rate is often anything but. "As it says in the small print," notes U.S. PIRG's Mierzwinski, "it can be changed at any time and for any reason at the issuer's discretion—including if you're not using that card as often as you did in the past or if you start charging more on a competitor's card, which they can learn by reviewing your credit report."

And it's done all the time, he adds, because the only thing a card issuer must legally do before raising a so-called "fixed" rate is give you 15 days' notice. "They typically bury that notification in promotional material or other junk mail that most people don't read," adds Mierzwinski.

In one common ploy, a low "fixed" interest rate offered on a new card entices you to apply for that card, or to move a balance from another card to that account. Once you've made the shift, however, that supposedly fixed interest rate miraculously shoots up—often just months later.

Your protection: If you notice a higher interest rate—you can detect one by scrutinizing each monthly invoice—do what most cardholders don't: Call and ask for a lower rate. One study by Mierzwinski's nonprofit group found that most of the cardholders who requested a lower interest rate from a credit-card company got it. Their rates dropped from an average of 16 percent to about 10.5 percent.

Here are the main criteria that dictated who received the lower rates: Being deemed a loyal customer who frequently used that particular card; having a high credit limit; and not "maxing out" that card or any others.

"Although it's not as easy as it used to be to simply call for a lower interest rate, it can be done—and often is," says Howard Strong, a California attorney who has handled several class-action lawsuits against credit-card companies.

"Tell them that you've received some offers in the mail that look attractive," advises Strong. "Then say, 'What can you do for me to stay with you?'" This ploy works best for cardholders who have a good credit history and make it clear they're not easily swayed by reward programs such as frequent-flier miles. "Banks issuing credit cards see reward programs such as free air miles as a gold mine," says Strong, author of *What Every Credit Card User Needs to Know.* "They think people will jump through any hoop to keep accumulating these rewards. But if you convince them otherwise—that there's a better offer out there, or that you're more interested in lower rates than in rewards—it can work in your favor."

Late-fee loopholes. If you're late paying your credit card bill—even by a few hours—you can be penalized in several ways.

- *You are charged* a late fee, which now averages $33—nearly three times higher than a decade ago.

- *A late payment* can wipe out any rewards—cash back or air miles, for example—you may have accumulated on the card. If it doesn't erase them altogether, the late payment may hold those rewards hostage until you pay a reinstatement fee, which can run as high as $100.

- *Less publicized* is the fact that a single tardy payment can trigger an automatic increase in your card's interest rate. In most instances your rate will jump 10 percentage points or more above its pre-late rate, but bleed-you-dry "default" interest rates of 30 percent are not unknown. "Some people see their interest rate triple after just one late payment," says Mierzwinski. "It usually stays at that higher rate for about one year."

Threaten to close your account and you can often get the late fee waived—especially if you have been a prompt payer until now. The punitive APR increase, by contrast, usually remains in effect—information not clearly stated, says Mierzwinski, to cardholders who get a late fee dropped.

Your protection: The easy way to avoid late-fee penalties is to pay on time. That's getting increasingly difficult, however, thanks to shortened payment deadlines; they now average 20 days from the date an invoice is mailed, down from 27 days a decade ago. No wonder an estimated 60 percent of cardholders were charged a late fee in 2004.

"Many issuers have also imposed strict hour deadlines for the due date," adds card maven McKinley. So even if your

---

Hate high late fees? Tell it to the U.S. Supreme Court! In 1996, when late fees averaged $5 to $10, the court lifted the restrictions then in place on late-payment penalties. Within months, most late fees doubled.

Credit-Card Counseling

SOME NINE MILLION Americans turn to credit counselors each year for help in whittling down the mountain of debt they have amassed. At any one time, two million are enrolled in active credit-repair programs.

But not every counselor is there to help. Some self-styled "experts" only compound your problems, offering improper advice, engaging in deceptive practices, or charging exorbitant fees. In fact, in March 2005 the Federal Trade Commission accused three consumer debt-services companies of cheating financially strapped clients out of some $100 million. Those companies—National Consumer Council, Inc. (in California), Debt Management Foundation Services (in Florida), and Better Budget Financial Services (based in Massachusetts)—paid a settlement of $6 million for promising easy debt relief that sometimes did the opposite: It forced their customers into bankruptcy.

So how do you identify a creditable credit counselor? The steps below should help you find one.

Don't get suckered by status. Nearly every agency in the business claims it has nonprofit, tax-exempt status. That doesn't mean a counseling firm won't charge you high fees, says the Consumer Federation of America (CFA), which did a pioneering study of the practices of credit counselors in 2003. Avoid any agency, says the CFA, that charges more than $50 in "set-up" charges for credit counseling. Likewise shun any outfit charging monthly fees above $25. The CFA also warns against using a counselor who works on commission—agencies may not reveal this fact—or any agency that claims to offer "voluntary" or sliding-scale payment; the likelihood is high it will later pressure you to pay "full price." All terms should be written out in your initial consultations.

Demand accreditation. The National Foundation for Credit Counseling is the largest and most respected network of credit counselors. The foundation requires its member businesses to undergo an accreditation process performed by a third-party organization such as the Council on Accreditation.

Many NFCC members operate under the name Consumer Credit Counseling Services (CCCS). For accredited counselors in your area, contact the NFCC at 800-388-2227 or visit www.nfcc.org.

Expect a careful review. Count on receiving individualized counseling. Any agency that takes less than 30 minutes to interview you or review your finances before developing a debt consolidation plan is not reliably deliberate; take your business elsewhere. In addition, resist being hustled into a one-size-fits-all consolidation plan pushed by the firm.

payment is received by the due date, you'll likely get penalized if the credit-card company doesn't process your payment by the due *time*—say, 11 a.m. or 1 p.m. of the due date. Some deadline hours come and go before the mail is delivered to that processing center, making the true due date a full day earlier.

Deadline hours may be posted on the invoice, or in the small print of your "terms and conditions" statement. But the best way to protect against any possibility of a late payment is to make two payments in a single one-month billing cycle. "I recommend making a copy of the invoice slip as soon as you get the bill," says McKinley. "Then, immediately mail in some payment—if only the minimum required to prevent a late fee. Send a second payment a few weeks later, closer to the due date." In addition to staving off late penalties, paying twice each month—even if the total amount equals a single payment sent later in the month—helps lower finance charges. Why? Because interest is calculated on each day you carry any outstanding balance—including purchases you make after the invoice is mailed.

- *You can also beat the clock* by paying with a phoned-in "demand draft," in which you provide your checking account number and the bank's routing number (that's the nine-digit number on the lower left of your checks). These payments usually post within two days—but some credit-card companies charge up to $15 for each one.

- *Give yourself at least three days* before the due date when making online payments, either directly to the credit-card company or through an online bank account.

- *Don't depend on beating late penalties* by sending an 11th-hour package via overnight delivery. "In the small print of your contract," warns Mierzwinski, "the card issuer often discloses that it doesn't accept overnight packages at the same address as snail-mail payments. You may need to call Customer Service to find the right address."

The universal default clause. Even if you pay your credit card bills on time, most issuers will raise your interest rate if

What the New Minimum Means

To the lucky minority of credit-card users who pay their balance in full each month, an increase in the minimum payment—which most issuers began in 2005—means little. But to "revolvers" who carry a balance, the higher minimum may be a welcome way to save you from yourself. Still, the card companies' motives may be less then altruistic: According to the Bankruptcy Abuse Prevention and Consumer Protection Act of 2005,

credit-card companies must post Surgeon General–style warnings on monthly statements, notifying customers how long they will remain in debt if they make no more than the minimum payment.

Let's say you have a $3,000 balance but have shelved the card in a fit of steely resolve to pay off the bill. If you pay only the minimum amount each month, here's the difference in how fast the old and new rates will get you to your goal:

2 Percent Minimum Monthly Payment			4 Percent Minimum Monthly Payment	
APR	Interest Paid	Time to Pay Off	Interest Paid	Time to Pay Off
17%	$6,447	32 years, 9 months	$1,558	10 years, 6 months
16%	$5,329	29 years, 3 months	$1,431	10 years, 3 months
15%	$4,456	26 years, 5 months	$1,302	10 years
14%	$3,755	24 years, 2 months	$1,180	9 years, 8 months
13%	$3,179	22 years, 3 months	$1,065	9 years, 6 months
12%	$2,697	20 years, 7 months	$ 956	9 years, 3 months
11%	$2,287	19 years, 4 months	$ 852	9 years
10%	$1,935	18 years, 2 months	$ 755	8 years, 9 months
9%	$1,629	17 years, 2 months	$ 662	8 years, 6 months
8%	$1,360	16 years, 3 months	$ 574	8 years, 5 months

you are late with other payments, such as those for your mortgage, insurance, car, or cellular phone service. That's because of the latest onerous ploy to be heaped on the back of the American consumer: universal default, quietly introduced by credit-card companies about five years ago after an intense (and successful) lobbying campaign of bank-friendly legislators. Universal default allows virtually any late payment reported to a credit agency to trigger across-the-board interest-rate hikes and added fees in bills sent to the late payor.

"A year ago, I'd say the most egregious penalty from being late with your credit-card payment was the tripling of its interest rate—which, if you carry a sizable balance, can add 10 years of interest payments," says Heather McGhee, a former employee of the New York public policy research group Demos. "Today, with universal default, if you're late paying your credit-card bill, your insurance, mortgage, or car loan rates can increase as well." Auto insurance premiums, to cite just one example of this outrageous practice, can rise as much as 50 percent in reaction to the fact that you have made a late payment to some other company. Why? Because, insurers maintain, more claims are filed by drivers with blemishes on their credit history. Indeed, most auto-insurance companies now check for late payments in the course of considering new customers for coverage.

Your protection: Make sure you mail your payment for every bill at least 10 days before its due date. Even online payments should be made three days before their deadline. Why such extreme caution? Because you don't want to give

---

Debt-Free Is 12 Steps Away

Compulsive overchargers and other chronic debtors can seek relief in 12-step programs tailored to their unique situation and needs. Both of the programs listed below are modeled after self-help groups such as Alcoholics Anonymous.

Debtors Anonymous, started in 1976, has some 5,200 groups worldwide. 781-453-2743; www.debtorsanonymous.org

Spenders Anonymous runs support meetings in select states. www.spenders.org

card issuers any excuse to exercise their universal default option—which, says Mierzwinski, more than doubles a credit-card interest rate after the second late payment made toward a mortgage, car loan, or other obligation. "Increasingly, however, credit-card companies are invoking the universal default clause after just one late payment," he says.

The only late payments that may spare you the indignity of universal default are those you might make to a utility; gas, electric, and water companies traditionally do not report late payments to the "big three" consumer reporting companies (Experian, Equifax, and TransUnion). Of course, their penalties may be even more painful: "They just shut off your service if you default," Mierzwinski adds.

Two-cycle billing. Never mind that you normally pay off your entire credit-card balance each month. Two-cycle billing can slam you with steep finance charges on those rare and unfortunate instances when you pay only a portion of the total amount due. With two-cycle billing, if you carry any balance at any time, finance charges are calculated over the previous two months—even if you had a balance of zero during the month previous.

Example: Let's say you start December with a zero balance, then begin using your credit card on December 8, in a new monthly cycle. In early January, when the bill arrives for that cycle, you opt not to pay off the entire balance.

Under the traditional method of computing average daily balance, the fact that you started December with no carryover balance would keep the interest clock from beginning to tick on January 1 with the new cycle. So the bill that arrives in early February would reflect charges levied only on the daily balance through the month of January, minus any payments.

Under two-cycle billing, by contrast, that February bill would include finance charges levied on your average daily balance going all the way back to December 8—the day your account lost its zero balance.

"Two-cycle billing doesn't mean you're paying double interest," says CardWeb.com's McKinley. "But it does mean you're paying extra interest; they're recapturing charges for carrying any balance from that previous month's purchases. If you don't consistently pay off your entire balance, avoid two-cycle cards." Two-cycle billing is usually noted in the "Terms and Conditions" statement of your credit card, and possibly on the monthly invoice. If you're unsure, contact your card issuer—and find a card with one-cycle billing.

Avoid Common Cardholder Mistakes

Be elastic with plastic. Credit-card companies want to make money from your use of their cards, but they have figured out a way to do that even if you keep your cards nailed to a board. If you haven't swiped your card for at least six months, expect an "inactivity charge" of up to $15. It's like a company fine for your fiscal discipline.

Keep tabs on the activation anniversary. Immediately upon receiving a new credit card with a low introductory rate, mark on your calendar the date that rate ends. "Some low introductory rates last a year or so," says McKinley, "but most typically expire within a few months. Credit-card companies count on your falling asleep at the switch when that low rate ends—and at least half of all cardholders do, then fail to bail out of that card when the rate goes up." The better-deal cards typically have an initial grace period of about 12 months, after which they may jump from a 0 percent introductory rate to only 8 or 9 percent. Less-attractive arrangements tease you with 0 percent for only three months or so, after which they zoom to 17 to 22 percent.

Because frequently canceling or switching charge accounts can damage your credit score, don't simply shred the card upon the expiration of its low introductory rate; instead, use it extremely judiciously once the higher rate takes effect.

Debit-Card Don'ts

Because a debit card lets you make purchases with money in your bank account, it offers the convenience of not having to carry cash and the security of not borrowing funds. But this particular plastic—which has surpassed the personal check in popularity and is rapidly eclipsing cash—has its own pitfalls, detailed below.

Lack of protection. If your credit card is lost or stolen and then used fraudulently, you could be liable for only $50 (most credit-card companies won't charge even that). If your debit card falls into the wrong hands, however, you're liable for up to $500 in fraudulent charges unless you notify your bank of the card's disappearance within two days. Meanwhile, the thief can drain your bank account via the nearest ATM, and the bank may require 10 days or longer to investigate and refund your money. During that time, obviously, your bank account may lack the funds needed to cover any number of checks you blithely wrote in the meantime. The result: a self-reinforcing cascade of bounced-check charges.

Hidden fees. When using debit cards abroad, expect to be hit with service fees on each purchase—but be aware they can be assessed domestically as well. A 2004 survey by the New York Public Interest Research Group found that nearly 9 in 10 banks charged debit purchasers as much as $1.50 for each "online" transaction—defined by the banking industry as any transaction that requires authorization with the customer's personal identification number, or PIN. This doesn't necessarily mean you'll be charged a service fee every single time you enter your PIN for a debit purchase, but New York PIRG found the fee unlikely to be assessed for "offline" transactions (those requiring a signature but no PIN).

Busting your balance. If you don't have overdraft protection on your bank accounts, making a debit-charge purchase that exceeds the funds available in your account—even by a few cents—will likely trigger a penalty of $25 or more. If you do have overdraft protection, by contrast, you'll still get penalized—but in those cases the penalty is usually much lower.

Aside from that minimal safeguard, says AARP consumer advocate Sally Hurme, overdraft protection is a decidedly mixed bag. "Banks are pushing people into loans via this so-called 'protection,'" says Hurme. "One easily overlooked liability of overdraft protection is that the bank often includes the amount of your overdraft protection in the 'available balance' figure it cites you. This encourages you to unknowingly tap into your overdraft balance, incurring both an overdraft fee and interest."

Even better, if you meet the provider's definition of a good customer—that is, you frequently use the card and you pay your bills on time—don't hesitate to call the issuer and explain that you need a lower rate in order to keep it as your primary-use card. Loath to lose a loyal, on-time customer, many an issuer will lower the increased rate in response to this plea.

Break into a credit union. Profession-based or company credit unions typically issue no-reward credit cards at interest rates 2 to 4 percent below those offered by banks, says McKinley. But a common misconception—that you must be in that profession or employed by that company to join its

▶ **A BETTER WAY**

Make Those Payments Pay Off!

Most credit-card holders are "revolvers," meaning they usually carry some balance from one month to the next. If you are among them, you probably know that paying only the minimum monthly amount of your outstanding balance gets you nowhere fast.

After federal agencies pressured the banking industry to boost minimum payments, many card issuers raised the minimum payment on account balances to 4 percent from the previous 2 percent (see sidebar, page 95). Even at the new, widely used (but hardly universal) 4 percent rate, it would still take nearly 11 years and $1,756 in interest payments to discharge a $4,000 balance on a card with a 15 percent interest rate. But that's a big improvement over

the 30 years and $6,123 in interest it would have taken to pay off that debt at the old 2 percent monthly minimum.

So how much should you pay each month? Obviously, the more the better.

"Paying 5 percent each month may prevent damage to your credit rating," says credit-card guru Robert McKinley, founder of CardWeb.com, a leading research firm. "But it will still take you a long time to pay off your balance."

McKinley's advice: Pay at least 10 percent of the balance every month; that will shave more than a decade from the time it takes to liquidate a four-figure account balance. To get real payoff numbers on your account, visit CardWeb's Card Calculator at www.cardweb.com/cardtrak/calc/payment.amp.

credit union—causes these great credit-card deals to go largely unclaimed. "The laws were changed a few years ago," says attorney Strong, "so just about anybody can join a credit union and get its lower-rate credit cards." Case in point: "I don't work at, nor did I ever attend, California State University, Northridge," notes Strong. "But I joined its credit union because it has good credit-card rates."

Most credit-union cards don't offer frills such as reward points, but at the same time they're less likely to include a binding mandatory arbitration (BMA) clause—a small-print loophole that forces consumers, often without their knowledge, to waive their right to sue. When bound by a BMA clause, you must settle any dispute with the card issuer at your own cost, through arbitration. "With BMA clauses," says attorney Ira Rheingold of the National Association of Consumer Advocates, "customers lose the opportunity to go to court—and credit-card issuers and other companies can continue their deceptive and fraudulent behavior and not be held accountable for it." Charge cards issued by credit unions—as well as the AARP credit card and some by smaller banks—are virtually the only ones that do not insert BMA clauses in their customer agreements.

Obviously, the first place to check is with your employer. Failing that, seek out a professional or trade association to which you or a neighbor belongs. Some credit unions, such as the one Strong joined, offer a "community" field of membership, so ask your neighbors which one they belong to, or check the Yellow Pages for credit unions in your community. In addition, the Credit Union National Association, which represents 90 percent of the nation's credit unions, offers a locator on its website at www.creditunion.coop.

Beware the balance transfer fee. It's a tempting offer: A letter arrives offering to let you move your credit-card balance from its current high rate of interest to a card that charges a lower rate. Look before you leap at that "great deal," however.

In particular, scrutinize the fine print that explains the fees associated with the shift.

"I fell victim to this blandishment myself when I got an offer for a 0 percent balance transfer," says credit-card expert McKinley. "I used it to transfer the maximum $5,000 amount allowed, but failed to notice the small-print $35 transfer fee. When I got my first statement, I realized that fee had put me over the credit limit—which in turn triggered an additional $50 penalty." These fees—typically $35 to $50—should first be subtracted from the amount you plan to transfer, especially if it's the maximum allowed. In addition, that irresistible 0 percent rate applies only to the balance transferred—not to any new charges you put on the new card.

"Rewards" That Don't

Don't get railroaded by free airplane miles. Among the most popular "reward" cards are those that promise free air miles—typically, one mile earned for every dollar charged. But if you're one of the 2 in 3 Americans who carries a credit-card balance, this popular plastic may be taking you for a different kind of ride.

According to McKinley, airline-sponsored reward cards typically charge interest that is 6 percentage points higher than the no-reward cards issued by the same bank. Their annual fees are higher, too—by an average of $51. It all adds up: If you carry a $3,000 credit-card balance for two years—the time it takes the average consumer to accumulate enough miles for a free ticket—you will shell out nearly $500 more in fees and finance charges than if you had made the same purchases on a no-rewards card.

Not much better are reward cards that offer free miles on the carrier of your choice. Although they routinely offer lower interest rates and annual fees than cards sponsored by a specific airline, they impose more restrictions on redeeming the reward. "You often have to accumulate more miles to get a

In the parallel universe that is the credit-card industry, a "deadbeat" is a customer who pays his or her bill in full each month. This deprives the card issuer of interest that accumulates on unpaid balances.

free ticket on those cards," says McKinley. "For instance, you might need 100,000 miles/points on a generic card, compared with 40,000 for a card sponsored by a single airline, before you can 'earn' a complimentary international ticket. They also tend to come with additional restrictions, such as blackout dates, bans on overseas flights, or refusals to grant nonstop tickets."

Your protection: If you pay off your balance each month, free mileage cards can be a good way to score some R&R payback on your plastic purchases. If you tend to carry a balance, however, fly a different route—that is, switch to a lower-rate, no-rewards card.

Retreat from cash advances. Some credit cards tantalize you with the seeming convenience of a cash advance. You may be able to obtain this loan—that's what it is, after all—simply by flourishing your credit card at a bank or ATM. Another common way of accessing this easy money is by redeeming checks mailed to you by the card issuer.

The cash advances described above are handled differently from credit purchases, and they can hurt you in three ways:

- *You can be charged a fee* of 2 to 4 percent of the borrowed amount.

- *You are socked with* a substantially higher interest rate—10 percent higher or more—on that borrowed money than on your credit purchases.

- *Payments made on your account* are often applied first to the lower-rate credit purchases and outstanding balance; only after that balance has been paid does any portion of your payment chisel away those more profitable (to the bank, that is) cash advances.

Your protection: Cash-advance fees net the credit-card industry some $6 billion each year. The best way to avoid them is—you guessed it—never to use your credit card for

By 2009, predicts market researcher Packaged Facts, 85 percent of credit cards will offer some reward for use.

Which type of card is truly rewarding? Cash-back programs trump those that confer frequent-flier miles. The former typically have no redemption restrictions, they allow for easier tracking of rewards, and—unlike mileage points—they tend not to expire.

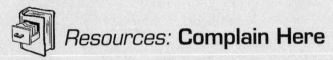

Resources: Complain Here

IF YOU BELIEVE you've been the victim of excessive interest-rate hikes or other penalties, try to resolve the situation with your credit-card company first. If that doesn't work, you can file a complaint with your state attorney general's office, or contact one of the following agencies.

For cards issued by state banks that are members of the Federal Reserve System:

**Federal Reserve Board
Division of Consumer
and Community Affairs**

Mail Stop 801
Washington, D.C. 20551
202-452-3693
www.federalreserve.gov

For cards issued by state banks that are not members of the Federal Reserve System:

**Federal Deposit Insurance Corporation
Consumer Response Center**

2345 Grand Boulevard, Suite 100
Kansas City, Missouri 64108
800-378-9581
www.fdic.gov

For cards issued by banks with "national" or "N.A." in their name:

**Comptroller of the Currency
Customer Assistance Unit**

1301 McKinney Street, Suite 3450
Houston, Texas 77010
800-613-6743
www.occ.treas.gov

For cards issued by federal savings and loan associations and federal savings banks:

**Office of Thrift Supervision
Consumer Programs**

1700 G Street NW
Washington, D.C. 20552
800-842-6929
www.ots.treas.gov

For cards issued by finance companies or stores:

**Federal Trade Commission
Consumer Response Center**

600 Pennsylvania Avenue NW
Washington, D.C. 20580
877-382-4357
www.ftc.gov

For cards issued by federal credit unions:

**National Credit Union
Administration
Consumer Complaints**

1775 Duke Street
Alexandria, Virginia 22314-3428
703-518-6330
www.ncua.gov

pocket money. Instead, land a lower-rate loan from your bank or credit union.

That $6 billion a year reaped from cash-advance fees isn't the only reason credit-card companies gladly send you those courtesy checks. Knowing that many cardholders consider them to be junk mail and will likely toss or shred them, these checks can be great places to bury notifications of unpleasant changes to your account. "The card issuer sends a letter saying, 'Here are some bank checks you can use for your convenience,' says McKinley. "Then, in smaller print, they casually mention they're raising fees."

Instructing a credit-card company never to send you cash-advance checks is a good idea—for two reasons. For one, this opting out robs mail-stealing or Dumpster-diving identity thieves of an easy way to plunder your account. (Consequently, always shred—never toss—all cash-advance checks or other pre-approved credit offers.) For another, it forces the card issuer to notify you of any changes to your account in more prominent notices mailed with your bill. To cancel the double-edged "convenience" of these checks, simply notify the card issuer. You can also opt out of preapproved credit offers by calling 888-567-8688 (888-5-OPT-OUT).

Shop with co-branding. It happens every day at America's

PROTECTIVE DETECTIVE

Using Plastic Abroad

A once-reliable axiom—that plastic is your best friend abroad—may be going the way of human telephone operators. Although charging your way through a foreign country offers fewer hassles—both during your travels and afterward in the event there's a problem or you want to make a return—extra fees may erase any possible savings.

Many credit-card issuers now impose a 2 percent fee on card purchases made outside the United States. That's in addition to the 1 percent currency exchange fee levied by Visa and MasterCard. Meanwhile, debit-card issuers charge up to a 2.5 percent fee for debit purchases—and a service fee as high as $3 each time a customer uses a debit card to get cash from an overseas ATM. These fees vary from bank to bank.

The new advice: When traveling abroad, use credit cards for major purchases—they offer better security. for virtually everything else, pay cash or use traveler's checks. Some merchants and smaller hotels offer discounts for cash-paying travelers.

malls and shopping meccas: Items in hand, a customer heads to the register, there to be greeted with a "great opportunity" from the sales clerk: If the consumer signs up for a store credit card on the spot, everything purchased that day—sometimes that entire week—will be discounted 10 to 20 percent. Ten minutes later, the shopper leaves the store with a new line of credit, buoyed by promises of reward points or other sales incentives—and burdened with one of the highest interest rates in the land.

The average interest rate on store-issued credit cards is a whopping 21 percent. Some exceed 30 percent—a usurious rate that quickly wipes out those "signing bonuses" if you carry a balance. Accumulating a fistful of store cards can also harm your credit score: It makes the credit-scoring formula "believe" you have access to too much credit—even if you come nowhere near to maxing it out.

Your protection: Check out lesser-publicized "store" credit cards that are specifically co-branded with Visa or Master-Card. Often these offer the same store-loyalty rewards, but at far lower interest rates. In early 2005, for instance, Target's regular store credit card was hovering around 21 percent interest; its co-branded card with Visa, meanwhile, was at 9.9 percent—one-half the rate of its regular store card. The only downside, according to McKinley: "The regular store cards may make it easier to return merchandise or learn about special closed sales."

TELEPHONE SERVICE

Be a Talking Tightwad

WHEN THE FEDERAL GOVERNMENT set out to deregulate phone service in 1984, experts predicted that the increased competition would drive down costs. In a way, they were right. Average long-distance rates have fallen from 51 cents per minute (adjusted for inflation) to about 10 cents today. Local calls, too, have dropped slightly in price—the result of competition that remains fierce, with smaller service providers fighting to wrest business from telecom titans.

Why, then, have phone bills increased 200 to 400 percent in some U.S. states since 1984? Largely because of the government-mandated breakup of "monopolistic" AT&T, which ushered in a slew of regulator-blessed surcharges and add-ons that pad your phone bill.

From the first page of that bill to the last, once-standard services seem to have morphed into privileges. Take the seemingly simple step of dialing directory assistance. No longer covered by your overall monthly bill, a single request to locate a telephone number can now cost you more than a long-distance call. Telephone "rental"—another service provided free of charge in the halcyon days before deregulation—can add hundreds of dollars to your annual outlay for telephone service. Yet approximately one million consumers continue to pay this monthly charge to lease their telephone from a phone company. Perhaps most egregious of all are those official-sounding line items—"Universal Service Charge," "Carrier Cost Recovery Charge," and so on—designed to hide the fact that the phone company is charging you for its own business costs. These and other surcharges, you've no doubt noticed, can easily add $20 a month to a "landline" calling plan advertised as a flat rate of, say, $59.99 a month.

It doesn't end there. If you request a single bill for your landline and cellular service from the same provider, count on paying an additional "Single Bill Fee" for the convenience. If you don't use all the long-distance minutes on your service plan, you may be charged for those calls anyway, thanks to the "Monthly Minimum Usage Charge" assessed on some bills. And who can forget the "Monthly Service Fee," a charge you pay simply for subscribing to certain long-distance services, regardless of how many calls you make?

Unless you name the long-distance calling plan you want, your phone company will charge you its highest per-minute rate. Your inaction can cost you three times more than had you specified a plan.

All of these surcharges are perfectly legal, but rarely are they mentioned to consumers shopping for telephone service. Perhaps the providers don't wish to spotlight some sobering arithmetic: These added fees can raise the typical monthly phone bill by up to 35 percent.

In addition to such licit scalping, you'll want to watch out for the wealth of unlawful billing scams perpetrated by budding "en-trap-eneurs." Many of these have flourished in the laissez-faire environment born of deregulation. They range from dollars-per-minute "trick" numbers to the illegal acts known as "slamming" and "cramming," in which your phone bill is inflated with unauthorized or bogus charges.

The very latest way to get taken for your talk: The bountiful options and complex pricing plans of cellular service can easily swell a "$59 monthly calling plan" to $100 or more—thanks to another set of surcharges and extra costs that hinge on how and when you use your cell phone.

As a result of these and other market forces, telecom analyst Bruce Kushnick estimated in 2005, 15 to 25 percent of the households in any given state are signed up for the wrong telephone package. Here's the 411 to keep you from joining them.

Save on Stamps—and Money

Instead of writing a monthly check, pay your phone bill with a credit card or other automatic deduction to save money—beyond the cost of a stamp. Phone firms get faster and more regular payments this way, so they save on manpower and mailing costs. Some will waive monthly service fees or discount the long-distance rates of customers who charge their monthly bill to a credit card, PayPal, or other automatic-deduction plan.

These cost-saving options do not get the marketing attention of the latest rates or calling-plan offerings. Contact your service provider to find out what alternative payment options it offers.

Another bonus that accrues from paying by credit card: The money you spend on phone service can earn you "cash back" or frequent-flier miles tied to that card. "If there's a problem with your phone bill, your credit-card company can help you resolve it," adds phone service watchdog Marc-David Seidel, Ph.D., of the University of British Columbia's Sauder School of Business.

Post-Deregulation Surprises

Do your own directory assistance. When Ma Bell was still alive, local and long-distance directory assistance was included in your monthly service. Nowadays it costs $1.25 to $3.49 per call for both cell phones and landlines to get a number from a 555-1212 service or AT&T's 0-0 Info. There's an additional charge of up to $1 to automatically connect you to the number you request, according to Consumer Action's *2005 Telephone Rates Survey.* True, laws in some states and localities mandate that a few directory-assistance calls can be made each month at no charge. But elsewhere you pay as you go, and dialing for directory assistance just once a week via this popular method can raise a typical monthly bill by about 25 percent.

Your protection: One way to save more in directory assistance is to dial fewer numbers: Dialing 411 is typically less expensive than dialing the area code followed by 555-1212, because it reaches your local service provider rather than a national directory. The exception: Dialing 800-555-1212 to get directory assistance for a toll-free number is always free.

If you are without computer access, try calling your credit-card company's toll-free customer-service number. "Many credit-card companies provide a free concierge service as part of their premium-level (gold or platinum) perks," notes phone-service expert Marc-David Seidel, Ph.D., of the University of British Columbia's Sauder School of Business. "Not only do these services look up phone numbers free of charge for premium-card holders, but some do a more detailed search." Rather than simply locating a shoe store nearby, for instance, a concierge service may do the first round of shopping for you, ascertaining brands and sizes of shoes in stock before you ever set foot in the store. And according to Seidel, many gold- or platinum-level cards levy no annual fee.

Don't let wiring trip you up. Another freebie before deregulation—in-home wire maintenance to ensure no-cost repair by the phone company —now costs $2 to $5 a month, depending on your carrier. It is essentially insurance against a costly repair if the phone lines inside your home flake out. Statistically, says Bruce Kushnick, this expense is unnecessary because of the very low incidence of problems with internal wiring. Yet it is often charged automatically unless you say you don't want it.

"Unless you have termites or mice inside the walls of your home or live in a hurricane-prone area," says Kushnick, "studies show that in-house

Let Your Fingers Do the Clicking

For free directory assistance, use your fingers on a computer keyboard, not the dial pad. Some companies that charge you for directory assistance by phone provide it free online. They include Verizon's www.superpages.com and www.bigbook.com, as well as AT&T's www.anywho.com.

Here are some other websites that offer to locate residential and business phone numbers at no charge to you:

www.people.yahoo.com

www.switchboard.com

www.whowhere.lycos.com

www.whitepages.com

ww.infospace.com

www.phonenumber.com

wiring breaks or has problems about once every 16 years. Yet many people, especially senior citizens, continue to pay wire-maintenance charges, unaware that they are an added expense because they used to be a free part of their monthly service."

Your protection: Read your bill or call your phone company to determine if you're paying for this overwhelmingly unnecessary charge. Then simply opt out of it.

Stop phone-leasing agreements. It's hard to believe, but millions of Americans continue to pay for another pre-deregulation freebie: renting their telephones at an annual fee of $54 to $250, depending on the phone model. They may not even be aware of the extra cost, says Kushnick, who founded TeleTruth, a phone-service advocacy group, upon discovering his elderly aunt was paying $1,119 in yearly rental fees for her outdated rotary phone. "We find many people were used to their phone being included as part of their monthly service and never noticed the added charge. And the phone companies certainly don't advertise how expensive phone-leasing is."

Your protection: A careful review of your phone bill will detect a line item for "phone rental" or "leasing." If you spot it, consider canceling it and buying a no-frills phone. They cost as little as $10.

About 93 percent of U.S. households have telephone service. The market penetration is highest in Utah and Washington (97 percent for both) and lowest in Mississippi (87 percent).

Get wise to the name game. With deregulation, the Federal Communications Commission gave phone companies a green light to tack on numerous surcharges. "These companies have become experts," says AARP phone-service expert Christopher Baker, "at fooling consumers with an array of confusing fees, which in some cases are represented as taxes and other official charges."

Granted, some of these charges are legitimate taxes. They include state and local sales taxes, the 911 service fee that pays for emergency phone dispatching in your community, and the infamous federal excise tax—a 3 percent tax, first levied in 1898 to fund the Spanish-American War, that continues to be

The 411 on 911

You needn't subscribe to cellular service to make emergency calls. Just buy or use an old cell phone—with no service contract. Then, if you need to dial 911, you will be connected—and free of charge, thanks to the 911 tax assessed on everyone's monthly landline bills.

Of course, only 911 calls can be made this way, but it's a no-cost insurance policy for those who want to keep a cell phone handy for medical and other emergencies. And naturally you have to keep the phone's battery charged.

assessed on all telecommunications services today.

Other charges, by contrast, are added by the carriers as hidden rate increases, dressed up in glorified language to make it seem as if they are required by some government agency. The official-sounding "Property Tax Allotment," for instance, simply allows the carrier to recover the cost of its own property taxes without having to include that expense in the advertised price of a calling plan. The "Local Number Portability Charge (LNP)" is allowed by the FCC so local telephone companies can recoup the cost of permitting customers to keep their old phone numbers when they switch to a new service provider. Each carrier can choose whether or not to add this cost; some, such as Verizon Wireless, have stopped collecting a line-item charge for LNP and now either absorb the cost or include it in their advertised rates, says Baker. That's good news for consumers: It means one less surprise on their monthly bill.

Your protection: Before switching phone companies— whether for your residential or business landline or cellular service—do what most consumers don't: Ask for a sample bill so you can compare surcharges. "The names of these surcharges change all the time," notes Baker. "But with a sample bill in hand, you can better determine what you're really going to pay—beyond the advertised rates." Although some companies may refuse to give you a sample bill, it's the key to performing a line-item comparison. "Certain firms advertise low calling rates, only to tack on numerous surcharges," Baker notes. "Others may levy fewer surcharges, but they roll these allowed costs into their actual rates." Be especially leery, he cautions, of generic-sounding charges—those labeled as a recurring "monthly fee" or "service charge."

Fend off phony feds. Among the most underhanded (and costliest) line-item surcharges on phone bills is the cunningly named "Federal Subscriber Line Charge." You may also find it listed as "Federal Line Charge," "FCC Charge for Network Access," "Federal Access Charge," "Interstate Single Line Charge," or "FCC-Approved Customer Line Charge."

Despite its official-sounding moniker, this line item does not fund the FCC—nor any other government agency. Instead, it's an extra fee levied by every phone company to offset its own costs of doing business. After years of being capped at $6.50 per month for the first telephone line and $7 for each additional line, this charge now threatens to rise to $10 a month. You can thank industry lobbyists for the proposed hike.

"In our research," says Kushnick, "we found that some companies offering lower per-minute long distance make up the difference by charging a higher FCC line charge." That's why it's important to press the provider about this particular surcharge as you shop around for telephone service. Phone companies cannot exceed the cap, but you'll notice that the charge for this line item varies from one carrier to the next by as much as 50 percent. So if you use long distance only sparingly, be aware that you may be able to save money by choosing service that features a higher per-minute rate and a lower "federal" subscriber charge.

Long-Distance Savings

Look small to save big. You may have seen television commercials preaching the latest save-big calling plan from AT&T, Sprint, or the Baby Bells (the latter are regional companies such as Verizon, Bell South, or Qwest). But for the real deals, seek out offerings from AireSpring, Acceris, Covista, and other lesser-known companies that routinely offer long-distance service for half the cost (or less) of larger providers.

Do lower prices mean lesser service? Not really. Most of the smaller providers are discount resellers; that means they buy long-distance service in bulk from the bigger companies, obtaining tremendous deals on per-minute rates. The resellers combine these rates with their lower marketing costs and pass the savings along to the consumer. "In essence, the bigger network providers simply sell their excess capacity to informed consumers at a discounted rate," says business school professor Seidel. Some of these smaller companies also have lower (or nonexistent) charges such as monthly service fees, saving you even more.

How do you learn about these deals? A good place to start is at www.tollchaser.com, a website that Dr. Seidel founded with two friends (one a network administrator, the other a former teacher and current graduate student). Here you can compare the services available in your state based on your specific calling needs. Some resellers operate only in select states, but many offer service for about half the cost of the "majors." Other websites to compare reseller rates include www.saveonphone.com and www.calling-plans.com.

Pay in advance for big savings. Another lower-cost option for landlines is to enroll in a prepaid long-distance plan, such as those offered at www.onesuite.com, www.pincity.com, or www.talkloop.com. Rather than paying a set monthly rate, you buy blocks of prepaid service charged to your credit or debit card—at one-third the going rate of large service providers, and with no monthly fees, says Linda Sherry of Consumer Action, the consumer advocacy group that does an annual survey of telephone rates.

Sherry should know; she has used the service for several years to make several long-distance calls a day. "I tend to talk for a long time," she says, "but I get about three months of service for $25." The only drawback: Customers must access

Don't buy wireless phones or service from a mall kiosk, warns a San Diego consumer-advocacy group.

Many mall kiosks are owned by independent agents, not the service provider. According to the Utility Consumers' Action Network, most of the cellular complaints it receives involve false claims made by workers at these kiosks.

Hidden Cell Phone Charges & Penalties

It's bad enough that a monthly cellular service plan advertised for $40 includes an additional 20 percent in extra taxes and surcharges—not to mention those hefty activation and cancellation fees. But here are some "hidden" costs that can raise your monthly cell bill even more:

Home rate area. If you use your cellular telephone outside your immediate "home rate area," such as when traveling, you can be billed the full per-minute charge specified in your service agreement—even if you have "free airtime."

800 and directory-assistance calls. These calls are always charged as calls made outside your "home rate area," even when the numbers are toll-free.

Roaming charges. Although many monthly plans no longer charge an additional cost for roaming calls—those made outside your home area—some still charge rates as high as 69 cents per minute for long distance. Verizon Wireless and Cingular are the two largest companies offering plans with no roaming charges.

Text messaging. Unless you subscribe to this additional service—an option that may set you back only $3 a month—figure on paying as much as 10 cents for each text message sent or received.

Penalties for early termination. The vast majority of cell-phone plans in the United States require new customers to sign a long-term contract (usually two years) for service. Cancel a contract before that period ends and you'll have to pay a penalty that averages $170 (but can easily go much higher).

Minutes used. You are charged for all time you talk—both incoming and outgoing calls. Having someone call you doesn't save you minutes.

an 800 number, then enter a PIN before dialing the phone number. Preprogrammed speed dialing can shortcut dialing the extra 14 numbers, as can the other shortcuts detailed on Onesuite's website.

Also investigate buying clubs. Costco, for example, sells MCI prepaid calling cards that translate to less than 3 cents per minute, and those minutes never expire. Other buying clubs, such as BJ's Wholesale Club and Sam's Club, likewise routinely offer discounted calling cards.

For those who don't care to be shackled by one- or two-

Those Notorious "Other" Charges

WHATEVER RATE YOU PAY for landline or wireless phone service, you should figure that an additional 15 to 35 percent in "other charges" lurks on your monthly bill. Most of these are not required by law; instead, government agencies tolerate them to allow phone companies to recoup their own business costs—at your expense.

The exact charges may differ depending on your service and where you live. Regrettably, you can do little about them. Some companies may avoid one surcharge only to collect that money by charging more for another. But here's what you can expect to see on your local, long-distance, or wireless phone bills—and the reason for it.

TAXES IMPOSED BY GOVERNMENTS

911 Service Fee (or Emergency Telephone Users Surcharge Tax) is a fixed fee that typically appears under local telephone charges imposed by regional governments to help pay for the technology to connect you to emergency telephone services for fire and rescue.

Federal Excise Tax is a 3 percent tax mandated by the federal government and imposed on all telecommunication services, both landline and wireless. It was originally enacted to fund the Spanish-American War.

City, county, or state taxes may be listed as "utility taxes," "sales taxes," or as a "gross receipts tax." These vary depending on where you live—and may not be charged at all—but are essentially user fees imposed by local or state governments.

SURCHARGES LEVIED BY PHONE COMPANIES

FCC Subscriber Line Charge, instituted after the breakup of AT&T in 1984 to cover the costs of the local phone network, goes by many names. Some of the most common are "FCC Charge for Network Access," "Federal Line Cost Charge," "Interstate Access Charge," "Federal Access Charge," "Interstate Single Line Charge," "Customer Line Charge," or "FCC-Approved Customer Line Charge." Most phone companies bill you for this as a separate line item. Although the FCC caps the charge at $6.50 a month, phone companies are lobbying to raise it to $10. Despite its official-sounding name, it is not a government charge or tax.

Local Number Portability Charge (LPN) is a way for local telephone companies to recover costs when customers keep their phone numbers, at the same location, when switching from one provider to another. Some but not all companies charge this.

Monthly Minimum Usage Charge is charged by some carriers if your chosen rate plan requires you to make a minimum number of calls. For instance, if your plan requires you to make phone calls worth at least $10 a month, you will be charged that amount even for those months when your dialing finger is on vacation. To circumvent this charge, change your calling plan.

Monthly Service Fee is another charge on some, but not all, calling plans. It is assessed simply for subscribing to that long-distance service—regardless of how many calls you make—and it is in addition to the actual cost of those calls. If your calling plan has a monthly service fee of $4.95, for example, and you make $10 worth of phone calls, you will be charged $14.95 (exclusive of other fees).

State Subscriber Line Charge is a charge by some state public service or utility commissions. In theory, it's another way to partially compensate the local phone company for the cost of providing telephone lines.

Telecommunications Relay Services Charge is a state-mandated charge to pay for the relay center that transmits and translates calls for hearing- and speech-impaired people.

Universal Service Fund or Universal Connectivity Fee helps offset the cost of phone service to low-income customers, and to schools, libraries, and rural health-care providers. This rate, on most bills, can be levied as separate line items on both local and long-distance service.

Property Tax Allotment is a charge imposed by some phone companies to pay taxes on their properties.

Carrier Cost Recovery Fee is a catchall phrase to describe operating expenses incurred by the phone company; these are essentially being passed along to you as nondescript charges.

Single Bill Fee is a charge assessed on subscribers who receive landline and wireless phone service from the same company—and have the temerity to request that the company send them a combined bill.

▶ A BETTER WAY

Do the Math for a Better Bottom Line

There are various long-distance calling plans, from per-minute rates to "unlimited" options in which you're charged a set fee. How do you determine the optimum one for you? "Your best bet is to review the last three months of phone bills and calculate the average number of long-distance calls and their average length," says telecom analyst Bruce Kushnick. "Then do some math."

A plan that charges 5 cents a minute may sound enticing, but consider additional monthly service and minimum-usage fees. If you make 20 minutes of long-distance calls and you're charged a $5 monthly fee, that nickel-per-minute suddenly costs six times that rate—and more if there is an additional minimum-usage charge. Plans with a higher per-minute rate tend to have lower or no monthly fees, making them a cheaper choice for many lower-usage customers.

No matter how you figure your net cost for long-distance service, says Kushnick, you're paying too much if it exceeds 10 cents per minute.

year cellular contracts, prepaid cell phone plans are increasingly popular.

The plus: These plans are convenient—you buy a cell phone, pay an activation fee, and purchase a phone card good for a certain number of minutes. Phone cards in denominations of $10, $20, or $30 can be picked up in convenience and grocery stores. Some prepaid programs also occasionally offer special deals on cellular phones, no activation fee, and other incentives such as free minutes.

The minus: These plans can be expensive—as much as $1 per minute. They are also likelier to impose strict expiration deadlines; you may lose all unused minutes upon the expiration date, in which case you will have to pay another activation fee.

Interpret the terms. Calling plans for wireless service tend to be much more confusing than those for landlines. Specifics of wireless calling plans vary from one provider to the next, but in general there are three primary levels of service:

- *Local or "home rate area" plans.* Traditionally the cheapest calling plans, these plans usually allow calls made only in your local area—typically defined as your home city or county, or those surrounding it. Call outside that area and you will be charged additionally.

Many so-called "national" plans limit cell-to-cell calls or "free" long distance made from your home area.

- *Network national plans.* With these plans, you may be able to call anywhere for free—so long as you stay on your company's network, that is. Call someone on another network and you could be socked with high roaming charges.

- *Full national plans.* These allow you to make calls to any network as dictated by your allocated minutes and contracted terms. You may still be charged for long-distance calls when you venture physically outside your home calling area. However, Verizon and Cingular have started the trend of offering national plans with no roaming charges.

More than half of the 1.3 billion carrier-held telephone numbers in the United States have yet to be assigned to customers.

Let yourself in on a secret. Once you sign on the dotted line for wireless service, you're stuck with that commitment for at least a year or two, right? Not necessarily. If service does not meet expectations—if, for example, you experience poor call quality or frequent dropped calls—all wireless customers have a trial period, usually 14 days, in which they can walk away from a new contract without having to pay that triple-digit cancellation fee. (Even if they cancel within that grace period, however, they still must forgo the $35 to $50 activation fee they paid.)

What are the chances you'll receive your first bill within two weeks of activation? Slim to none. That means you will be unable to scrutinize bill-raising surcharges before you decide to keep or cancel the service.

Your protection: Although the cellular-service salesman may mention this 14-day trial period, understand that it is not carved in stone. "Actually," notes phone-service watchdog Baker, "the cellular industry trade group recommends that each carrier offer new customers a trial period of *at least*

14 days." Some carriers (Cingular is one) give customers 30 days in which to test the waters—er, airwaves—without being charged a cancellation fee.

Cellular customers should never enter a new agreement expecting to be able to cancel it without penalty—but it has been known to happen. "The dirty little secret in the wireless industry," says Baker, "is that if customers with a new contract threaten to complain to the FCC because of poor service or because their contract terms were not spelled out clearly, the company will often allow them to cancel the contract within 30 days or so without being penalized—even after the free trial period expires. There are no guarantees, of course, but it's worth a shot if you need to get out of your contract."

Were it not for those hefty—and hated—cancellation fees, half of all cell-phone users would switch service carriers "as soon as possible." In 2005, reports national consumer advocacy group U.S. PIRG, cancellation fees averaged $170.

Master the 1010 game. The advertisements have died down, but 1010 numbers are still very much alive. With this service, also known as "dial-around" plans, you dial 1010 (some companies use 1015 or 1016), then a three- or four-digit number, then finally the 10-digit phone number itself. This finger-cramping sequence routes the call around your existing long-distance carrier to give you a supposedly lower rate. 1010 calls are normally made from your home telephone; they appear on your phone bill as a separate line item.

Does all that extra dialing truly deliver more savings? "Generally, you can save a lot when making international calls with a 1010 service," says Rich Sayers, who operates www.1010phonerates.com, a website that tracks such calling plans. "You can also save with 1010 calling plans if you make a lot of long-distance calls within your state, if you happen to live in a state with high intrastate long-distance rates. But typically, dialing state-to-state long-distance calls with a 1010 plan winds up costing more money than with regular long distance."

It's all in the fine print: Although these plans—and there are scores of them—charge as little as 3 cents per minute for long-distance service within the United States and Canada, many tack on per-call connection fees that start at 39 cents, as well as monthly fees that can climb to several dollars for "low-usage" customers. Not only that, but per-minute rates tend to vary from state to state, so a per-minute charge of 5 cents in one state may cost you 30 cents in another. (Per-call connection fees vary too.)

And don't forget the biggest factor of all: Some rates are charged on a set block of time—say, 99 cents for each call that lasts up to 20 minutes. "If you get an answering machine or the call lasts only five minutes," explains Sayers, "you still pay the full 99 cents." His advice for using 1010 plans:

- *Before using a 1010 plan,* call the provider to find out about *all* additional fees or "hidden" fees. Then check rates of your regular long-distance carrier, and check how long your calls typically last. "If you're paying more than 5 cents per minute for in-state toll calls or state-to-state calls, 1010 service may save you money."

- *Be alert to rate changes.* 1010 companies are known to advertise new, lower rates—only to go right on billing you at higher ones. You can always call and get switched to the lower-rate plan.

Common Phone Scams

Allowed extras, superfluous surcharges, and tacky tack-ons can make you feel scammed when you open your phone bill each month, yet they are perfectly legal. At the same time, there is no scarcity of dirty dealings that qualify as outright ripoffs. Here are some of the most notorious bogus deals to watch out for:

The call-forwarding scam. This is a true con in that it is often pulled by prison inmates—typically those in lower-security facilities with round-the-clock access to pay phones. *The ploy:* To persuade unsuspecting customers, usually

Parents of teens, take note: Insurance plans to replace lost or stolen wireless phones average $4 a month—a worthwhile investment, given the youthful propensity to mislay the devices.

Before you can make a claim, however, you'll probably have to file a police report or plead your case with the carrier or insurance provider. Even then, you'll receive only a "comparable" phone, not the latest model.

called at random, to activate their call-forwarding service so scammers can make long-distance calls at the victim's expense. "They'll pose as phone-company repairmen and say they need to test the lines," says Tiffany Nels of SBC Communications, a "Baby Bell" providing phone service in 13 states. "Or they'll say a family member has been in a car accident, then offer to patch you through to the emergency room."

The ruse is to have victims first dial *72 or 72# and then another number—often that of their prison payphone, or that of a phone belonging to an accomplice on the outside. For business phones that require dialing 9 first to get an outside line, call forwarding is activated by dialing 90# and the other number. This "forwards" your incoming calls to that second number—and gives scamsters the opportunity to charge long-distance or 900 "sex line" phone calls to your account.

"When you hang up, they stay on and make their calls," says Nels. This continues until the call-forwarding service—usually "bundled" with Caller ID or voice mail—is deactivated, usually by dialing *73 or 73#. Because many victims are unaware they have activated call forwarding, they learn they've been scammed only when their bill arrives with hundreds (even thousands) of dollars in unexplained phone calls. It's then up to the phone company to decide whether or not to charge you—and, unless you put up a fight, some will.

A call made from a correctional facility is nearly always preceded by a recorded message indicating its origin and is then made "collect." But the scammers easily get around that. "They first dial collect to someone on their approved call list, such as their spouse," explains Michigan Department of Corrections spokesman Russ Marlan. "That person then initiates a three-way call to the victim to bypass the recorded message. Inmate and accomplice work together to trick victims into forwarding calls to the accomplice's number." This transfers the per-minute collect charge—up to 84 cents at Michigan facilities—from the accomplice's line to the victim's.

Your protection: Never dial *72 or another call-forwarding

ID Theft from a Camera Phone?

Did you hear the one about the cell phone whose built-in camera is used to commit identity theft? Posing as an obnoxious type who talks on his cell phone while waiting in line, the cyber-crook in this scenario furtively takes a picture of a stranger's credit card in mid-purchase. Then, having captured the account number, the malefactor embarks on a buying spree at the victim's expense.

Mind you, the Federal Trade Commission has no reports of identity theft occurring this way. (Part of the FTC mandate is to track such incidents.) Even police agencies warning the public to beware camera-phone-wielding perps are hard-pressed to cite specific instances. And the language of many such alerts reads identically, suggesting it came from a single source—and reinforcing its likely status as urban myth.

What do experts say about the validity of this "scam"?

"I've tested this capability myself using several camera phones," says camera-phone expert Alan Reiter, "and it's urban legend—for now. With the camera phones currently available in the U.S., you'd have to get close enough to the other person's credit card to be able to read the number. Both camera and card would have to be held rock-steady, and the lighting would have to be good enough for a clear shot. Basically you'd have to *help* someone take the picture to get a clear shot at the number."

Stores in Japan sell camera phones whose lenses can provide an accurate picture of credit-card numbers from a few feet away. "These phones may come to the U.S.," adds Reiter, who consults businesses on telephone technology, "but probably not for several years." Until then, unless the sneaky geek went phone shopping in Japan, the more realistic peril is being photographed nude—the reason why many health clubs ban camera phones from locker rooms.

number at the request of a stranger. Legitimate phone workers, police, or emergency personnel never ask customers to use call forwarding to patch them through to another number.

The Caribbean calling scam: You get an e-mail, voice mail, or page instructing you to call a phone number to claim a prize or inheritance, or to receive news of a "sick" relative.

The ploy: To give you a vacation from your money. The area code of these phone numbers is for a Caribbean country, where the per-minute rate is often $3 or more—at least 10 times the cost of long-distance service in the U.S.

Because these numbers have American-sounding area codes, "you may think you're dialing an area code in the U.S.," says Sprint spokesman James Fisher. "In reality, you are dialing outside the country—and paying the price for it. After they've lured you to make the call, the scam is to keep you on the line by making you go through a series of transfers; that runs up the charges. A 10-minute call to one of these numbers, which is not uncommon, can cost $35 or more."

Your protection: Beware of faux-American area codes, such as 809 (Dominican Republic), 284 (British Virgin Islands), or 876 (Jamaica). Others—all for various Caribbean countries—include 246, 441, 473, 664, 758, 784, and 868. Overseas phone numbers fall outside the jurisdiction of the FCC, so their owners can charge whatever they want on a per-minute or per-call basis. You can always check an area code via directory assistance or at www.areacodes.org. For other free sites, google the phrase "area code lookup."

> **PROTECTIVE DETECTIVE**
>
> ## Terminate Telemarketers
>
> Joining the National Do Not Call Registry, maintained by the Federal Trade Commission, is supposed to prohibit most telemarketers from calling you. But even after registering—which can be done online at **www.donotcall.gov** or by calling **888-382-1222**—you will likely still get unsolicited calls. Exceptions to the no-call rules include charitable organizations, pollsters, or even commercial companies with which you have "an existing business relationship."
>
> If you receive unauthorized calls from other types of business, you can file a complaint on the Do Not Call Registry website, subjecting the caller to steep fines. To file a complaint, your number must have been listed on the registry for at least 31 days. You'll have to supply the date of the unauthorized call, and either the name or the phone number of the company that called you.

Fat-finger dialing. In this scam, unscrupulous companies deliberately buy phone numbers that differ by just one digit from those of legitimate phone service providers.

The ploy: To reap big money from fumble-fingered dialers trying to make a collect call. For instance, you may be trying to call 1-800-CALL-ATT but instead dial 1-800-CALL-LAT; or instead of punching in 1-800-COLLECT, you might dial 1-800-COLECCT. Your call goes through, but there's no cue you've misdialed. The net result of your "fat finger" dialing is telephone charges at least three times higher than those you would normally pay. "You don't know that you've misdialed until the bill comes and you discover you've been charged an incredibly high rate," says Fisher.

Your protection: Although the major phone companies continue to bring legal action against fat-finger operators, this scam still flourishes. Be careful when you dial commonly advertised "collect" services. Legitimate collect-call services notify callers or recipients of the charges; if you don't get a per-minute rate, warns Fisher, or if you are asked to accept collect charges, hang up at once—it's likely a fat-finger scam. For instance, when using 1-800-CALL-ATT to make a credit-card phone call, you'll always get a "Thank you for using AT&T" recording before you dial the rest of your call.

Slamming & cramming. "Slamming" occurs when your long-distance service is switched without your knowledge. It can result from a seemingly innocent action on your part, such as submitting an entry form for a contest or a survey, or cashing a check for a small amount that arrived unsolicited in your mail. On both documents, barely legible fine print "authorizes" a change in your long-distance company, or enrolls you in expensive phone services.

Your protection: FCC anti-slamming rules are the reason why that automated or third-party service comes on the line to verify your carrier choice when you select or change your long-distance provider. "If you don't get this verification," says Fisher, "chances are you're being slammed."

If you've been slammed or you suddenly receive invoices from an unfamiliar long-distance company, you don't have to pay anything—so long as you contact the slammer and your "real" long-distance carrier within 30 days of receiving the

Outwit pesky telemarketers by having your last name listed in the phone directory as your mother's maiden name or some other pseudonym. You can make the switch with a single call to your phone carrier.

If your last name is Smith and your mother's maiden name was Jones, any telemarketer who asks for Mr. Jones has no business contacting you—and is in violation of Do Not Call Registry guidelines (assuming you've enrolled).

The Future of Phone Service

IF YOU ALREADY HAVE a high-speed broadband or cable Internet connection—as do 1 in 3 U.S. households—you're a prime candidate for a technology that may redefine the way the world communicates: VoIP, or Voice over Internet Protocol services.

With this technology, a special adapter allows phone calls to be routed like e-mails, obviating the need to shunt the calls through the telephone company's network. You can use your existing telephones, including additional phones on the same line, but broadband phones will also serve the purpose. Here are some pluses and minuses of the technology, now offered by many traditional phone companies as well as newly minted VoIP-specific companies:

ADVANTAGES

Cost: Companies such as Vonage, which pioneered this technology, offer unlimited VoIP local and long-distance calling plans for as little as $25 a month—about half the cost of similar phone-company plans. Other VoIP providers may charge even less.

Features. Call-forwarding, call-waiting, voice mail, caller ID, and other services are often included in VoIP service at no additional charge. Many VoIP providers also allow customers to choose their own area code—no matter where they live.

Portability. You can easily unplug the adapter and make and receive phone calls when you travel, as long as you have a high-speed Internet connection (such as via your laptop or in a hotel room).

DISADVANTAGES

Cost: If you don't have high-speed Internet service—and the majority of Americans do not—you'll need it in order to use VoIP. The typical cost for Internet service is $20 to $50 a month, depending on your service provider, and that does not include the cost of the VoIP service itself. It will cost you about $5 per month to rent a high-speed modem from your Internet service provider, or you can buy one for approximately $100. Either way, you'll still pay a monthly fee for that broadband or cable Internet service.

Some companies bundle both Internet and VoIP service for a lower combined cost, but the savings usually last only a limited time. Also be aware that if you purchase your own modem and it causes problems with your service, your service provider will not repair it.

Emergency 911 calls. Traditional phone service can trace the location of a call made to emergency personnel; VoIP cannot. That means if you live in one state but are using VoIP when traveling to another (the portability advantage), ambulance, fire, or police personnel in your local area might be sent to your empty home.

Equipment. Your computer must be VoIP-capable. Information about the minimum hardware you will need can be found on the website of any VoIP company.

Inconvenience. The majority of VoIP service providers will not send you a hard copy bill via the U.S. Postal Service.

Quality. Some VoIP users complain about the service defect known as latency, in which the user may experience a slight delay between the time when he speaks and the time when the party at the other end of the line actually hears what has been said. There's no surer way to sabotage spontaneity in a conversation.

Reliability. In the event of a blackout, a power surge, or a cable interruption (a commonplace occurrence for those with cable modems), VoIP service will not work with landline telephones. Although corded telephones on landline service can be used during a blackout, cordless phones cannot. Not only that, but not every high-speed connection can handle VoIP calls; to find out if yours does, visit www.testyourvoip.com.

Security. Like your home or business computer, VoIP is susceptible to worms, viruses, and hacking. VoIP companies are working on encryption to prevent these problems.

Sound quality. Although some improvements have been made, the sound quality of VoIP may fall below that of landline service. This is because data transmitted over the Internet often arrive scrambled and must then be reassembled. The same technology that transfers written e-mails is also used to send and decipher voice data.

bill. After that, you must pay charges at your authorized company's rates. If you've already paid the bill, the slammer must not only pay you 50 percent of those charges but also reimburse the phone company 100 percent.

"Cramming" involves the addition of unauthorized, misleading, or deceptive products or services to your phone bill. It can result from the same ploys as those that trigger slamming. More often, it is set in motion by a call you make to an 800 number advertised as a free date line, a psychic hotline, or a sweepstakes-entry line: Your phone number is captured, then billed at exorbitant rates for a one-time call or a monthly "club" membership fee. Until that sky-high phone bill hits the mailbox, most customers are unaware of these charges.

"Sometimes, people call 800 numbers thinking they are toll-free, but then they're asked to press 1 and they're switched, without their knowledge, to a 900 number that is especially expensive," says Sprint's Fisher. (By law, 900 numbers costing more than $2 a minute must reveal the charge to callers, who then have three seconds to hang up; crammers flout this regulation.) Services that begin with 011 or 500 cram you with international charges that can be even higher.

The ploy here is to keep you on the line as long as possible. Like the Caribbean scam, says Fisher, crammers use transfers and other stalling tactics to delay, delay, delay. This runs up your charges—which, conveniently for the crammer, are dictated by the owner of the telephone number.

Your protection: It's up to you to spot charges and report them. So probe and parse your phone bill as you read it. Cramming charges are often hidden inside vague terms such as "service fee," "service charge," "membership," or "club fee." Getting reimbursed for cramming charges is a tougher proposition, so it's best to nip these charges in the bud.

COLLEGE

5

Get Schooled on Scholarship Tools

FOR EVERY HIGH SCHOOL phenom offered a free ride to Harvard or Princeton, thousands of others—along with their parents—take a bumpier route to those ivy-covered walls: sweating over getting in—and sweating even more over how to pay for it. With each year bringing a record number of applications, admission is tougher than ever at "choice" colleges. What's even harder is paying the bill, approaching $30,000 per annum at the typical private university—with predicted annual increases of 5 percent. Public universities, considered the financial bargain by many, average about $10,000 per year, but some have recently raised tuition by 10 percent or more annually.

Although more financial aid is now available than ever before—more than $122 billion a year—the lion's share of it continues to take the form of student loans that must be paid back. So where does this leave the typical American college-bound student, a middle-class kid with some of the right stuff but not likely to be the school valedictorian, star athlete, or other spotlighted wunderkind?

Perhaps surprisingly, it leaves him or her with a very good chance at billions of dollars available from universities, corporations, and other sources in no-payback, performance-based merit scholarships. Though much of it goes to students with top grades and test scores, don't underestimate other

IN THIS CHAPTER

Start Early for Payoff Later

University-Funded Scholarships

Private Scholarship Money

Essays That Excel

129

The less money you have in a student's name, the better it is for getting income-based financial aid.

According to the Expected Family Contribution formula that is used to calculate need-based assistance, families are expected to spend 35 percent of the student's income earned from part-time jobs. For money saved in parents' bank accounts, by contrast, the expected contribution is only 6 percent.

criteria worth thousands of dollars a year per lucky recipient: Wearing a tux or gown made of duct tape to the high school prom. Being a C+ skateboarder who's better at Ollies than algebra. Being left-handed and planning to attend a specific school in Pennsylvania. Being 5-foot-10 or over; being 4-foot-10 or under.

For many students, getting scholarships is a matter of good marketing—that is, finding a way to show how that student stands out in some way, whether it's inside the classroom or beyond it. Although no single formula can seek out and secure these awards, strategies abound to increase the odds of getting them.

Start Early for Payoff Later

Hit the hallways running. College may not really register on the mental radar of many high schoolers until their junior year, but the marketing strategy for scholarships should be hatched years earlier. "It really begins when students start 9th grade," says John Midgley, a school counselor at Methacton High School in suburban Philadelphia, where a recent graduating class of 350 students garnered more than $3 million in merit scholarship offers. "Colleges don't see a student's grades before that, but they see *everything* from freshman year onward."

Translation: Because the most generous merit scholarship offers come from universities themselves, "Parents can boost their student's chances of landing scholarships down the road by helping him or her pick the right courses from the very start of high school. That often means getting them into the most challenging classes that they can tackle successfully," adds Midgley. "Assuming the student can handle a demanding course load, going for tougher 'honors' and similar classes early on indicates to colleges that here's a student who isn't afraid of hard work and is committed to their education, a student they want on their campus."

Not only do tougher courses make students more attractive to those granting admission and scholarship funds—even if they don't necessarily score an "A"—but these academically-intensive classes are often a prerequisite for high school Advanced Placement (AP) courses, which may be accepted as college credit. At some colleges, a student's overall high school course load—including AP classes—plays a bigger factor in admission than do SAT or ACT scores.

And there's the real reason for an early start on harder classes: "When the transcript indicates that a student hasn't taken more challenging courses until later grades, some colleges might interpret these kids as having the ability, but not the desire, to apply themselves," says Midgley. "That doesn't help in getting scholarships."

To find out how particular colleges weigh course load versus standardized test scores, call that school's admission office or check with the high school guidance office.

Millionaires' School Daze

Does an Ivy League education guarantee admission to the Millionaires' Club? Doubtful. A study of 1,300 American millionaires found that most were college graduates—and half held advanced degrees—but few had attended the country's most prestigious universities.

That may be because they couldn't get in, reports Thomas Stanley in *The Millionaire Mind*. The average SAT score of millionaires he surveyed was 1190—better than the national average of 1026, but not enough to qualify for admission to Ivy League or other "most selective" schools. Nor could those scores secure them entree to many "highly selective" public or private universities.

And with a typical grade-point average of only 2.92 (roughly a C+), most future millionaires hardly distinguished themselves as scholars once they were admitted. So just what, in their own words, did they learn at college?

"Hard work was more important than genetic high intellect in achieving."

"Learning to fight for our goals because someone labeled us as having 'average or less ability.'"

"To properly allocate time and make accurate judgments about people."

Do practice application forms. Most students never fill out application or scholarship forms until the moment they actually apply. Bad move. "As with everything else, there's a learning curve in doing these applications," says Ben Kaplan, who attended Harvard on two dozen scholarships totaling $90,000 and authored *How to Go to College Almost for Free.* "You don't want to hurt your chances when it's really important by tackling them cold."

Kaplan's counsel: By requesting admissions applications well before it's time to apply, students can get a better idea of the types of essay questions they are likely to be asked. This gives underclassmen plenty of time to practice. "Start doing practice applications in middle school or early in high school," Kaplan advises, "so you can master this process before the time really comes. This prepares you better for the real deal. It also gives you plenty of time to get feedback from teachers and others if you are writing essays."

An early dry run can also snag later scholarship money in several learning programs for younger students, such as the Toshiba National Science Teachers Association ExploraVision Awards for grades kindergarten through 12. "In this case, a two- to four-person student team projects a vision of technology 20 years into the future and does a report on it. Each member of the winning team receives $10,000," says Kaplan, founder of www.ScholarshipCoach.com, a website that gives tips to students who want to win scholarships. "And there's a snowball effect. Once you have a few awards, even small ones, it gets easier to win larger ones: You

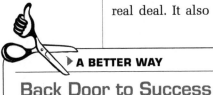

▶ **A BETTER WAY**

Back Door to Success

Admission to the satellite campus of a large public or private university may be easier for marginal applicants than getting into that school's main campus. Many schools have lower SAT or GPA requirements at their smaller, suburban campuses—which, as a bonus, typically offer a lower student-to-teacher ratio. The social activities may not be quite as abundant, but the quality of education is just as good, say university officials. After two years, most "farmed-out" students typically transfer to the central campus—and the degree awarded makes no distinction about the road taken to attain it.

can list those early awards on your application to show colleges you are worthy."

Climb those other ranks at school. "Getting merit-based scholarships starts with grades, but it's not only a student's grades and class rank that matter," says Chuck Hughes, a former Harvard admissions officer who now runs a Boston-based college admissions-consulting firm. "Students fare much better for admissions and scholarships when they demonstrate a relevant set of experiences that portray them as a leader, even if it's outside the classroom."

For many students, that means getting involved and climbing the ranks of extracurricular activities. "While colleges want to see the student's involvement in school activities, they don't necessarily want the kids who join every club as much as they want those who stay involved in a select few over time," adds Midgley. "What's more impressive to many colleges is that student who joins a particular activity in 9th grade and becomes an officer or team captain by 12th. They don't have to be president, but becoming some type of officer conveys leadership and personal traits that colleges want to see: maturity, responsibility, commitment, passion, and especially stick-to-itiveness."

Being selected as these leaders may be a popularity contest, but that too bodes well: It signals that the student is well-liked and respected by both peers and coaches.

Aim for versatility. Budding Spielbergs need not focus solely on running the Video Club. "Colleges especially like well-rounded kids," says Midgley, "and it helps to have extracurricular activities that show varied interests and versatility." That can mean deliberately mixing it up. "Select" activities ideally include one sports team, an arts group such as band, and an academic club or student government. That conveys a more evenly balanced applicant than one who excelled in just one area.

Pop quiz: You have a choice of saving for retirement or saving for your child's college education. Which do you choose?

The former, many financial planners recommend. Whereas there are good rates for education loans, no loans are available for retirement.

How the Kirchheimer Kids Did It

ONE SON WANTS to create computer animation and film special effects; the other wants a more energy-efficient world. These aims anchor opposite ends of the career spectrum, yet we found a common way to fund them: Both students got five-figure-per-year merit scholarships from prestigious universities.

It's a good thing, too, because the Kirchheimer clan is solidly middle-class. With two incomes, we apparently earn too much money to qualify for need-based college assistance money. Yet we lacked the pelf to pay for their educations unaided—especially with their kid sister preparing for her own matriculation.

How did my boys do it? They got good grades in high school—but not as good as classmates who landed less scholarship assistance. They took Advanced Placement classes and were active in extracurricular programs, but others took more Einsteinian course loads and achieved Bigger Man On Campus status. My kids worked hard on their applications and essays, searched for outside scholarships, and got good faculty recommendations. But so did umpteen others. What were our secrets?

A picture is worth 1,000 words (and they showed why). "Admissions officers want to know who you are, where you come from, and where you're going," says Chuck Hughes, a former admissions officer at Harvard who founded the admissions-consulting firm Road to College. "Show us what you're about."

We did that, literally. Along with compelling-but-faceless essays and other application paperwork, both boys added a videotape showing their "big-scene" theater performances and other school activities, demonstrations of hobbies that influenced their intended major, a "tour" of home life, an on-camera endorsement from a favorite teacher, and a brief concluding monologue explaining "Who I am" and "What I will bring to your school"—mentioned by name in each video.

Outcome: Some tapes may have been tossed, but at least one school viewed it and passed it around. Or so went the story we heard when the college offered my oldest son, Lang, a half-tuition scholarship. (He eagerly accepted it.)

Meet alumni. In addition to attending those cattle-call summer campus tours, we asked short-listed schools about less-publicized chances for applicants to meet with past graduates "to learn more about campus life." At one event, where the alumni-to-applicant ratio was a favorable 2 to 1, Lang struck up a conversation with a past graduate. Twenty minutes later he had gleaned some valuable insights about school life, scholarship-boosting tips for his high school "résumé" (which he "happened" to bring along), and the alum's business card (essential for that next-day thank-you note).

Outcome: Several weeks later, an additional $1,000 "alumni" scholarship was offered on top of nearly $50,000 over four years. Guess which grad had recommended the extra loot?

Get a plug from the boss. Colleges expect to receive glowing recommendations from favorite teachers. But what about someone who may be even better at predicting an applicant's success in the workplace? Dan asked his summer-job boss of three years for a recommendation, but he tailored his approach. Aware of the boss's hectic schedule, Dan offered to draft some "sample" recommendation letters that stressed such traits as attitude, integrity, and work ethic. The boss edited each sample as he saw fit, then printed them on company letterhead. The kicker: Dan asked his boss to include a personal phone number "should additional comments be needed about this outstanding young man."

Outcome: Each school receiving the boss's letter offered Dan admission. One top-notch institution extended nearly $23,000 a year in scholarships. Among the reasons it cited for its generosity was the "relatively rare" endorsement from an employer with in-depth knowledge of the student's performance in a real-world job setting. Although Dan ultimately opted for another school, the recommendation detailing his summer work—maintenance and light construction at the boss's properties—likely played no small role in securing a part-time, well-paying job on campus building and breaking down stage sets.

Keep a log of volunteer work. Dan also netted two freshman-year scholarships given for "good grades and showing outstanding character with community service." He's a do-gooder, no doubt about it, but that would have meant little, fiscally speaking, had no one noticed. Throughout high school—and especially during his senior year—he kept his teachers and guidance counselor aware of his steady but not all-encompassing volunteer work, especially when it had nothing to do with school-sponsored activities.

This "civic activities résumé" made it easy for his high school to document his community service for a $2,000 corporate scholarship requiring school-issued paperwork. A smaller award resulted when the local alumni chapter of his selected college called the high school to ask about worthy recipients—and Dan's volunteer work dossier was on hand.

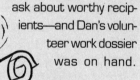

Consider weekend activities. A student's "outside" life—again, ideally throughout high school—can be equally important in snagging scholarship money. Part-time jobs not only show initiative and work ethic—both rank high on the wish list of scholarship awarders—but some burger chains and convenience stores offer generous scholarship programs for their high school employees. Membership in a Scout troop, participation in a weekend soccer league, or experience collecting donations for cancer research can likewise reap rewards.

"College admission is based on applications," says Kaplan. "But scholarships are awarded to people, and those who get them are able to paint a portrait of the whole person—not just the student. It's especially useful if you can show in this portrait how your outside-of-school interests apply to your intended career goals."

Kaplan scored some of his bounty by combining his intended career goal—to become a writer—with a proven scholarship-garnering attribute: community service. "When I was in high school, I contacted the local Meals on Wheels chapter and said, 'I'd really like to become a writer. Is there any way I could help you out?' I wound up writing their public service announcements for radio, which impressed some scholarship awarders" (to say nothing of Harvard admissions officers).

These outside interests should telegraph at least one key trait that traditionally earns the bestowal of many nonacademic merit scholar-

Tax Breaks from a 529 Savings Plan

State-run "529 plans" offer several advantages over other college savings plans. In at least 32 states, the account owner (usually a parent) is eligible for a full or partial state income-tax deduction for money contributed to the plan. Some plans permit the purchase of credits at today's prices that can be used years later—no matter how much tuition costs rise between now and then. These plans were originally tailored to students who want to attend college in their home state, but many now allow all contributions to be used at out-of-state universities as well. Call your state Treasurer's office for information about your own state's 529 offerings.

ships: Hard work, individual initiative, teamwork, civic responsibility, or a long-standing commitment to a particular passion.

University-Funded Scholarships

Cast a (relatively) wide net—and let that fact be known. Over-applying to colleges—usually defined as approaching 10 schools or more—may harm an applicant's chances of landing a university-funded scholarship, traditionally the most generous individual award, because it suggests a lack of commitment to that particular school. But under-applying may be even worse.

"The very worst thing a student can do is to apply to only one college, no matter how prestigious it is," says Hughes, author of *What It Really Takes to Get into the Ivy League and Other Highly Selective Colleges.* "It leaves you with no bargaining power when it comes to discussing aid."

The expert consensus is that most students should apply to no fewer than three schools, and usually no more than six. Above all, complete the often-omitted section of admission forms that asks applicants to list contending schools. "Colleges don't necessarily know the family's value judgment about attending one school over another," says Hughes, founder of Road to College, an admissions-consulting firm. "But they do know what their competitors charge, and what they typically offer similar students in scholarships and other aid. It pays to let them know you're shopping around." This sometimes makes them work harder, Hughes explains, to draw desirable students to their campus with scholarships.

Try this better mix. An all-too-common student stratagem is to apply to one "dream" school that's a bit of a stretch (such as an Ivy League or other big-name institution), along with several more realistic contenders. There's also that all-important "safety" school—often the local state university.

College students get high marks when it comes to handling their own credit.

Students are more than twice as likely as other adults to pay off their monthly credit-card balance, reports the Georgetown University Credit Research Center. While in school, 88 percent of students pay their student loans as scheduled—about the same rate as recent graduates.

The FAFSA Factor

THOUGH PRIVATE SCHOLARSHIPS are often awarded solely on the basis of a student's perceived "merit," other forms of financial aid are determined by the Free Application for Federal Student Aid, better known as FAFSA.

Failing to submit a FAFSA each year prevents any federal and most school-offered aid (such as student loans, work-study awards, and "need-based" grants) from being given to incoming students or those already in attendance. The FAFSA form can be attained at most schools, many libraries or other public buildings, or online at www.fafsa.ed.gov. Based on information supplied on the FAFSA, you will receive a Student Aid Report (SAR) that indicates the Expected Family Contribution (EFC)—how much a household is expected to pony up for the student's education bill.

Yet many working but cash-strapped families who submit a FAFSA are surprised to learn that they are deemed to qualify for little, if any, assistance. Among the reasons:

Timing. Filing a FAFSA begins on January 1 each year. The best financial awards—heavier on no-payback grants and lighter on loans—are generally given to those who file early. Some states have filing deadlines in March or April; miss that cutoff and no aid will be offered, regardless of need.

Income. The EFC is calculated largely by the family's income—both taxable money (wages, pensions, and capital gains) and nontaxable funds (child support, tax-exempt interest, and money contributed to IRAs and similar savings plans). In addition, nearly 6 percent of money saved in parents' bank accounts is considered in the EFC calculation, meaning that households that sock away more money (even if it is not earmarked for a college education) tend to have a higher EFC—and therefore less opportunity for student aid.

Students who hold part-time jobs to save for college get hurt even more. Some 35 percent of their income is expected to be applied toward college—regardless of their other expenses, such as car insurance—so paycheck-earning students often get lower aid packages than those who do not hold jobs.

The school's cost. Usually, more generous aid packages are offered at schools with higher tuition and living costs. As a general rule, financial need is determined by each school by subtracting the EFC from its Cost of Attendance (tuition, fees, room and board, books, and other expenses). So attending a lower-cost public university will usually yield a lower financial-aid package than if that student went to a pricier private school.

But there's a better recipe, and its chef, Mark Kantrowitz, is founder of FinAid (www.finaid.org) and director of advanced projects for FastWeb (www.fastweb.com), two popular websites that offer free information about scholarships. To improve an applicant's chances of initiating a bidding war, reveals Kantrowitz, "I usually recommend that the typical student also apply to at least one school where they will really stand out. For the typical student, that usually means a second- or third-tier small, private university that they may not have previously considered."

These smaller, private schools usually have to work harder to attract good students. They are therefore more likely to offer scholarships to those they fear may go elsewhere. "Because tuition is so much cheaper at public universities," says high school counselor Midgley, "more students are applying to state schools than in the past, and smaller, private colleges

Deciding on Early Decision

About 10 percent of the nation's nearly 2,500 four-year colleges and universities offer "early decision" plans. These allow students to apply for admission and to be informed of the institution's decision up to six months before the usual notification date.

Because this is done primarily at elite schools—which tend to be "more accepting" of early-decision candidates—anxious applicants can chill out for the remainder of their high school career, secure that they have cracked their "dream school." That's a psychic edge, mind you, not a fiscal one: Early decision typically freezes any opportunity to negotiate a nice financial package.

"If money is not a factor for your family," says financial-aid expert Anna Leider of Alexandria, Virginia, "early decision is a good idea. The admissions criteria widen, and you stand a better chance of getting into the most elite schools. But you have no bargaining power when it comes to securing university-offered scholarships or other financial aid. If admitted early, you agree to accept whatever they offer—and schools may have no incentive to offer you anything."

Leider's advice is to apply for early decision only if you're rock-solid certain you want to attend that school—and, of course, if you can somehow pay the full sticker price.

are really hurting. They're getting fewer applicants. At the same time, many state schools consistently rank high on the *U.S. News & World Report* and other 'Best Colleges' lists, so these smaller schools know they will lose kids to those respected state colleges unless they make them a scholarship offer." It's not uncommon for these smaller colleges to volunteer scholarships generous enough to lower their effective tuition rate closer to what is charged at public universities.

Applying to a smaller school where the student will stand out may also increase the odds of getting money from competing private institutions. "When you get a scholarship from at least one source, it does tend to boost your chances of receiving others," says book author Kaplan. "There's something of a herd mentality; one offer can lead to another because of this 'You're worthy' factor."

Be aware of B-average awards. Although the big money is handed out for straight A's, hundreds of colleges and universities offer automatic awards of $1,000 to $5,000 to students who have maintained a 3.0 or better average throughout high school. These awards—usually called "Dean's Scholar," "Presidential Award," or something equally generic—may also be bestowed on students who meet certain SAT or class-rank criteria.

"Some schools mention these scholarships on the admissions application, but a lot of them don't," says Anna Leider, the author of *Don't Miss Out: The Ambitious Student's Guide to Financial Aid,* published annually. "Often it's a matter of calling the school's Office of Loans and Scholarships to find out what's available." While you're at it, ask that department about other programs—such as unique "club" awards, scholarships from local "booster" club or alumni associations, discounts for enrolling in an honors program (often entailing nothing more than writing an additional essay), having siblings attend the same school, or special scholarships for "legacies"—the children or relatives of past graduates.

Familiarizing your college-bound kid with the financial challenges of higher education can be an excellent form of education in and of itself.

In addition to www.finaid.org, the website of the College Board, www.collegeboard.com, offers a good section specifically for students, entitled "Paying for College."

Contact the coach. Touch base (ha ha!) with those running the college athletic, theater, art, or music departments. Don't neglect the sponsors of the campus debate team, volunteer group, or any other activity your student pursued in high school. True, star athletes are more likely to receive athletic scholarships, but even enthusiastic second-stringers can score some university ducats.

"Once you get beyond the football and basketball scholarships at elite sports schools," says Leider, "hundreds of coaches of other sports still need to field a team. Even if your ability does not get you an athletic scholarship, your interest in participating may well help you on the admissions end, and in getting some aid. You want to persuade the coach to say to admissions and financial-aid officers, 'We really want this kid to come here.'"

How? When applying to a college, she advises contacting the coach or other activity head—either with a phone call or by a visit during a campus tour. "Introduce yourself and mention your interest in continuing your high school participation with them," says Leider. "By telling or showing the coach or department or club people what you can offer, you may be able to enlist their help in getting a better financial-aid package."

That's because many schools use "preferential packaging" in deciding how to distribute need-based financial aid. For instance, two students with similar family incomes may both

Educate Yourself on Scholarship Scams

Scholarship scams account for less than 2 percent of all fraud pulled on the American public, but federal officials say they are increasing: In 2004, nearly 5,000 complaints were lodged against more than 1,000 companies offering financial-aid awards for a fee. (That was up dramatically from 670 only a few years earlier.) All this comes in spite of the College Scholarship Fraud Prevention Act, enacted in 2000 to establish strict sentencing guidelines for criminal financial-aid fraud and to mandate public-education programs.

Although some bona fide counselors help in other aspects of nabbing scholarships—coaching students to write essays that win awards, say—a legitimate scholarship requires no up-front fees. (Repeat the preceding phrase until it's encoded in your parental DNA). Never pay a fee touted as covering administrative or processing costs, "memberships," or to "ensure that only serious candidates apply."

Don't Pay to Get Money

Here are some red flags that signal "Scholarship Scam Ahead!"

Up-front funds. Any request, tied to a scholarship or not, that requires you to pay an advance fee for obtaining a low-interest educational loan (sometimes hawked as an "origination" or "guarantee" fee). Real student loans always deduct any fees from the disbursement check. Real student loans never require an application-processing fee.

Fees for services. Beware any request for a payment that will allegedly grant you access to scholarship-matching lists of "secret" or otherwise enticing awards, such as those offering "guaranteed winnings" or "millions of dollars in unclaimed scholarships." These services usually offer the same opportunities available for free at websites such as www.finaid.org and www.fastweb.com—yet they charge $400 or more for the added hype. (P.S. Not one scholarship in the United States "guarantees" winners, nor is there any surplus of unclaimed scholarship money.)

Compensated "counselors." Services that promise to apply for scholarships or student loans "on your behalf," sometimes under the guise of financial-aid seminars, can be a front to sell overpriced loans or glean personal information such as bank account or Social Security numbers. Conversely, legitimate admissions consultants (often former university admissions officers) work one on one with students or schools to provide guidance on admissions and scholarship applications and essays; they do not get involved in loan applications.

Unsolicited offers. Only after you ask about a scholarship should you receive details about it. "Any scholarship offers or applications that come to you from out of the blue are likely bogus," says high school counselor John Midgley, "especially when they arrive via e-mail." Scamsters buy students' e-mail addresses and spam them with bogus scholarship offers, most requiring up-front fees.

Any offer with one of these phrases:

• *This scholarship is guaranteed or your money back...*

• *You can't get this information anywhere else...*

• *We need only your credit card or bank account number to hold this scholarship...*

• *We do all the work...*

• *You've been selected as a finalist in a scholarship contest, and we need only a small handling fee...*

If you suspect that you have been the victim of a scholarship scam, report it to the Federal Trade Commission. To file a complaint, log onto www.ftc.gov/scholarshipscams, or call 877-382-4357.

qualify for $10,000 a year in financial aid. Whereas one may be offered $8,000 in loans and $2,000 in grants, an endorsement from a coach or club sponsor may "rewrite" that allocation to a more palatable $2,000 in payback loans and $8,000 in free grant money. Timing is crucial, Leider says, so make your approach concurrent with the application or just after submitting it. "The coach or sponsor will not want to speak on your behalf unless you're going to apply there and are really interested in participating in their program."

Private Scholarship Money

Do frequent searches at scholarship websites. There's a trick to using free scholarship-search websites such as Fast-Web, FinAid, CollegeQuest by Peterson, Collegenet, or even the College Board: Revisit them every few weeks in order to tap opportunities untouched by one-time visitors.

"People don't realize that some of these databases don't give you all the scholarships at once," says Kaplan of Scholarship Coach.com. "They trickle them out, to get you to keep visiting the site. What they usually offer first are well-known scholarships or those that pigeonhole applicants into a specific category, such as grade-point average." But the more frequently you access the sites, Kaplan adds, the deeper your search goes—unearthing lesser-known scholarships that may or may not include broader application criteria.

"Profile" unique hobbies. Do what many students don't: Complete the profile section that often appears on scholarship databases. These student profiles seek information about the applicant's hobbies, employment history, fraternal organizations their parents belong to, and even their religion. "Unfortunately," says FinAid's Kantrowitz, "many students rush through this profile, or completely skip the hobbies section."

That's shooting yourself in the pocketbook. Whereas certain scholarships are visible to all website visitors, programs that attract fewer applications are matched by keywords supplied in the student profiles. "If you play the bagpipes," notes Kantrowitz, "list that under your hobbies! Certain college scholarships are awarded for playing the bagpipes—and virtually everything else that makes a student unique. But you won't find them unless you enter the keywords."

Follow the yellow-click road. Another way to ferret out scholarships is with smart keyword searching on an everyday search engine. "If you go to Google and type 'scholarships,'" says Kaplan, "you'll get too many hits."

Instead, type "Coca Cola Scholars" or another sought-after scholarship. "This generates hits for high school and college guidance websites across the country that list not only that particular scholarship but others as well—including some that may not be in the materials at your own high school or on scholarship databases." This strategy is especially useful in uncovering the smaller, lesser-known awards—typically $1,000 or less—that tend to draw few applicants.

Make nice with that crosstown rival. Another productive trail to follow is the one that leads to other schools in your area. "When I was in high school," says Kaplan, "I would visit the high school across town and check out the scholarships listed on the bulletin board in their guidance office. I found several small, local scholarships that no one in my school knew about—one had only three applicants—and I wound up winning them. Staffers at the 'rival' school were willing to help me because they admired my proactive search."

Essays That Excel

Do some detective work. To determine the type of essay that earns scholarships awarded by corporations or civic associations, research what has worked in the past. "Before writing your essay," advises scholarship coach Kaplan, "contact

the organization and ask for samples of essays that won in the past. Winning essays and profiles of their applicant authors are often published in corporate newsletters or on the company website."

In reviewing past winners, the point is not to copy those topics. "They'll spot that in a minute," Kaplan warns. "But you should note how it was written—the theme, the points made, the overall structure.

"The chances are high that your essay will be reviewed by the same people who have decided past winners," adds Kaplan. "This strategy may seem obvious, but our research indicates that 97 percent of applicants writing scholarship essays to corporations or civic associations never read the winning essays from previous years. Yet when they do, we find, it doubles their chances of winning."

While you're at it, visit the "About Us" section of the association website for clues to why they sponsor the award. If they note a "proud tradition of serving the community," an essay highlighting the student's involvement in a local civic or volunteer group might fit the bill. If you find out that the corporate officers attended small colleges, it could be a deft move to write about being an average, everyday kid who possesses big dreams—and the ability to reach them. If the scholarship sponsor is a patriotic group, an essay about a proud veteran in the family or neighborhood will obviously fare better than an antiwar screed. "You need to ask yourself this fundamental question: 'What is this scholarship's definition of the ideal applicant?'" says Kaplan. "The answer is often on their website or in the company mission statement."

▶ **A BETTER WAY**

College Advice: Is It Wrong to Pay for It?

In the spring, many high schools hold informative—and free—seminars for college-bound students and their families. During these sessions, college admissions and financial-aid officers provide gratis much of the same advice offered by paid college counselors on how to apply for aid, write an essay, or complete admissions forms.

If you opt to hire a private counselor, be leery of any who request that ongoing payments be charged to a credit card. Instead, their fee should be a one-time charge.

Showcase Accomplishments

AN ACCOMPLISHMENTS RÉSUMÉ lets university and scholarship reviewers examine a student's achievements outside the classroom. (A mythical applicant is profiled below.) The intent here is to paint a portrait of the "whole" person, focusing on the student's talents as a time manager. Hand the accomplishments résumé to any teacher you ask to write a recommendation; it eases their task.

List specific rank when in top 10% of class.

Jane Q. Public
SS #123-45-6789
Current class rank: **16 of 362** (Top 5%)

Any leadership positions are a gold star; "climbing the ranks" may be even more attractive by showing "earned" status over popularity.

High School Activities

Springfield High School Theater Company - Grades 9, 10, 11, 12
Served in every school fall drama and three spring musicals as actor and stage crew/set design. **Club president in 12th grade and vice president in 11th.**

Listing sports "specialties" is important for coaches who need to field a team.

Springfield H.S. Swim Team - Grades 9, 10, 11, 12
Junior varsity in freshman and sophomore years; varsity thereafter. **Competed in 50- and 100-meter backstroke events.** Also swam for Springfield Sharks Swim Club in summer.

Technology Students of America (TSA) - Grades 11, 12
Competed in seven engineering-oriented projects on a regional or state level under guidelines specific to each event; medal winner in two. Served as club secretary for two years.

Community service of any kind is the key to securing many corporate-awarded scholarships.

National Honor Society - Grades 11, 12
Led fund-raising drive to support local homeless shelter.

Environmental Club - Grades 9, 10
Helped design and landscape a working pond and self-sustaining ecosystem on school grounds, along with other club activities to curb pollutants in our environment.

Organization and commitment to mundane events tells colleges you can endure even "boring" classes.

Spanish Club - Grade 10, 11
Helped tutor freshman students and **organized the annual Spanish dinner event.**

Work Experience

May 2004 to present
Big Burger Barn Restaurant
123 Main Street
Springfield, North Carolina 12345
Supervisor: **Joe Smith (Phone: 919-555-5678)**
Worked 16 hours per week during school and 32 hours during summer; shift manager since October 2004.

Summers 2002-2004
Springfield Day Camp
Camp director: **Bonnie Jones (Phone: 919-555-8765)**
Hired at age 13 as the **youngest counselor** in history of township-run day camp for 160 children, ages 5 to 12. Responsible for planning, organizing, and running activities for all age groups in all-day summer program (8 a.m. to 5 p.m.).

Awards

Received three scholastic and five community-service awards since Grade 8 grade for overall academic excellence, writing, science, mathematics, art, and volunteer work, including:

The "S" Award for Springfield district middle and high school students who maintain an overall 93 percent or better grade point percentage throughout the year, and an "A" in each subject in every marking period. Received three times.

Presidential Scholars Award given in recognition of Outstanding Academic Excellence

Girl Scouts of America—Gold, Silver, and Bronze awards

Part-time jobs show ambition, responsibility, and perseverance. To colleges and scholarship awarders, the more you do, the more you can do—and the more deserving you are.

It's unlikely colleges will call references, but listing them suggests you've been a good employee. Get permission from supervisors beforehand.

A "can-do" attitude at a young age gets notice.

List any national, state, or district-wide awards you may have received by name. Because they are more competitive, they are considered more substantial achievements.

Don't climb every mountain. No matter whether the essay aims to accomplish university admission or a scholarship, it's best to avoid that oldest chestnut of an essay topic: *Describe an obstacle you faced and how you overcame it.* "Every essay should be self-reflecting—that's true," says essay coach Hughes. "Yet I generally caution applicants against writing anything overtly depressing in a college essay.

"Why? Because it can backfire easily unless the student is a truly great writer. And most aren't."

College and scholarship reviewers are often looking to be inspired, so they may be predisposed against these "downer" topics. Not only that, but some essays—such as failing to make the freshman basketball team, but then becoming a starter on varsity years later—can reveal an applicant's tendency to overestimate the true relative magnitude of an obstacle.

Although such exaggeration is understandable—it typically stems from a genuine lack of life experience—it may suggest to an admissions officer that the applicant is likely to be "high maintenance" once he or she arrives on campus.

Even life-transforming obstacles—dealing with an illness, death, or divorce, for instance—are generally better handled in a teacher's letter of recommendation, suggests guidance counselor Midgley. (Example: "While his mother fought breast cancer, Johnny shouldered the burden of caring for his younger siblings. Yet even under these trying circumstances,

> **▶ SCAM ALERT!**

A Target Population

College life lends itself to identity theft. About half of all campuses still use Social Security numbers as student identifiers; many universities even post those IDs outside classrooms to convey test grades "anonymously."

In addition, reports the U.S. Department of Education, half of all enrolled students regularly receive solicitations for credit cards. These can easily be intercepted and used to establish a bogus credit line in the student's name.

Your defense: At some schools, students can request an alternative ID number, such as a string of nine random digits. For incoming mail, they should list their home—not campus—address, and authorize their parents to destroy credit-card offers. To prevent the theft of any vital personal data the university may send via e-mail, students should change their computer log-in name and password every 30 days.

he managed to maintain great grades and a positive attitude in my class.")

Seek unusual role models. Another common essay topic—*Who is your role model and why?*—also is a trap just waiting to be sprung. "Contrary to popular belief," says Kaplan, "the answer isn't about the role model—it's a way to learn about the values you choose in *recognizing* a role model. Most people doing this kind of essay pick obvious role models—Martin Luther King, Jr., or Gandhi. If you choose those universal heroes, you're going to knock yourself out of the running unless your essay is remarkably original."

A better strategy is to pick an obscure role model: the volunteer soccer coach who missed meals to teach you after practice how to kick with your left foot; the single parent who worked two jobs but still made it to those Saturday soccer games to cheer each left-footed goal; John Lloyd Wright, inventor of Lincoln Logs (and son of the famous architect), whose toy sparked your dream of becoming an architectural engineer. "A university admissions or scholarship officer reads thousands of applications in a given year," says Kantrowitz. "And after the 20th essay espousing the deep philosophy of a 17-year-old, it all becomes a blur. The essays that get noticed are those that reveal who you are and what you believe in *from a truly personal perspective.*"

Share your character uncharacteristically. The real purpose of many essays is to allow applicants to display themselves as unique individuals. "One of the most memorable and enjoyable essays I ever read," says Hughes, "was from a girl who worked part-time in a fish cannery in a small Alaska town. While many kids applying to college have part-time jobs or come from small towns, it's not every day you read an essay about a kid who works in a fish cannery *and* comes from a small Alaska town."

In other words, an applicant with dreams of becoming a

veterinarian can be expected to write about his lifelong love of animals, but the essay that gets noticed is from the neighborhood St. Francis who went door-to-door trying to reunite a lost puppy with its owner—only to have second thoughts about relinquishing Fido as the mission was accomplished. The high school drama queen is certain to discuss the thrill of being center-stage, but the essay that stands out is the one describing her experience as an extra in the crowd scene of a Hollywood movie. "You have to be who you are," says Hughes. "But you'll stand out if you're someone who can show uniqueness from the pack."

Say it before you write it. No matter the essay topic, students should make a practice run before writing even the first sentence. "I recommend they always use a tape recorder," says Kantrowitz, "because most students are more comfortable speaking than writing. The typical student can speak about 200 words a minute—about five or six times more than typing them. With a tape recorder, you get your thoughts out more quickly, and it's easier to transcribe a tape and massage those thoughts into an essay than to try to write them out cold."

Of course, a good essay isn't simply a matter of transcribing thoughts. It should be polished several times. Better yet, do as many rewrites as necessary to maximize the essay's chances of impressing its influential readers.

TRAVEL

6

Go More Places for Less

DOMESTICALLY AND ABROAD, travel has become big business. Travel spending within the United States topped $600 billion in 2004, and the Travel Industry Association of America expects that figure to reach $700 billion in 2007.

Already the travel industry is responsible for more than seven million jobs in the U.S., with an annual payroll of about $162 billion. Across the country, travel generates $100 billion in tax revenues for local, state, and federal governments; in 29 states, it ranks among the top three industries. California, Florida, Texas, Pennsylvania, and New York are the most common destinations. Most trips are short—two nights or less—and summer remains the busiest season.

Globally, meanwhile, the travel industry pumps $3.5 trillion into the world economy each year.

Travel can also generate some world-class headaches, of course, with snafus ranging from disasters unleashed by Mother Nature to those delivered by surly service-providers. Overall, many travelers' most frequent complaint is simply the cost of getting from point A to point B. Case in point: Skyrocketing jet-fuel prices spurred many airlines to raise their fares repeatedly in 2005—and that was before Hurricanes Katrina or Rita disrupted Gulf Coast oil production.

What's the answer? Many travelers turn to the Internet, which allows you to better compare costs—but not always to

IN THIS CHAPTER

Airlines

Hotels

Rental Cars

Cruises

secure lower prices. That's because airlines update their fares throughout the day, often resulting in a practice known as "fare-jumping." These sudden price surges afflict both online travel agents—Expedia, Orbitz, and Travelocity, to cite the most-trafficked examples—and the airlines' own websites. Meanwhile, hotel and car-rental costs may strike you

▶ **A BETTER WAY**

The Inside Scoop on Online Booking

For all their popularity and reputation, the Big Three online travel agencies—Expedia, Orbitz, and Travelocity—may not give you the best deals in airline, hotel, or rental-car reservations booked online.

These websites make it easy to compare prices, yes—but they include only select companies, and they don't provide all their lowest rates. Meanwhile, lesser-known sites such as SideStep (www.sidestep.com), Mobissimo (www.mobissimo.com), and Kayak (www.kayak.com) act as true search engines. These relative newcomers—launched in 2000 or later—occasionally display bargains not found on competing third-party websites. SideStep, for example, has free software that scours the websites of various airlines—including JetBlue, which does not release its fares to independent sites. Even when the newer sites quote rates equal to those on the Big Three, the smaller search engines customarily charge lower service fees for booking online.

"In my experience, with the latest iteration of these sites," says Norie Quintos, who edits the "Smart Traveler" section of *National Geographic Traveler* magazine, "you save time and money because the newer sites search more for you. I think they're the best first step in comparing prices."

But when it comes to booking, your best bet is usually with the airline, hotel, or car-rental company's own website, says corporate travel consultant Joel Widzer, author of *The Penny Pincher's Passport to Luxury Travel: The Art of Cultivating Preferred Customer Status.* Because travel providers must pay a commission to these third-party websites—which also tack on their own fees—more providers now post their best rates on their own websites.

In his own research, Widzer compared 63 identical air routes. "In nearly every case, the lowest rate was posted on the airline's website," he says. Another advantage to booking online with the provider itself: "Because of manpower costs, more airlines are now adding a surcharge when you make reservations by phone," adds Quintos.

as consistently higher online because these third-party websites must charge mark-ups in order to turn a profit. Finally, the low rates trumpeted on television and in print may elude you when you call to claim them: Travel service providers never mention precisely how many fares, rooms, or rental cars they are offering at those discounts.

By following the advice in this chapter, however, you should be able to sidestep high costs and heinous hassles in both business travel and recreational escapes. Read on to learn some insider trip tips.

Airlines

Wise up to night-owl reservations. You've seen those enticing advertisements for low-fare flights. But what happens when you try to reserve one? You're told they're sold out.

You can thank the lax regulatory environment, which allows airlines to ballyhoo bargain fares without disclosing the exact number of discount seats available on any given flight. So what's your fastest route to an inexpensive ticket?

One way is to make your reservation as a midweek night owl, advises Peter Greenberg, chief correspondent for Discovery's Travel Channel and author of *The Travel Detective* and *Flight Crew Confidential*. "Starting from one minute after midnight to about 1 a.m. on Wednesday," he says, "all airline computer systems are flooded with low-fare reservations that were booked during the previous weeks but never paid for." That's when these unclaimed reservations get canceled—then immediately go up for grabs at discount rates.

This one-hour window of bargain prices—which can be nabbed for hundreds of dollars less than full fare—varies according to where you live and where your target airline is based. If you live in New York and you're booking with American Airlines, whose hub is the Dallas–Fort Worth airport, start calling the reservation phone line at 1:01 a.m. Eastern Standard Time. If you live on the West Coast and want to fly

Before leaving on any flight, program the airline's toll-free number into your cell phone.

If your flight is delayed or canceled, the upshot could be faster trouble-shooting than is possible by waiting in line at the airport ticket counter.

an East Coast-based airline (Atlanta-based Delta, for example), you needn't lose as much sleep to use this tactic; you can start calling at 9:01 p.m. (PST, of course) on Tuesday. Meanwhile, if you're booking on an airline's website, understand that specials for weekend deals are typically posted the previous Monday and fares are raised on Friday.

Consider the calendar. In addition to the hour you make reservations, the day on which you make them can play a big role in snagging a deal, says John W. Frenaye, Jr., director of marketing and business development at Capital Travel Center in Annapolis, Maryland. "For the very best deals, make reservations 21 to 45 days before your departure date," he advises. "On the 20th day before travel, airfares typically increase. They increase further on the 14th day before departing, and again seven days before." At three days before departure, however, rates on unsold seats usually drop like a rock—especially for those midnight callers, says Frenaye.

Fly small to save big. You don't need to fly a low-fare airline to save money. Their mere existence may help you.

First, when an airline such as Southwest or JetBlue comes to a particular airport, says Greenberg, "the fares of larger competitors serving the same airport suddenly drop an average of 43 percent—and usually stay low to remain competitive."

These and other low-fare carriers serve some major hubs, but they are more likely to be found in smaller airports near or in a major city—and that's where the deals can be, even if competing larger carriers are there too. Case in point: Booking a flight from Los Angeles to New York three days before departure, Greenberg found that flying a round-trip on American Airlines would be $800 cheaper if he left from the Long Beach airport rather than from Los Angeles International (LAX). The reason: Low-fare competitor JetBlue operates from Long Beach, but not from LAX. "Yet the difference between both airports is only a 20-minute car ride," Greenberg notes.

The next time you call about airfares, ask: "How much for first class?"

"The overwhelming number of tickets sold are for coach seats," says travel expert Joel Widzer, "so there may be special fares for unsold first-class seats. They're not mentioned unless you ask." In one case, that question got him a first-class seat for $250 less than the last-minute coach fare on the same flight.

What Else Is on the Web?

The Web allows you to do much more than ferret out low travel costs. The websites listed here investigate some less-publicized aspects of the travel experience that are nonetheless crucial to your comfort on the road.

SeatGuru (www.seatguru.com) shows the best and worst seats, by airplane model, for dozens of carriers. The site lets you compare seat pitch, width, and amenities such as power ports between first class, business class, and coach.

AirlineMeals.net (www.airlinemeals. net) includes photographs and passenger reviews of thousands of onboard meals served by most air carriers operating in the United States and other countries.

Security Checkpoint Wait Times (http://waittime.tsa.dhs.gov) is operated by the federal government's Transportation Security Administration. Type in the day and time of your planned departure to receive an estimate of how long you will have to wait at security barriers in most U.S. airports.

FlyerTalk (www.flyertalk.com) offers an array of useful message boards and forums for air travelers.

Great Circle Mapper (http://gc.kls2. com) allows you to plot your intended air route and calculate its length in miles.

Exchange Rate Calculator (http://corp orate.visa.com/pd/consumer_ex_rates. jsp) allows Visa cardholders to determine the foreign currency exchange rate when making credit-card purchases. This website also includes a section on the bank fees you're likely to incur when using plastic abroad.

So for bargains (whatever your preferred carrier), consider flights serving Providence rather than Boston, Chicago's smaller Midway Airport instead of O'Hare, Oakland over San Francisco, Fort Lauderdale as opposed to Miami, and so on.

Get a heads-up on back-to-back ticketing. Fares are generally lower if your trip includes a weekend stay (this explains why business travelers who are on the road Monday to Friday typically pay more). But if you're planning a trip that doesn't involve the required weekend stay for automatic savings, says David Rowell, publisher of The Travel Insider website

The Road to Ripoffs

Travel scams consistently rank near the top of complaints to the Federal Trade Commission and many state attorney general offices. We're not talking petty larceny here: Trusting consumers get bilked an average of nearly $500 per incident.

What should you be on the lookout for? Here are four of the most common dodges:

"Free vacations." These offers may arrive via snail mail or e-mail. Either way, they announce that you've been selected to win a free vacation. The catch: To claim the "gift," you must pay a "processing fee" that typically exceeds the cost of a similar trip. Not only that, but the travel dates are limited.

Sometimes, the phone number by which you can purportedly redeem your "prize" is a 900 number or one outside the United States—a ruse to generate sky-high long-distance charges. "Basically, any offer for a free vacation that comes to you unsolicited is a scam," says Norie Quintos of *National Geographic Traveler*. Although some time-share facilities do indeed offer free trips, plan to endure an entire day of high-pressure sales pitches to buy vacation time at that resort.

Discount travel clubs. This scam tenders a "membership" costing several hundred dollars in exchange for a certificate that supposedly entitles you to re-duced rates for travel. "However, re-deeming the certificate may be next to impossible," says travel agent John Frenaye, a member of the Communications Council of the American Society of Travel Agents (ASTA). "The typical scenario is that the certificate is good only for certain dates—and expires before it can be redeemed."

"Become a travel agent." Another ploy promises you the same discounts offered to accredited travel agents: After you pay a fee, the company grants you "credentials" that supposedly let you access travel-agent freebies and discounts. However, says Frenaye, hotels, airlines, and other travel-industry operators do not recognize these credentials because they bear no relation to the legitimate discount-granting privileges extended to members of organizations such as ASTA, the International Airlines Transport Association (IATA), or the Cruise Lines International Association (CLIA).

Pricing too cheap to be true. It's all in the fine print: Read it closely and you'll discover that many low-cost fares are one-way only—meaning, of course, that you must double them to get an accurate idea of your expected outlay.

Frenaye's advice: "Be sure to read all fine print" before you click that 'Buy' button online or agree to a phone-in reservation.

(www.travelinsider.com), "There's a cure for the airlines' Saturday-night fever, and it can save you plenty": Buy two discounted round-trip tickets—each including a weekend stay—and use only the first half of each ticket.

Rowell cites a favorite case study: "Let's say you want to fly from Denver to New York on Monday and return to Denver on Friday. If you buy one round-trip ticket, you may pay $800 because it doesn't involve an overnight weekend stay. But if you buy one round-trip ticket that leaves Denver on that Monday and returns a week or two later, and a second round-trip leaving New York on that Friday and likewise returning a week or two later, those round-trip fares might be only $250 each. Use the first half of the first ticket to get to New York and the first half of the second ticket to get back to Denver, and you'll save $300 because both tickets include the required weekend stay for substantial savings."

Airlines dislike it when customers employ this tactic. They claim it violates airline policy, says Rowell. And if an airline catches you in the act of using back-to-back tickets, it can seize your tickets and bar you from boarding its plane. You may also be stripped of all frequent-flier miles you have accumulated with that airline. So make sure you understand the risks inherent in this stratagem before you decide to undertake it.

Your protection: "The best way to avoid problems," says Rowell, "is to buy each discounted ticket with a weekend stay on a different airline. Also, never use frequent-flier miles to secure either ticket."

A similar ploy, called "throwaway ticketing," can be utilized to sidestep pricy one-way airfares, which often exceed the cost of a round-trip that includes a weekend stay. "Simply buy a round-trip flight that includes a weekend stay," Rowell recommends, "and throw away the return flight portion." If you are flying abroad (to tour Europe or Southeast Asia, say), ask about an "open-jawed" ticket: This lets you arrive at one location and depart from another, obviating any doubling back to your original arrival point.

To survive the cooped-up cabin environment, suggests flight attendant James Wysong, bring these two key items on board: a small vial of lavender lotion and a pair of disposable ear plugs.

Dab the former below your nostrils to combat odors from the galley, lavatories, or unsavory passengers—"especially important in the summer," notes Wysong, who as A. Frank Steward wrote The Plane Truth: Shift Happens at 35,000 Feet.

Uncover "hidden city" savings. Lower competition for lightly traveled routes means flying into a small city can cost you big. To beat these little-town blues, choose a route that makes a layover stop at the town that is your true destination. If you want to fly to Syracuse, for example, seek a flight that stops over there before continuing on to, say, New York City.

"When the plane arrives at Syracuse for its layover," says Rowell, "you simply walk off the aircraft and out of the terminal. Though airport security will not admit you to the gate area unless you hold a ticket to board a flight leaving that airport, they do not check the tickets of deplaning passengers.

This tactic is useless if you need to check your luggage. If you can't carry it onboard, use a baggage-transportation service such as Luggage Express (www.usxp.com) to ship your bags to your final destination. Expect to pay at least $60 per piece.

Fly off-peak to pocket savings. Although there are no hard-and-fast rules, the busiest times for airline travel are usually the most expensive. What does that mean? "Flying out of an airport early in the morning or late in the afternoon, the peak times for business travelers," says Rowell, "is ordinarily the costliest window for other travelers as well. The busiest and typically most expensive days to fly are Monday and Friday."

Hop the same-routed flight leaving a particular airport between 10 a.m. and 2 p.m., by contrast, and you may find the fare discounted hundreds of dollars—especially Tuesdays, Thursdays, or weekends. "At the very least," notes Rowell, "there tend to be more discounted seats on flights during those 'off-peak' times than during the rush-hour flights."

Avoid "fortress" hubs. Another saver's strategy is to book a flight that doesn't transit through that airline's "fortress" hub. For an American Airlines flight, for instance, this means shunning any route that involves a mid-flight stop in Dallas–Forth Worth; for a U.S. Airways flight, it means eschewing a layover in Philadelphia. "Because that airline dominates at that fortress hub," says Rowell, "its flights through that airport tend to be more expensive than those of other airlines traveling there, or flights by that airline to other hubs."

Be late for a better seat. When you manage to snag a bargain-basement fare, it often comes with a dreaded middle seat—and on most planes, B and E seat assignments indicate that you'll be sandwiched between the aisle and the window. Of course, you can always request a specific seat assignment when making your reservation. But don't abandon hope if you're told the more desirable aisle and window seats are already taken. Instead, delay getting a seat assignment until the last possible minute—or simply arrange to be the last

> ▶ **A BETTER WAY**

Faster Flier Miles

Credit-card programs that earn you one airline mile for every dollar you charge can get you nowhere fast—or somewhere expensively. Before you start congratulating yourself on having converted 25,000 reward points into a "free" air ticket, pause to consider that you may be holding, essentially, a $25,000 ticket to Akron.

Fortunately, says Matthew Bennett, publisher of FirstClassFlyer.com, there's a quicker way to fly courtesy of your plastic purchases: Any American Express cardholder enrolled in a Membership Rewards program in the United States can buy 1,000-mile reward increments for $25 a pop. Up to 500,000 points can be purchased per account each year, and these can be transferred to the frequent-flier reward program of at least 13 airlines.

If you can't quite bring yourself to buy frequent-flier miles—even at those steep savings—consider the Starwood Preferred Guest™ credit card from American Express, suggests Bennett. With each 20,000 miles you accumulate, you receive a bonus of 5,000 miles, netting you 1.25 miles for each dollar you charge. And as Bennett points out, "the rewards can be used on 30 different airlines."

Topping it off, the Star Points card—which historically has waived its $30 annual fee for the second year—offers free car-rental damage insurance, extra points for hotel stays, and other travel perks.

Fees of Flying

They all seem to have their palms out for a cut of your airfare: Telephone-reservation clerks, baggage handlers — even Uncle Sam.

Here are some of the many ancillary charges that can make you feel the sky is not the limit when it comes to plane costs:

Government fees & taxes. These add as much as $50 to a round-trip ticket that costs $200, according to the Air Transport Association. Here's what that money has to cover:

• The U.S. government's 7.5 percent passenger-ticket tax.

• A "segment" fee of $3.10 for each leg of a flight, levied by the Federal Aviation Administration.

• A $4.50 passenger facility fee, charged at each stop in 200 of the nation's 500-plus airports.

• A security service fee capped at $10 per round-trip from the Transportation Security Administration.

Calling fees. Phone in to make your reservation rather than book it online and you may be slapped with a surcharge of $5 to $20 for the "privilege."

The additional outlay is necessary, the airlines claim, to offset the cost of human operators and supervisors, the expense of the "toll-free" phone call, and facilities rent. Online costs, by contrast, are likely to remain fixed—until computers learn to request pay raises.

High-priced paper. At some airlines, a paper ticket can cost as much as $50 more than an e-ticket.

When change is bad. Change fees to modify or cancel an already made non-refundable reservation cost $100 at most major airlines.

Burdensome bags. Expect to pay $40 to $80 for checking a third bag; other fees may be imposed if your luggage is deemed "too heavy." The industry-wide standard luggage-weight limit is 20 kilograms (44 pounds) per bag, so if you're planning to overpack, check with your airline.

Onboard meals. Once complimentary, these will now set you back $5 to $10 on many airlines.

Kid costs. Unaccompanied minors often are charged $40 or more for the luxury of flying alone—more when traveling overseas.

Usurious upgrades. Some airlines charge fees as high as $250 each way for frequent fliers who want to use their miles to upgrade an inexpensive coach-class fare to business class on an international flight. That's in addition to redeeming the 25,000 miles required for the trip.

passenger to board the aircraft. That's the advice of James Wysong, a longtime flight attendant who has written two books about air travel under the name A. Frank Steward. (Get it?)

"A lot of the best seats on every flight aren't assigned until the day of the flight," says Wysong. The reason: Seats are typically assigned from the back of the plane to the front. Passengers who book the earliest therefore often wind up sitting near the lavatories or in the rear of the cabin. In being the last to board, you can scope out any unoccupied seat and claim it as your own. Because flight attendants will rarely check your boarding pass once you enter the cabin, you are unlikely to be denied the seat you choose in this spontaneous fashion. The one hitch in the plan is that 11th-hour arrivals cannot count on finding space in the overhead compartment for carry-on bags.

Why not Y-Up? Many airlines, says Wysong, typically overbook reservations by 15 percent to compensate for the historical rate of no-shows. As a result, the economy-class passengers who show up for any flight may outnumber the economy seats available on it. But the airline is legally obligated to accommodate them, so it must decide which coach passengers will be granted first-class seating. This is why savvy travelers who pay full fare for an unrestricted economy seat often specifically request a so-called "Y-Up fare." Although it usually costs 10 to 15 percent more than regular "economy coach," Y-Up passengers are the ones most likely to be offered a free upgrade to first class.

Dress up for upgrades. After considering Y-Up passengers, according to Wysong, most airlines base their upgrade selections on one simple criterion: the passenger's wardrobe.

"All things considered," he says, "a passenger wearing a suit will always be offered a free upgrade over someone in shorts and sandals—whether or not they are traveling on business. It dates back to the days when passengers dressed

Block That Pickpocket: Bob Arno's Advice

BOB ARNO is a professor of purse snatching, a thespian of thievery. To demonstrate one danger of traveling overseas, the Stockholm-born comic pickpocket steals the show—and the wallets of audience volunteers who venture onstage—with his masterly sleight of hand. Arno has spent nearly 40 years studying, photographing, and disclosing the tricks of the trade used by professional street criminals around the world. Below he reveals some common pilferage ploys—and your best defense to parry them.

● Men should ideally keep their wallets in a breast pocket; if not, tight jeans offer the best protection. Don't try the old trick of wrapping a rubber band around your wallet. According to professionals, that only makes the wallet easier to lift—or "break," in pickpocket argot. A front pants pocket is just as vulnerable as a back one.

● Women should wear a handbag diagonally across the chest—ideally held securely just below the underarm. To make the handbag more resistant to being severed with a knife, it should have a wide strap. The clasps should lock securely; purses that feature locking closures are better than those with metal snaps. Wallets should be buried deep in the handbag, never in one of its outside pockets.

● Unless you sport a safety pouch—worn under shirts or pants—carry only a small amount of cash and no more than two credit cards when traveling through busy public places abroad. "Always keep at least one credit card in the hotel safe, in case you are victimized," recommends Arno, author of *Travel Advisory! How to Avoid Thefts, Cons, and Street Scams While Traveling*.

● When walking at night, carry a "throwaway" wallet with a few dollars and some old hotel key cards. "Drug addicts often prey on American tourists," says Arno. "If you're approached, you can throw that wallet to avoid a mugging. When he sees it contains some money and cards that might be credit cards, he's happy and runs off."

● Most often, pickpockets operate in tightly choreographed teams: One thief distracts the victim, a second lifts the wallet, and a third carries it quickly from the scene.

POCKET-PICKING PLOYS AROUND THE PLANET

Here are some patterns to watch out for in seven popular international destinations:

London. Be cautious on public transport and in shopping districts—"particularly around Regent Street and Oxford Street," says Arno, who frequently counsels local law enforcement on how to foil Fagins.

Italy. In Rome, pickpockets tend to travel on crowded public transportation. As one diverts a passenger—often by asking for directions—another who has been "squeezed" next to the victim lifts the wallet.

Arno's advice: "Do what Europeans do—keep your hand over your wallet-containing pocket whenever you're on public transportation." In Naples, pickpockets also work the streets, where they target tourists sporting jewelry or expensive watches.

France & Germany. These two countries have little pickpocketing in the streets themselves. Aboard trains and inside train stations, however, are notorious hot spots.

Russia. "Be aware of people who loiter in lobbies and follow you outside," Arno advises. Their goal is to accost you several blocks away—beyond the range of hotel security cameras or police patrols. An accomplice waiting there may drop a map or other item in front of the victim, or "mark"; as he or she bends over to pick it up, the follower bumps the mark and lifts the wallet or opens a purse. St. Petersburg is a pickpocket's haven, says Arno, especially in the vicinity of museums such as the State Hermitage.

Scandinavia. Pickpocketing can be problematic during the summer months, when gangs from Eastern Europe migrate here to fleece American tourists. "They tend to operate around or inside hotels—especially in Copenhagen," says Arno.

Here's a common scenario: A female tourist waiting in line to pay her bill will be diverted by the polite conversation of an attractive stranger. This makes it easy for the man's accomplice to open her handbag and filch her wallet.

The United States. Stadiums, amusement parks, public transportation, and shopping malls are all hot spots. Here again, the modus operandi is the same: As one thief distracts, the other dips. "However," warns Arno, "traveling gangs also work the supermarkets and other businesses near retirement communities; they stay 10 to 15 days before moving on." Seniors tend to be especially vulnerable, Arno explains, because of their looser-fitting clothing and their occasionally delayed reactions.

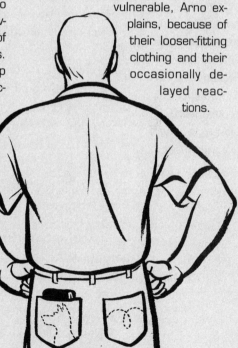

up for travel; even today, airlines want their first-class passengers to look the part." When allocating these free upgrades, he adds, some airlines value a passenger's dress more than his or her membership in its mileage club.

Cite 240 for a quicker exit. When your flight is delayed or canceled for any reason other than severe weather, you needn't spend hours on end waiting for that airline's next available departure. Just mention to the ticket agent or other bearer of that bad news that you're aware of Rule 240—essentially a list of an airline's "conditions of carriage," or dos and don'ts, filed with the U.S. Department of Transportation.

Before airline deregulation, Rule 240 was a federal mandate. One condition of carriage was that airlines had to put ticket-holding customers on the next available outbound flight—even if it was offered by a competitor. Whereas this is no longer a government decree, says Greenberg, who also serves as travel editor for the *Today* show, most airlines still adhere to the rule. Although the specific conditions vary from one airline to the next, most airlines will typically also provide meal vouchers (and limit the amount of compensation they give customers whose flight is delayed). A copy of your airline's conditions of carriage should be available at every ticket counter or on the airline's website.

Airlines aren't thrilled by the prospect of placing their own paying passengers on a competitor's flight: It robs them of revenue. "But if you mention it," says Greenberg, "they have to comply."

The exceptions: Rule 240 pertains only to airlines with competition agreements—carriers such as American, United, U.S. Airways, Delta, and Northwest. Smaller carriers such as JetBlue and Southwest, lacking any agreement to honor competitors' tickets, do not have to abide by it.

If you're told that Rule 240 does not apply, you may still contest a scrubbed flight. For example, says newsletter publisher Rowell, you can challenge an airline that cites weather

Enhance your safety by requesting a room above the ground floor. Higher foot traffic makes hotel rooms nearest elevators generally the safest.

as the cause of cancellation while its competitors are still flying. "The weather has to be really bad," he says, "and it has to affect many flights—not just your own."

Hotels

Shop, but don't book, online. Don't assume you'll get better hotel bargains by booking online. Orbitz, Expedia, Travelocity, and hotels.com typically buy rooms from hotels at a discount price; they then turn around and charge website users a markup of 24 to 48 percent for making a reservation, says travel editor Greenberg, author of *Hotel Secrets from the Travel Detective: Insider Tips on Getting the Best Value, Service, and Security in Accommodations from Bed-and-Breakfasts to Five-Star Resorts.*

Instead, do an online search for rates—but then phone the hotel directly. "If you see a hotel room advertised online for $100 a night," Greenberg advises, "call the hotel directly and offer $85. At the typical markup, you have to figure that the hotel is offering that room to the discounter for $65. So the hotel still stands to make a $20 profit by booking it through you rather than through the website."

With whom you negotiate—and how—makes a big difference: Ask to speak with the on-duty manager or sales director, who is authorized to make "cold call" deals that would be out of bounds for a lower-level reservations operator or desk clerk. "Explain that you understand the hotel is offering a discount on the Web, but you're looking for a better deal because you want to cultivate a relationship with that hotel and intend to stay there again in the future," says Greenberg. "The manager is more likely to give you a deal because of the prospect of your repeat business."

Booking directly with a hotel has other advantages, adds Joel Widzer, who runs a travel consulting firm in southern California and writes a travel column for Tripso.com. "Because the hotels have to pay a commission to these third-party websites, they are less likely, if at all, to upgrade your room when they see the reservation was made through that website. And if there's ever a problem with the reservation once you arrive, you may be directed to get it solved through the website that made it—rather than through the hotel itself."

Practice the upgrade shuffle. Try this tactic to maximize your odds of a room upgrade: Make your initial reservation for a standard room, but at check-in ask to be upgraded to a suite. Depending on occupancy, this move may cost you nothing—or you may be informed that it will set you back as

▶ **A BETTER WAY**

Alternative Lodging Options

If you want to save money—and experience distinctive accommodations—consider these alternatives to hotels:

Home exchange services let you swap lodgings with other travelers in the United States and abroad. For an annual fee of $50 to $100, you get access to other homes at low (or no) cost; in exchange, you agree to make your own home available for others' shelter for a similar time period. To learn more, check out www. homelink.org, www.intervac. com, www. homeexchange.com, or http://singles homeexchange.com. Traveling educators can visit a site of their own at www.teacherhomeswap.com.

Hospitality exchanges may not require you to reciprocate. Instead, you can stay with a local family for free (or for just a few dollars) in exchange for shouldering household chores. For more informa-

tion, check out www.globalfreeloaders. com or www.couchsurfing.com.

Apartment and villa rentals are often designed for extended visits of several months—at 20 percent or more below the rates charged by local hotels. See www.vrbo.com or www.interhome.us.

Other options: For as little as $30 per night, visitors of any faith can stay at an Italian convent; you'll find additional information at www.santasusanna.org/com ingToRome/convents.html. For the bucolically inclined, the European Federation for Farm and Village Tourism at www.eurogites.com offers links to associations in 19 countries offering housing that is off the beaten path. Many universities in Europe (and some in the U.S.) offer cut-rate dormitory housing in summer; to determine availability, contact colleges in your travel destination.

much as $100. Still, as Widzer points out, a single Benjamin is far cheaper than the hundreds more you would have paid to book a lavish hotel suite from the get-go.

This strategy may not work at truly tony facilities—their suites are often reserved far in advance. But, says Widzer, author of *The Penny Pincher's Passport to Luxury Travel: The Art of Cultivating Preferred Customer Status,* it does often succeed at slightly less palatial facilities, such as certain mid-level hotel chains. You stand the best chance of a hotel upgrade in the early afternoon of your arrival date, before business travelers check in and snap up those rooms.

Buddy up to bellhops. Never underestimate the power of the lowly baggage porter when you're looking for any type of favor—including a room upgrade. "In my experience," says Widzer, who travels some 100,000 miles a year, "bellhops often wield more influence with the hotel staff than the concierge does. They know the inner workings of the hotel, and they know everybody in it. They are familiar with every guest room—and when each is available."

Case study: On a trip to Hawaii, Widzer asked the hotel's front-desk clerk for an oceanfront room at check-in. "But when I got to the room," he says, "it was pretty average. So I pulled two $20 bills from my wallet and asked the bellhop carrying my bags if he thought I could get an upgrade. But I didn't give him the money… yet. He knew a nice tip was coming his way, so he got on the phone in my room and said, 'Can we get Mr. Widzer into Room X?' The next thing I knew, I was headed to that upgraded oceanfront room, which cost me nothing more than the tip." The bellhop left with dual Jacksons—and a mental note to meet that guest's needs on any future visit.

If this suggests that money talks, so be it—but bear in mind that some answer its call more graciously than others. When a friend of his tried to tip his way to an upgrade at the front desk of another hotel, Widzer recounts, "The clerk took his $50 tip—then gave him an average room. Hence my advice:

Never hand over a tip until the goods have been delivered."

Double-check those charges. If you truly want to "spend a night, not a fortune," as the ad slogan has it, get wise to some common hotel flimflams.

One is "double-dipping," which occurs when you're presented with a room-service charge on a slip resembling a credit-card receipt, with space left conspicuously blank for a delivery tip. But if you read the receipt carefully, warns Greenberg, you may note that in addition to the cost of that overpriced meal and mandatory state and local taxes, many hotels already add a service charge (usually about 2.5 percent) and an automatic gratuity of 15 to 20 percent for delivering your nosh. To protect your wallet, read the room-service menu carefully for any mention of automatic gratuity charges.

Another unwelcome surprise may be waiting if you have a fax or overnight-courier package delivered to your room. "The desk will ring you and ask if you'd like the item brought up, and most likely you will tip the person who makes the delivery," says Greenberg. "Not until check-out, however, do you discover that the hotel has tacked on a surcharge of $3 to $5 for every fax or package received." In either case, he suggests politely complaining to the manager on duty. Nine times out of 10, in Greenberg's experience, the hotel removes the charge upon request. (Your own success rate may vary.)

Also be aware of "resort fees" quietly tacked on to your bill. "Hotels realize that many people aren't tipping the staff, so many now add a $10-per-day surcharge to your room rate," notes travel agent Frenaye, who also writes a column for Trip so.com. At check-in, he recommends, ask about this surcharge to ensure you won't be tipping twice for the same service.

Fail to check in once you've made a reservation and you'll most likely be charged for the room anyway; most hotels stipulate that you must cancel a room reservation at least 24 hours before your scheduled arrival time. Indeed, many are moving toward a 48-hour minimum advance notice. Similar

If your hotel room does not offer a room safe and you're hesitant to use the hotel office safe, don't leave valuables in the first places that thieves look: Dresser drawers or under the mattress.

Better: Bring a sealable waterproof bag and hide small items inside the toilet tank (you can hang them from the flush bar with a twist tie). If your room has a ceiling of acoustic tiles, lift one of the panels and conceal the items overhead.

charges may bracket your stay at the other end: Leave at least a day before your reservation is up and the typical busy hotel will slap an early-departure charge of at least $50 on your bill. To avoid paying these no-show or early-go fees, says Widzer, you must produce some unassailable reason, such as the sudden illness of a family member.

Compare amenities to rates. A common mistake of many hotel guests, says Widzer, is choosing lodging solely by room rates. "People assume they have to stay at the Holiday Inn because the Four Seasons costs too much. You may pay a little more at a nicer hotel—and sometimes don't have to, depending on occupancy—but you usually get more too: That free breakfast, low-cost or free Internet access, or complimentary on-site gym can make up the difference. No luxury hotel wants to be seen as a discounter, but many include amenities not found at less costly hotels—and those can make the overall cost comparable."

Rental Cars

Reject "fare-jumping." The fare-jumping that bedevils airfare web-sites is just as likely to befall travelers who attempt to rent a car online. And strange as it may seem, says David Rowell of *The Travel Insider,* the result may be higher prices for customers who enter special promotional discount codes.

While shopping the Hertz website for rates in 2005, Rowell reports, he was offered an initial "anonymous" rate. But when he entered his Hertz "frequent-renter" membership code, which should have entitled him to a discount of 10 to 20 percent (depending on the rate plan), the rate suddenly spiked about 10 percent higher. "When I tried another discount rate for being in the travel industry," says Rowell, "it was lowered a bit—but even that rate was higher than the one I was first quoted as an anonymous shopper.

"I called Hertz for an explanation," Rowell continues, "and

was told there must have been a computer glitch. But when I wrote about it in my newsletter (www.thetravelinsider.com), several people contacted me saying the same thing had happened to them at other rental-car websites."

The theory: Frequent car-renters are the ones most likely to join a car-rental company's reward program. They are also apt to be business travelers—who, because they journey on the company's dime, typically pay more for many travel arrangements. Rental-car companies may therefore assume that frequent renters are better able to afford high rates—or less likely to squawk about them.

Your protection: Though fare-jumping may afflict anyone booking a rental car—or making other travel plans online— you will do best to note the initial rate offered, then call for reservations. Unlike airlines, rental-car companies do not impose a surcharge for reservations made by telephone. Only after you have verified the initial low rate with the agent at the other end of the phone line should you mention any promotional code discounts; these may reduce the price even more.

Ensure you need that "insurance." Most veteran travelers have weathered the following "counter encounter": The rental-car agent aggressively pushes you to elect extra "insurance" coverage, adding approximately $15 to your daily rate.

Why does this happen? Many travelers believe the extra expense is unnecessary, and that the tactic serves primarily to make money for the rental company.

That's true—to a certain extent. The extra coverages aren't really insurance at all, but rather "waivers" to indemnify you from any damage caused to the rental while it is in your possession. Although many drivers may be covered by their own personal car-insurance policy, do some research before you automatically waive the extra coverages. *Important:* If your current car-insurance policy provides no collision or comprehensive coverage on your older personal vehicle, that policy will not cover a fender bender on your rental car, either.

How to shorten that maddening wait for valet parking to return your car?

"When the waiter hands you the check, hand him the parking stub," suggests Mark Brenner, author of Tipping for Success. *"Then say, 'As I tally the bill, would you mind giving this to the parking-lot attendant so my car is ready when I leave?' The waiter knows you're about to tip him, so he'll do it. And it's a very James Bond–like move."*

Another way to dodge a car-rental company's costly coverages is to pay for the rental with a gold- or platinum-level credit card, some of which automatically furnish the coverages offered at the counter. Here again, though, exceptions abound. Although that prestige plastic is more likely to protect you from damage done to a garden-variety sedan, rarely will it cover damage to a rented SUV, a truck, a van, or a luxury car.

One place where a car-rental company's default waivers may be a good idea indeed is at locations abroad. Imagine a scenario, suggests travel consultant Joel Widzer, in which you're involved in an accident in Ireland or France: In both countries, you could be socked with stiff penalties unless you opted for the rental-car company's collision insurance. And in Italy, theft insurance is mandatory for car rentals.

Fight the attack of the tack-ons. The rental-car industry is notorious for add-on charges that go unmentioned when you're quoted the rental price. These include airport taxes, sales taxes, concession fees, and "vehicle leasing" fees. Taken together, the tack-ons may increase your quoted rate by as much as 50 percent.

If you pick up your car at an airport rental facility, for example, you will likely pay 10 percent more than if you retrieve the vehicle at a "downtown" or other off-site location run by

PROTECTIVE DETECTIVE

Rental Car Roadblocks

If you're 65 or older and intend to rent a car outside the United States, you may be headed for a discrimination dead-end. Older drivers are blocked from renting cars in a score of countries worldwide—even if they have already made reservations.

Each country sets its own upper age limit. The precise figure is usually dictated by the nation's government or its insurers, says a Hertz spokesperson, who acknowledges age limits in Hertz franchises in 13 foreign countries. These include Egypt (age 69); Gibraltar, Kenya, and Morocco (age 70); Tahiti (age 75); and Ireland, where the 75-year-old ceiling can be waived.

Avis spokeswoman Alice Pereira admits that her company's franchises refuse to rent to older drivers in 10 countries, including Belize, Honduras, and Costa Rica. In Ireland, the age ceiling ranges from 65 to 74, depending on car class. There are no upper-age restrictions in the United States, but most U.S. companies will not rent to drivers younger than 25—or, if they do, it is only at inflated rates.

the same company. In some cases, it may be less expensive to take public transportation to another rental facility. Often this allows you to return the car to the airport franchise at no additional cost.

When it comes to international rentals, surprise taxes often add 10 to 30 percent to the price of getting the same car type in the United States. To avoid this particular strain of culture

Tips on Tipping

It's an international protocol, yet few Americans seem to have mastered it. Follow this advice from the American Society of Travel Agents and you will know how much to tip in any situation:

At airports and train stations, $1 per bag is appropriate for porters (double that if your luggage is very heavy).

Cab and limo drivers should be tipped 10 to 15 percent of the fare. Shuttle van or bus drivers, often overlooked, should be tipped $2 per person.

Cruise personnel are generally tipped on the last night of your voyage: Dining-room waiters receive $3.50 per person for each day, whereas the busboy should receive $2 per person per day. The dining-room maitre d' gets 35 cents per person per day, while the head waiter gets 15 cents per person per day (the rates are so much lower for these two individuals because they are tipped by all patrons and do not necessarily provide individualized service). Room stewards receive $3.50 per person per day.

At hotels, bellhops typically get $1 to $2 per bag; maids get $1 to $2 per night; the concierge receives $5 to $10 for special favors. For room service, a 15 percent tip is standard if the gratuity has not already been included in the bill for the meal (see page 168 to better determine if it has). A $1 tip is the norm for doormen who hail cabs but carry no bags.

At restaurants, waiters and bartenders should get 15 to 20 percent of the total bill. Note, however, that in Europe and Asia the tip is often included in lunch and dinner bills. At fancy restaurants, tip the maitre d' $5 to $10 if he snags you a table—more when the restaurant is full and you show up sans reservations. Tip $1 when you check your coat and 50 cents to $1 for restroom attendants. Wine stewards typically receive 10 percent of the wine bill.

Tour guides usually get $1 per person for a tour lasting half a day and $2 for a full-day tour.

shock, ask that all international charges be disclosed in the price quote. Here and abroad, companies may also impose an "extra driver" fee—a surcharge if you want to share driving duties with a travel companion. One final pothole to dodge: Return the car with less than a full tank and you may be charged twice the going per-gallon rate.

Your protection: Ask about all additional fees when you reserve a car. At the same time, request that written confirmation of your bottom-line costs be sent to you; that way (theoretically, at least), you can't be socked with nasty surprises at the pickup counter.

By the same token, if you need a child seat, make that fact clear at the time you book your reservation. The industry is notorious for issuing child seats on a first-come, first-served basis, so you may be unable to secure this essential item unless you take pains to reserve one at the time you reserve your car. Many companies have only a squishy grasp of the word "reservation." Some of them—Hertz included—have formalized the process whereby agents must inform customers (at least three days in advance) when a previously "reserved" car seat becomes unavailable.

Hint: When you get a car seat, don't install it in the vehicle yourself. Instead, make sure a representative of the rental company tends to this task. This relieves you of any liability that might result from improper installation.

Cruises

Put bad publicity to good use. It doesn't take a genius to understand that news of the latest virus or other illness outbreak on a cruise ship yields an immediate cornucopia of deals because of canceled reservations. "Probably the best time to save money on a cruise is right after there's been such an onboard-illness scare," notes online travel columnist Widzer. He might have added that this may also be the *safest* time to cruise: The negative publicity born of a "Bacilli on Board!"

If you must fly to the port of departure for a cruise, arrive a day beforehand to avoid missing the boat—literally.

Many cruise lines will not refund your money for a missed sailing if airline reservations were made by you, a travel agent, or a website other than their own.

alert typically spurs the affected cruise line (and its competitors) to achieve squeaky-clean sanitary conditions.

As cruises have ridden a rising tide of popularity in recent years—in 2004, a record 10.5 million people traveled this way—great deals on last-minute bookings have become more difficult than ever to find. In fact, the best cruise deals now result from booking at least six months ahead of time.

Hint: Although reservations for the busy spring and summer cruise season once had to be made by January, insiders now recommend booking passage by the previous fall.

PROTECTIVE DETECTIVE

I Don't See *That* in My Phrasebook!

Be careful how you hurdle the language barrier when traveling abroad. The familiar (to us) hand gesture for "Okay!"—joining your thumb and index finger, with the other fingers fanned out—is a supreme insult in South America, Germany, and Russia, where it indicates you have a rock "bottom" opinion of the person to whom you display it. In France, it suggests you regard another as a worthless "zero." In Japan, by contrast, the gesture carries no such cross-cultural baggage: There it simply signals you want your change from purchases in coins, not currency.

Shop the new ships. By 2007, there will be 15 additions to the cruise industry's fleet, which numbered approximately 150 vessels in 2004. As each new ship comes on line, says Quintos of *National Geographic Traveler,* its sponsor typically offers a special "introductory rate" that can deliver substantial savings. To learn about these new vessels and the savings available, Quintos suggests contacting individual cruise lines to get on their "alert" mailing lists. You can also check out websites such as www.cruise-news.com or www.cruisenewsdaily.com for the latest on new ships.

Book with a specialist. Although travel agents still book about 90 percent of all cruise vacations, online bookings have made enormous headway in recent years. But with literally hundreds of such websites in existence—including online titans Travelocity, Expedia, and Orbitz—what is your best course of action?

As with human travel agents, choose websites that specialize in cruises. Worth looking into are www.cruise411.com, www.cruisesonly.com, www.cruise.com, and www.cruise value.com. You can find local specialists at www.cruising. org, a website operated by the Cruise Lines International Association (CLIA), a trade group that works with approximately 17,000 travel agencies in the United States. For those who want information on where to go, which lines to take, and other questions frequently voiced by novice cruisers, check out www.cruisemates.com, www.cruisecritic.com, www. cruiseopinion.com, or www.cruisereviews.com. Note that prices sometimes tend to be higher on a cruise line's own website.

Exclusive deals are available for AARP members through the AARP Passport program, which is provided by Travelocity. For details call 888-291-1757 or visit travelocity. com/AARP/home.

Factor in the extras. As with other aspects of travel, the quoted price for a cruise often omits "extras" that are anything but, such as:

- *Port taxes and fees,* which can add an additional $100 per person per cruise.

- *Airfare* to and from the port destination (this may cost less if you book it yourself).

- *Services* such as spas, shore excursions, and medical care.

- *Certain foods and drinks*—including soda and ice cream served at "parlors" rather than in the dining room.

Gratuities may also be automatically added to the quoted "base" price without being identified as such; inquire if this surcharge is included on your bill before you tip waiters, stewards, or other cruise staff at the end of your trip. Also note that on many ships, the onboard doctor is typically a foreign national who doesn't carry the same malpractice insurance as U.S. doctors. If that's the case on your cruise, ask the cruise line to spell out its policy on medical liability.

PROTECT YOUR HEALTH

MEDICAL ERRORS
Avoiding Common Mistakes

MEDICAL ERRORS KILL more Americans every year than diabetes, pneumonia, Alzheimer's disease, or kidney failure. In fact, if this category was included in the Centers for Disease Control's annual list of the nation's leading causes of death, it would rank as high as number 3—behind only heart disease and cancer.

According to a July 2004 study of 37 million patient records, often-preventable errors made in U.S. hospitals claim 195,000 lives a year. Another finding, published in the *Journal of the American Medical Association,* estimates that 225,000 deaths occur annually in hospitals from "iatrogenic causes"—those resulting from a specific health care–administered medical treatment. Neither estimate includes mistakes that are not readily reported, such as those made in doctors' offices, private pharmacies, or at home.

Half of all medical errors occur from unexpected reactions to medication. Patients bear some of the blame: They often fail to tell caregivers such crucial information as the other drugs they're taking (a potential source of harmful interactions), their past medical histories, or any allergies they may have. Culpable too are the drug companies, which give divergent drugs similar names—Lamictal is an antiepileptic drug, whereas Lamisil is an antifungal—and have delayed warning doctors and pharmacists about certain products.

IN THIS CHAPTER

Survive a
Hospital Stay

Prevent
Procedure Errors

Avert
Medication
Mishaps

Get More
from Doctors

The United States has a higher rate of medical errors than other industrialized countries, says a November 2005 Commonwealth Fund survey.

One in three Americans report being victims of medical errors—a higher ratio than befell residents of Germany, Australia, Canada, New Zealand, or the United Kingdom.

But there are also plenty of misplaced decimal points, wrong abbreviations, and mislabeled information when drugs are repackaged that result in the dispensing of wrong drugs (or deadly doses of the right ones). Patients also have much to fear from hospital-acquired infections, incorrect diagnoses, and unnecessary surgeries. Even "treatment" of the wrong body part is not unknown: In 1998, comedian Dana Carvey's surgeon bypassed the wrong artery during open-heart surgery.

Nor, if you poll the public, is the situation improving. One in 3 people in a 2004 survey conducted by the Henry J. Kaiser Family Foundation, the U.S. Agency for Healthcare Research and Quality, and the Harvard School of Public Health reported that they or a family member had been subject to a medical error at some point. Many respondents claimed the mistake had caused "serious health consequences." And twice as many respondents believed medical care had worsened from the past as those who believed it had improved.

But it often takes only simple measures—by you, if not by your health-care providers—to protect yourself from the hazards of healing.

Survive a Hospital Stay

Check for hands-on detective work. Hospital deaths caused by medical error stem from a wide variety of causes. Perhaps most alarming is this statistic: 40,000 people die in hospitals each year because patients received the wrong drug, had unnecessary surgery, or were on the receiving end of other errors. Many of these errors occurred because hospital workers failed to follow the golden rule of medical safety: Properly identify your patient.

When you're hospitalized and a strange face enters the room, the first thing it should do is look at your hand—to examine the name-inscribed wristband issued to all admitted patients. "But many hospital workers don't," says Harvard School of Public Health researcher Robert J. Blendon, Sc.D.

His survey of 1,300 doctors, published in the *New England Journal of Medicine,* found that 1 in 3 physicians reported medical errors occurring in their own or a family member's care. "With so many hospitals hiring temporary nursing staff these days," cautions Dr. Blendon, "it's absolutely essential that you are properly identified before any medication or procedure is administered." What to do: If a nurse or doctor doesn't immediately check your wristband or ask your name during an initial meeting, introduce yourself to make sure you get the proper treatment. This is also a perfect time to ask about all medications you are scheduled to receive. You'll want to list them and compare that tally to the medications brought to you each day.

Harp on hygiene. About 80,000 Americans die each year from infections acquired in hospitals. One easy way to protect yourself is to ask all staff entering your room when they last washed their hands or changed their gloves. The Agency for Healthcare Research and Quality, the federal government's watchdog for health- care safety, reports that when patients ask this, doctors, nurses, and other staff usually wash their ungloved hands more often and use more soap—not just when treating them, but as a matter of habit.

Consult the calendar. Here's something to keep in mind if you're heading to a hospital in the summer for a nonemergency procedure: Training doctors traditionally start their

---

How Deadly Errors Occur

How does the medical establishment explain the estimated 225,000 iatrogenic (doctor-caused) deaths that stem from medical errors in U.S. hospitals each year? According to Johns Hopkins researcher Barbara Starfield, M.D., M.P.H., writing in the *Journal of the American Medical Association:*

106,000 deaths result from unexpected reactions to medications.

80,000 deaths result from infections acquired in hospitals.

20,000 deaths result from "other" nonclassified errors.

12,000 deaths result from unnecessary surgery.

7,000 deaths result from incorrect drugs or dosages given in hospitals.

internships and residencies around July 1, unsheathing a double-edged sword as they immediately plunge into hands-on patient care.

"You may get more personal attention, but the skill level and experience will not be there," says David Sherer, M.D., a risk-management specialist and author of *Dr. David Sherer's Hospital Survival Guide*. "That's fine if you need a routine test or something else that's not high-risk. But if you're having elective surgery that can wait, it's wise to postpone it for a few months."

Until they get their feet wet, the majority of interns are allowed to do nothing more responsible in an operating room than hold retractors and cut sutures. (They may conduct medical tests and other procedures.) This helps explain why studies in academic centers have shown that medical errors are not more common when the interns are green in July. Still, a postponement, when possible, may increase your comfort level. "I certainly wouldn't want to be the patient at a teaching hospital who gets open-heart surgery on July 2," says Dr. Sherer.

Identify your "lead" provider. You may be treated by a slew of hospital personnel during your stay, but only one doctor—your "primary attending physician"—has ultimate responsibility for your personal care. However, the identity of the primary attending physician may change throughout your hospital stay, so ask who this is every day.

Why? Because it's this doctor to whom you should directly address key concerns about your treatment. When this final-say doctor is not around, jot down any questions that occur to you about the care you are receiving.

Show you're a popular patient... Want more TLC from nurses and other frontline support staff? Having frequent visitors is one way to gain a psychological edge that could translate to better care, says Vincent Marchello, M.D., medical

Adverse drug events cause over 770,000 injuries and deaths annually.

director of Metropolitan Jewish Geriatric Center in Brooklyn, New York. "If a nurse is caring for 10 or 15 patients, the one who always has relatives or other visitors around tends to get more attentive care."

. . . And why. You attract more than just bees with honey. "I don't want to give the message that you have to be nice to be treated nicely," says Marc Siegel, M.D., of New York University Medical Center. "It's expected that patients who are sick will be irritable. But those patients who, despite their illness, manage to remain cheerful, friendly, and positive to the staff often receive an extra level of response."

That's because a smile and some polite schmoozing shows that patients are concerned about the staff—and that concern is more likely to be reciprocated.

Call staff before you need them. Don't make the common mistake of assuming that buzzing for the nurse will result in an immediate visit. In the course of an average shift, the typical nurse must simultaneously juggle a dozen patients. "When you notice your IV bag has about 2 inches left, that's when you should call the nurse—not when it's almost empty," says Mary Lorrie Davis, who worked as a licensed vocational nurse for 20 years before writing *How to Survive a Stay in the Hospital without Getting Killed.* "If the IV saline solution or medication gets too low, you may incur the pain of having to start a new intravenous line."

Preventable Adverse Drug Events (ADEs) cost the American health-care system—or its patients, to be precise—about $2 billion every year.

Prevent Procedure Errors

Go surgeon-shopping. When you need surgery, you want a doctor with plenty of experience in performing that specific procedure. But what exactly should you look for? "Unless it's an extremely rare procedure," says Dr. Sherer, "you want to be involved with someone who has done the procedure hundreds or even thousands of times." This applies particularly to "routine" procedures performed on multiple patients in a single day—cataract or LASIK surgery, many cosmetic or orthopedic procedures, and screening tests such as a colonoscopy or mammogram. "For many of these common surgeries and tests, I'd say that a doctor's experience in the 500 to 600 range is a nice, comfortable level."

Most doctors are proud to talk about their high numbers. You should expect lower figures, however, for more complicated (and therefore less frequently performed) procedures such as organ transplants. "Still," warns Harvard's Dr. Blendon, "I wouldn't go with anyone who is talking single digits in a given year."

Call ahead. Numbers also matter when it comes to choosing the facility where you'll be treated. Ordinarily, of course, patients must go to a hospital where their surgeon has operating privileges. In some cases, however, a facility may be chosen on the strength of its expertise in treating your specific ailment, in which case a doctor will be assigned to you. In either event, call the hospital administrator and ask him or her these two questions:

1) How often, in the previous 12 months, was your specific procedure performed there?

2) What was the outcome?

Seriously consider those health centers with the higher numbers and the higher success rates. "Most patients opt for the facility recommended by their primary care doctor or the designated surgeon," says Dr.

PROTECTIVE DETECTIVE

I.D. Your Body Parts

What's the one item many savvy surgeons carry into presurgery checkups? An 89-cent permanent marker, used on the patient's skin or bed sheets to note the correct surgical site or procedure. This 10-second protective measure against wrong-site surgery is especially important when your surgeon, like many, performs a consecutive string of operations in a given day.

So play doctor yourself—bring your own marker to the hospital. "If you're having a knee replacement," advises Vincent Marchello, M.D., medical director of a New York City geriatric center, "write, 'Replace this knee' or some other explicit indicator." You can also write the name of the procedure, such as "angioplasty" or "appendectomy." But be careful of your phrasing: If you're getting surgery on the left side of your body, use the word "correct" (as opposed to "right") to avoid confusion.

Blendon. "Or they choose the hospital that's closest to them." Statistically, though, you're likely to fare better at a teaching hospital affiliated with a medical school: These facilities are usually better equipped, and their higher volume translates to a lower per-patient error rate. Again, an institution that undertakes only a handful of procedures each year is a clear signal to keep shopping around.

Be the early bird. A surgical team often must complete a succession of identical or similar procedures within the time it has reserved the operating room. Does your order in that line-up matter? "I don't think that physicians are any less competent later in the day," says New York cardiologist Evan Levine, M.D., author of *What Your Doctor Won't (or Can't) Tell You.* "But they may be more rushed because they're lagging behind. Given a choice, I'd rather be the first procedure of the day than the fourth or fifth."

The diseases most likely to result in court-issued awards in medical-malpractice lawsuits are cancer, heart attack, and appendicitis.

Pick paper or plastic. For less pain and lower risk of infection, insist that bandages and IV lines be secured with paper or plastic surgical tape—not the more commonly used silk tape. "As you get older," says Dr. Sherer, "the skin thins and becomes more delicate, especially in women. When silk tape is pulled off such skin, it tends to leave a rash or even rip the skin. Plastic or paper tape won't do that." All hospitals and outpatient facilities stock the more gentle surgical tape, but you usually have to ask for it beforehand.

Get a security blanket. Operating rooms are deliberately kept chilly—usually between 64 and 72 degrees F—in order to restrict bacterial growth. But increasing your comfort isn't the only reason to ask a nurse or orderly to give you an extra blanket before surgery. The added warmth also lowers blood pressure and dilates veins, making it easier to start IVs. "Chilly patients have more blood-pressure problems and arrhythmias," reports Dr. Sherer. "They tend to need longer recovery times."

▶ A BETTER WAY

Preparing for Surgery

There's a good reason not to look your best when preparing for surgery: Wearing cosmetics or jewelry can interfere with both the surgery and the recovery.

Skin moisturizers or lotions prevent surgical tape from sticking to your skin, making it difficult to secure bandages or IVs, says anesthesiologist David Sherer, M.D.

Makeup, lipstick, or mascara can rub off onto anesthesia tubes in your mouth and nose or get onto the surgical team's gloves, risking infection if the cosmetic enters your body.

Contact lenses should be removed before surgery; if not, they may dry out and stick to the cornea, creating intense pain.

Dentures need to be removed before surgery to prevent chipping or problems with intubation. Dentures can be swallowed while you're under anesthesia.

Nail polish or false fingernails can interfere with a pulse oximeter, the device placed on fingertips or toes to measure the amount of oxygen in your blood.

Jewelry, including wedding bands, should be removed because fingers swell during surgery. There's also a risk of skin burns with metal jewelry if your surgeon uses a "Bovie" electrocautery device to stop bleeding.

If your surgery will take several hours, ask about heated air mattresses (warming blankets inflated with warm air) and heated intravenous solutions as well.

Take a cue from sailors. Anyone who's ever had surgery under general anesthesia knows that nausea and vomiting can be the worst postoperative side effect. One way around the retching is to opt for local (or local-with-intravenous) anesthesia, both of which are less likely to induce such a reaction.

Even more important, postsurgery death and complication rates are lower with the "lowest" form of anesthesia. So whenever it's practical, opt for a local anesthetic (which numbs only a small tissue area) over one that is regional (which anesthetizes a larger area while you're still conscious) or general (which puts you under completely).

But how can you protect yourself in a surgical scenario that you know will require general anesthesia? Before your surgery, advises anesthesiologist Sherer, "Get a device called a Relief Band. It emits safe, mild vibrations to a specific acupressure point on the underside of your wrist that blocks impulses in the part of your brain that triggers the vomiting reflex. It really works."

The band, available at pharmacies and specialty retailers, is a high-tech, acupuncture-like version of the wristbands that cruise-ship passengers wear to stave off motion sickness.

Avert Medication Mishaps

Avoid early-month purchases. Whether you're getting a new prescription or renewing an existing one, you may want to avoid visiting the pharmacy pickup window during the first week of each month. That's the busiest time for many pharmacies, when sales surge to those who have just received their monthly Social Security checks.

After tracking nearly 132,000 medication-error deaths over a 21-year period, researchers at the University of California, San Diego, reported in the journal *Pharmacotherapy* that death caused by drug error is 25 percent more likely to occur during the first seven days of any given month. These odds held true regardless of age or income.

Keep tabs on new tablets. No matter when you get drugs, make sure they're the right ones. Keep a record of all the medicines you take every day—especially while you're hospitalized (when getting new drugs is more likely). This means noting, on paper, a daily log of each medication's name, dosage, color, shape, and frequency of being administered. "If ever there's a sudden change in what's given to you," says Dr. Marchello, "especially a differently colored or shaped drug, ask why before you take it." If your condition keeps you from maintaining this log yourself, designate a visitor to do

Hospital patients who suffer medication errors remain hospitalized 8 to 12 days longer than those who escape such mishaps. This adds an average of $16,000 to $24,000 to their bill.

it for you; he or she can get the information from the nurses' station (it's on your chart).

How's my handwriting? Nine in 10 medication errors—including those that don't cause death—involve patients getting the wrong type of drug or an incorrect dose of the right type, as opposed to dangerous interactions between two or more medications. The best way to avoid this is to make sure that your issued script isn't scribbled—sloppy handwriting by doctors was supposed to have gone out with house calls. If you can't read the script, chances are good your pharmacist won't be able to either. Ask that the doctor print out the drug name and dosage before the pharmacist fills the prescription. Many commonly prescribed drugs have similar-sounding

PROTECTIVE DETECTIVE

Speak Before You Swallow

Some 106,000 Americans die every year from "non-error adverse effects of medication" (unforeseen complications that arise when a patient receives the right drug). To reduce your own risk of this fate, ask the following questions—and get satisfactory answers to each one—whenever you are given a new medication or prescription:

• *What is the medicine for?* What specifically does it do?

• *What is its brand name?* Its generic name?

• *What does it look like?*

• *What is the drug's expected result?* When should that occur?

• *Are there alternative drugs to this choice?* If so, why prescribe this one?

• *When should I take it?* Does "four doses daily" mean taking it every six hours, or four times during waking hours?

• *How should I take it?* For how long?

• *What should I do if I miss a dose?*

• *What side effects are likely?* What do I do if they occur?

• *What does this drug interact with?* What food, drink, or activities should I avoid—and when? (Ask about milk and grapefruit juice in particular!)

• *Does light, heat, or humidity affect its safety?* If so, how should I store it?

Prescription Speak

How do medication errors occur? Often because doctors continue to write prescriptions with abbreviations based on Latin terminology—a practice discouraged by the Institute for Safe Medication Practices and other consumer groups.

Case in point: q.d.—the abbreviation for *quaque die*, meaning "every day"—can easily be misread for qid, the abbreviation for *quater in die*, or "four times a day." Here's a rundown of commonly used symbols:

Abbreviation	For the Latin	Meaning	Other terms to know:	
ac	ante cibum	before meals	ad lib	freely
bid	bis in die	twice a day	bib	with drink
gt	gutta	drop	h	an hour
hs	hora somni	at bedtime	IM	into the muscle
od	oculus dexter	right eye	IV	into the vein
os	oculus sinister	left eye	M	minimum
po	per os	by mouth	non rep	don't repeat
pc	post cibum	after meals	qAM	every morning
prn	pro re nata	as needed	qod	every other day
q 3 h	quaque 3 hora	every 3 hours	s.l	under the tongue
qd	quaque die	every day	sub Q or sc	under the skin
qid	quater in die	4 times a day	ung	ointment
tid	ter in die	3 times a day	c̄	with
			s̄	without

names, notes Dr. Sherer. You can't rely on the pharmacist checking with the doctor before filling your prescription.

Visit the copy machine before the pharmacy. Another safety precaution: At the doctor's office, ask for a photocopy of your prescription. Then take both the copy and the prescription to the pharmacy. Although the pharmacist will keep the original, you can compare the copy with the info on the pill-bottle label to make doubly sure you've received the correct brand and dosage. "This is probably the easiest thing you can do to reduce your risk of a medication error," says Dr.

Show & Tell at the Doctor's

YOU KNOW WHAT they want you to show them: your insurance card and payment. But what else should you *show* your doctors, not just tell them, to reduce your risk of dangerous drug interactions? Here's what the experts advise:

The common practice of telling a doctor which medications you take is risky. "Patients frequently mispronounce the names of their medications or don't know the exact doses they take," says David Sherer, M.D., a risk-prevention expert. "Also, many patients tend to forget drugs they may occasionally take, and rarely mention vitamin and other supplements."

Your protection: "Put all the medications you take into a brown lunch bag and bring it with you once a year to your primary care provider, or any time you see a new specialist—including vitamins and other over-the-counter supplements," he says. "That's because many vitamins and herbal products interact with prescription drugs." For instance, garlic, ginseng, and ginkgo biloba supplements can "thin" the blood, a potential problem for people taking Coumadin or similar drugs. St. John's wort also interferes with blood thinners and reduces the effectiveness of certain prescription and over-the-counter drugs— including cancer medications, birth control pills, antidepressants, and blood-pressure drugs.

Anti-inflammatory medications such as aspirin and corticosteroids deplete the body's stores of vitamin C, which can affect skin, immunity, and protection against harmful "free radical" molecules.

Diuretics to control high blood pressure can reduce potassium levels, necessary for heart and nervous system health and to ensure proper fluid balance within the body and its cells.

Hormone-replacement drugs such as Premarin and Estratab can lead to deficiencies in Vitamin B6—vital for nerve health and maintaining immunity; they also lower magnesium and zinc levels.

SSRI antidepressants such as Prozac and Zoloft may deplete zinc, selenium, and some B vitamins.

Over-the-counter laxatives containing mineral oil interfere with many nutrients by removing them from the intestines before they can be absorbed by the body.

This "brown-bagging" of medications is especially important if you're about to get surgery. "That's because to reduce the risk of problems, we like patients to be off certain medications— including blood thinners such as aspirin—for at least 10 to 14 days before they receive anesthesia," says Dr. Sherer, an anesthesiologist. "This includes some supplements such as garlic and ephedra."

Marchello. When you get home, file the copy with your other medical records; these should be brought to annual exams and any hospital admission.

Ask what drugs are "high-risk" for you. When a doctor is in the process of writing you a prescription, never withhold such critical details of your personal health as your age, pregnancy, or whether you smoke. In addition to sparking drug allergies or interacting with other medications, certain drugs are especially risky on their own. For example, at least 48 drugs should not be taken by those over the age of 65; these include oral estrogens, the antidepressant Prozac, the heartburn drug Tagamet, the painkiller Demerol, and even mineral oil. Pregnant women, meanwhile, should steer clear of certain antibiotics, the "blood thinner" Coumadin, ACE inhibitors for high blood pressure (during the last two trimesters), the popular acne medication Accutane, and other medicines; all can cause birth defects. Finally, smoking can raise the risk of dangerous side effects from birth control or other drugs. Even aspirin should not be given to children under the age of 12 unless directed by a doctor. It has been known to induce Reye's Syndrome—an often deadly disease that attacks vital organs.

> **PROTECTIVE DETECTIVE**
>
> ## Reaction Résumé
>
> To provide caregivers with consistent information about your medical history, keep a "reaction diary"—a list of those scary medical moments of yesteryear. "If you developed a rash 10 years ago after taking aspirin, your doctors and hospital need to know that," says Mary Lorrie Davis, a former nurse and author of *How to Survive a Stay in the Hospital without Getting Killed.* "What you remember to tell your OB-GYN may not be the same thing you need to tell your general practitioner or allergist."

Get More from Doctors

Gauge caring with a call... To predict the level of care you may get from a new doctor, test the waters with a simple phone call placed during normal business hours. How long does it take for a staffer to pick up? "If it rings off the hook or you get only voice mail or otherwise can't reach the doctor," says Dr. Levine, "that's a red flag that the doctor or staff doesn't respond well to patients. When a good doctor gets too busy, she or he hires extra staff. Usually there's no excuse for a phone to go unanswered beyond five rings." If the call is answered quickly, you can ask an innocuous question about office hours, make an appointment, or simply hang up.

Here are some other ways to gauge the caring capabilities of a medical staff:

The most common allegation made in a medical-malpractice lawsuit is a misdiagnosis that results in delayed treatment or incorrect diagnostic tests.

- *Can you get an appointment* reasonably quickly (generally within two weeks, depending on the nature of your visit)?

- *Can you get a timely response* from a doctor who cannot be reached when you call?

- *Does the practice have a policy* for advising you what to do when a doctor is unavailable? For example, does the staff reflexively send you to the emergency room? Or do they have an established system in place to evaluate you?

. . . And competency with paperwork. If you're scheduled to be the recipient of a pacemaker, implantable cardioverter defibrillator, or other high-tech medical gear, another test of your doctor's "caring quotient" is to make sure you also receive the paperwork associated with the device—including the often-issued wallet card that lists the make and model, serial number, battery information, and a toll-free telephone number for maintenance and programming issues. "You really should be issued that card, and carry it with you at all times," says Dr. Sherer. *Bonus:* Having this wallet card on hand may allow you to avoid x-ray and magnetic equipment while going through airport or other security checkpoints. (You'll still have to endure a pat-down inspection, however.)

Seek the right referral. An estimated 90 percent of patients, estimates Dr. Levine, choose their primary care physician and any specialist based on one of the following two factors: referrals from friends and family, or the doctor's office location.

For better behind-the-scenes insights, Dr. Levine suggests, ask local nurses to contribute their two cents' worth: "You'd better believe that nurses know who the best doctors are in your town." To solicit their opinions, contact area hospitals, a local nursing union or organization, or the nurses in your primary-care physician's office. Whether the nurses have worked with them or not, doctors—and their reputations for technical and personal skills—are a hot topic of conversation at both the hospital cafeteria and practice reception desks.

Look for extra initials. Before you examine those degrees on the wall, check the doctor's front door. If you see extra initials following the "M.D." or "D.O." in your doctor's title—usually starting with "F" for "Fellow"—that means he or she has completed one to six years of additional training based on the requirements of the Fellowship organization. Here are some examples:

- F.A.C.C. (Fellow of the American College of Cardiology)

- F.A.C.S. (Fellow of the American College of Surgeons)

How to Report Medical Errors

In addition to state agencies, you can report or get more information on medical errors at the following:

MedWatch, the U.S. Food and Drug Administration Safety and Adverse Event Reporting System
800-332-1088
www.fda.gov/medwatch

MERP, the Medication Errors Reporting Program, operated by the United States Pharmacopeia (USP) in cooperation with the Institute of Safe Medication Practices (ISMP)
www.ismp.org
www.usp.org/patientSafety/mer
800-233-7767

Maude, U.S. Food and Drug Administration Database for Manufacturer and User Facility Device Experience Database
www.fda.gov/cdrh/maude.html

National Coordinating Council for Medication Error Reporting and Prevention
www.nccmerp.org

- F.A.A.D. (Fellow of the American Academy of Dermatology)

- F.A.A.F.P. (Fellow of the American Academy of Family Physicians)

Many doctors are also board-certified, but that confers no extra initials.

"All things considered," says Dr. Sherer, "you're usually better off with a board-certified doctor—especially those with multiple certifications.

"If your doctor is not board-certified, try to find out if he or she is board-eligible. That means the practitioner has received (or is still getting) this additional training, but has not yet taken or passed the board exam for certification."

For young doctors, less time in the trenches may explain why there's no certification; for older physicians, you may want to ask why this seal of approval is missing.

"Google" with warm saltwater. An Internet search of your doctor's name (with M.D. or O.D.) also provides insights—both good and bad. Recent malpractice suits or other warning signs may be in published newspaper reports or legal filings. On the plus side, hits generated may reveal research the physician has published. Getting ink in prestigious medical journals (the *Journal of the American Medical Association* or the *New England Journal of Medicine*) is the gold standard. It often means the author is recognized for cutting-edge science or otherwise enjoys a stellar reputation.

A Web search may shine light on a doctor's academic or other affiliations—exceedingly useful information, given that only highly regarded practitioners are customarily invited to teach medical students, or to serve on medical association or governmental committees. Do not be swayed by any "best doctor" status that may have been conferred by a regional magazine or any other nonmedical publication;

In 2002, the average court-issued award in medical-malpractice lawsuits was nearly $185,000.

some doctors hire public relations firms to guarantee themselves good press.

For quick-glimpse, no-cost educational background on members of the American Medical Association, visit the AMA website (www.ama-assn.org) and click on the "Doctor Finder" link. By entering a doctor's name and the state of practice, you can learn what medical school he or she attended, where he or she completed residency and hospital training, and which additional certifications, if any, he or she has.

Doctors who are not AMA members (membership is voluntary, and noted on this website) may also be listed, but their education and training experience are not normally included. Commercial websites provide this information too—but usually for a fee.

Resources: **State Medical Boards**

THE SIMPLEST WAY to avoid medical errors is to steer clear of those doctors or hospitals that make them. "Some states require the reporting of all medical errors made in hospitals—and sometimes by individual doctors," says Robert Blendon, Sc.D., of the Harvard School of Public Health. "Getting this information is often a matter of contacting your state's medical licensing board or local health department." If you opt to go that route, use these contacts:

**Alabama State Board
of Medical Examiners**
Phone: 334-242-4116
Fax: 334-242-4155
www.albme.org

Alaska State Medical Board
Phone: 907-269-8163
Fax: 907-269-8196
www.dced.state.ak.us/occ/pmed.htm

Arizona Medical Board
Phone: 480-551-2700
or 800-822-5039
Fax: 480-551-2707
www.azmdboard.org

**Arizona Board of Osteopathic
Examiners in Medicine and Surgery**
Phone: 480-657-7703
Fax: 480-657-7715
www.azosteoboard.org

Arkansas State Medical Board
Phone: 501-296-1802
Fax: 501-603-3555
www.armedicalboard.org

Medical Board of California
Phone: 916-263-2382
Fax: 916-263-2944
www.medbd.ca.gov

**Osteopathic Medical Board
of California**
Phone: 916-263-3100
Fax: 916-263-3117
www.ombc.ca.gov

**Colorado Board
of Medical Examiners**
Phone: 303-894-7690
Fax: 303-894-7692
www.dora.state.co.us/medical

**Connecticut Department
of Public Health**
Phone: 860-509-7590
Fax: 860-509-7607
www.dph.state.ct.us

Delaware Board of Medical Practice
Phone: 302-744-4507
or 800-464-4357
Fax: 302-739-2711
dpr.delaware.gov/boards/
medicalpractice/

**District of Columbia Board
of Medicine**
Phone: 202-727-4900
Fax: 202-727-8471
dchealth.dc.gov

Florida Board of Medicine
Phone: 850-245-4131
or 888-419-3456
Fax: 850-488-9325
www.doh.state.fl.us.fl.us/mqa/medical

Florida Board of Osteopathic Medicine
Phone: 850-245-4161
or 888-419-3456
Fax: 850-921-6184
www.doh.state.fl.us/mqa/osteopath/os_home.html

Georgia Composite State Board of Medical Examiners
Phone: 404-656-3913
Fax: 404-656-9723
www.medicalboard.georgia.gov

Hawaii Professional and Vocational Licensing
Phone: 808-586-3000
Fax: 808-586-2874
www.hawaii.gov/dcca/pvl

Idaho State Board of Medicine
Phone: 208-327-7000
or 880-333-0073
Fax: 208-327-7005
www.accessidaho.org

Illinois Department of Financial and Professional Regulation
Phone: 312-814-6910
Fax: 312-814-3145
www.ildfpr.com/dpr

Indiana Professional Licensing Agency
Phone: 317-234-2060
Fax: 317-233-4236
www.pla.in.gov

Iowa Board of Medical Examiners
Phone: 515-281-5171
Fax: 515-242-5908
www.docboard.org/ia

Kansas State Board of Healing Arts
Phone: 785-296-7413
or 888-886-7205
Fax: 785-296-0852
www.ksbha.org

Kentucky Board of Medical Licensure
Phone: 502-429-7150
or 888-365-9964
Fax: 502-429-7158
www.kbml.ky.gov

Louisiana State Board of Medical Examiners
Phone: 504-568-6820
or 800-296-7549
Fax: 504-568-8893

Maine Board of Licensure in Medicine
Phone: 207-287-3601
888-365-9964
Fax: 207-287-6590
www.docboard.org/me/me_home.htm

Maine Board of Osteopathic Licensure
Phone: 207-287-2480
Fax: 207-287-3015
www.maine.gov/osteo

Maryland Board of Physicians
Phone: 410-764-4777
or 800-492-6836
Fax: 410-358-2252
www.mbp.state.md.us

**Massachusetts Board
of Registration in Medicine**
Phone: 617-654-9800
or 800-377-0550
Fax: 617-426-9373
www.massmedboard.org

**Michigan Department
of Community Health
Bureau of Health Professions**
Phone: 517-335-0918
Fax: 517-373-2179
www.michigan.gov/healthlicense

**Minnesota Board
of Medical Practice**
Phone: 612-617-2130
or 800-627-3709
Fax: 612-617-2166
www.bmp.state.mn.us

**Mississippi State Board
of Medical Licensure**
Phone: 601-987-3079
Fax: 601-987-4159
www.msbml.state.ms.us

**Missouri State Board
of Registration for
the Healing Arts**
Phone: 573-751-0098
or 866-289-5753
Fax: 573-751-3166
www.pr.mo.gov/healingarts.asp

**Montana Board
of Medical Examiners**
Phone: 406-841-2300
Fax: 406-841-2305
www.medicalboard.mt.gov

**Nebraska Board of Medicine
and Surgery**
Phone: 402-471-2118
Fax: 402-471-3577
www.hhs.state.ne.us

**Nevada State Board
of Medical Examiners**
Phone: 775-688-2559
or 888-890-8210
Fax: 775-688-2321
www.medboard.nv.gov

**Nevada State Board of
Osteopathic Medicine**
Phone: 702-732-2147
Fax: 702-732-2079
www.osteo.state.nv.us

**New Hampshire State Board
of Medicine**
Phone: 603-271-1203
or 800-780-4757
Fax: 603-271-6702
www.state.nh.us/medicine

**New Jersey State Board
of Medical Examiners**
Phone: 609-826-7100
Fax: 609-826-7117
www.njmedicalboard.gov

New Mexico Medical Board
Phone: 505-476-7220
or 800-945-5845
Fax: 505-476-7237
nmmb.state.nm.us

**New Mexico Osteopathic
Medical Examiners Board**
Phone: 505-476-7220
Fax: 505-476-4665
www.rld.state.nm.us/b&c/osteo

New York State Medical Board (Licensure)
Phone: 518-474-3817, ext. 560
Fax: 518-486-4846
www.op.nysed.gov/med.htm

New York State Board for Professional Medical Conduct
Phone: 800-663-6114
Fax: 518-402-0745
www.health.state.ny.us

North Carolina Medical Board
Phone: 919-326-1100
or 800-253-9653
Fax: 919-326-1130
www.ncmedboard.org

North Dakota State Board of Medical Examiners
Phone: 701-328-6500
Fax: 701-328-6505
www.ndbomex.com

State Medical Board of Ohio
Phone: 614-466-3934
or 800-554-7717
Fax: 614-728-5946
www.med.ohio.gov

Oklahoma State Board of Medical Licensure and Supervision
Phone: 405-848-6841
or 800-381-4519
Fax: 405-848-8240
www.okmedicalboard.org

Oklahoma State Board of Osteopathic Examiners
Phone: 405-528-8625
Fax: 405-557-0653
www.docboard.org/ok

Oregon Board of Medical Examiners
Phone: 503-229-5770
or 877-254-6263
Fax: 503-229-6543
www.oregon.gov/bme

Pennsylvania State Board of Medicine
Phone: 717-787-2381
Fax: 717-787-7769
www.dos.state.pa.us/med

Pennsylvania State Board of Osteopathic Medicine
Phone: 717-783-4858
Fax: 717-787-7769
www.dos.state.pa.us/bpoa

Board of Medical Examiners of Puerto Rico
Phone: 787-782-8937
Fax: 787-792-4436

Rhode Island Board of Medical Licensure and Discipline
Phone: 401-222-3855
Fax: 401-222-2158
www.health.ri.gov/hsr/bmld/index.php

South Carolina Board of Medical Examiners
Phone: 803-896-4500
Fax: 803-896-4515
www.llr.state.sc.us/pol/medical

South Dakota State Board of Medical and Osteopathic Examiners
Phone: 605-334-8343
Fax: 605-336-0270
www.state.sd.us/doh/medical

**Tennessee Board
of Medical Examiners**
Phone: 615-532-4384
or 800-778-4123
Fax: 615-253-4484
www.state.tn.us/health

Texas Medical Board
Phone: 512-305-7030
or 800-248-4062
Fax: 512-463-9416

Consumer Complaint Hotline:
800-201-9353
www.tsbme.state.tx.us

**Utah Division
of Occupational Licensing**
Phone: 801-530-6628
or 866-275-3675
Fax: 801-530-6511
www.dopl.utah.gov/licensing.html

Vermont Board of Medical Practice
Phone: 802-657-4220
or 800-745-7371
Fax: 802-657-4227
www.healthyvermonters.info/bmp/
bmp/shtml

**Vermont Board of Osteopathic
Surgeons**
Phone: 802-828-2373
Fax: 802-828-2465
vtprofessionals.org/opr1/
osteopaths

Virginia Board of Medicine
Phone: 804-662-9908
or 800-533-1560
Fax: 804-662-9517
www.dhp.state.va.us

**Washington State Health
Professions Quality Assurance**
Phone: 360-236-4700
Fax: 360-236-4818
www.doh.wa.gov

West Virginia Board of Medicine
Phone: 304-558-2921
or 877-867-6411
Fax: 304-558-2084
www.wvdhhr.org/wvbom

West Virginia Board of Osteopathy
Phone: 304-723-4638
or 800-206-6625
Fax: 304-723-6723
www.wvbdosteo.org

**Wisconsin Department
of Regulation and Licensing**
Phone: 608-266-2811
Fax: 608-261-1803
www.drl.state.wi.us

Wyoming Board of Medicine
Phone: 307-778-7053
or 800-438-5784
Fax: 307-778-2069
wyomedboard.state.wy.us

HEALTH-CARE RIPOFFS

8

Shield Your Money & Your Life

YOU CAN'T PUT A PRICE on good health—yet the cost of maintaining it is enough to make you sick. Americans have traditionally spent twice as much on health care as do the citizens of any other industrialized nation, and those expenses have only gotten worse in recent times.

Since the year 2000, out-of-pocket health costs have risen at least three times faster than wages. The typical American now pays an average of $60 per doctor's visit, whose average length is 12 minutes. Millions forgo the drugs they need because they cannot afford them; millions also break federal law by shopping for cheaper prescription drugs from abroad (see warning, page 210). The typical hospital bill may contain hundreds, even thousands, of dollars in overcharges. Some of these are unwitting. Others are deliberate.

While 45 million Americans try to survive with no health insurance to cushion the costs of doctor's exams, medical tests and procedures, hospital visits, and other first-line health care, even the insured are digging dangerously deep into their pockets. Because of rising premiums and shrinking coverage, the overwhelming majority of Americans who spend at least 25 cents of every dollar they earn on medical expenses do so despite having employer-provided coverage.

Worst of all is the long-term prognosis. The U.S. spent 16 percent of its GDP on health-care costs in 2004, and that number is projected to reach 18.7 percent by 2013. Individual health-care expenses, meanwhile, are expected to climb 7 to 10 percent annually for years to come. In the following pages you'll find out how to effectively battle these trends.

Hospital Expenses

Ask for an itemized hospital bill—daily. Hospital overcharges total an estimated $10 billion per year and infect as many as three hospital bills in four. The average overcharge favors the facility by $1,200. One reason stems from what you may have noticed: The typical hospital bill is written in a series of codes, making it difficult for patients to decipher exactly which services they have received.

Another is that hospital bills are often calculated from a "block" of medical supplies, drugs, and services predetermined to be necessary for a given procedure or treatment. All too often, however, these goods and services are never provided—yet patients still foot the bill, says Charles Inlander, president of the People's Medical Society, a patient advocacy group in Allentown, Pennsylvania. If a doctor is scheduled to check on you twice a day but shows up only once, for instance, you're still billed for that "second visit." Why? For the simple but insufferable reason that the two visits were blocked.

Your protection: Separate genuine charges from blocked items that inflate your hospital bill by asking that an itemized list be delivered to your bed at the end of each day during your stay. If you ask for it, the hospital must furnish this

Broken Backs Break the Bank

Half of all declared bankruptcies occurring in the United States are caused by soaring medical bills. Typically these afflict middle-class working Americans *with* health insurance.

More than two million Americans experience medical bankruptcy each year—and 3 in 4 of them have health insurance at the onset of their debt-causing illness. But insurance offers "little protection," Harvard researchers reported in a February 2005 study published in *Health Affairs:* The average patient spends nearly $12,000 in out-of-pocket medical costs before filing for medical bankruptcy.

line-item listing of charges. The listing details every drug, test, or service that will wind up on your final bill while your treatment is still fresh in your mind, says Inlander, enabling you to better track exactly what you're getting on the bill received at discharge. Patients who cannot find competent visitors to perform this task—or, as happens occasionally, whose own mental faculties have been compromised during their hospitalization—should hire a hospitalist (see page 204) or secure a power of attorney.

Learn "hospitalese." Another advantage of reviewing your charges daily is that you learn the language some hospitals use to hide outrageous prices for everyday items. A *mucous recovery system*? That's hospital-speak for a box of tissues— hardly worth the $12 that was uncovered in a hospital-bill audit by Medical Billing Advocates of America (MBAA), one of many companies that scrutinize medical bills for overcharges and receive a percentage of any funds they recover for questionable or undelivered services.

"One of my favorites," says auditor Nora Johnson, who works for MBAA, "is a *fog reduction/elimination device* (FRED), which is relatively common and usually billed for about $60. That's a 2-by-2-inch piece of gauze treated with a cleaner and used to wipe off optical equipment in the Operating Room. Basically it's what you would use to clean your eyeglasses."

Other examples: A *thermal therapy kit* (bag of ice cubes) billed at $30 and a *portable urinal device* (a cheap plastic cup for bedridden patients) billed at $10.

When such items are not given such highfalutin names, they may be listed under the general category of "routine supplies." "That's where I once found a $1,004 charge for a toothbrush," says Johnson.

Johnson estimates that she has discovered gross overcharges (customarily defined as more than 25 percent above an item or procedure's reasonable and expected cost) on about

90 percent of the hospital bills she has audited. If you notice such charges on your bill, raise the issue at once with your hospital or with your insurance provider. Better yet, visit the MBAA website (www.billadvocates.com) to find a medical-billing advocate in your state who will agree to perform a "copyrighted compliance hospital-bill review."

BYOD (Bring Your Own Drugs). Hospitals are notorious for marking up the drugs they administer to patients. Some quadruple the price you would normally pay for both prescription and over-the-counter (OTC) medications. To avoid shelling out $5 per pill for a postoperative antibiotic, cholesterol-lowering statin, or OTC pain reliever you normally take, consider the following course of action:

In addition to packing an adequate supply of your routine regimen on the eve of an expected hospital stay, ask your doctor beforehand what drugs you will be likely to need following your procedure. "Then fill those prescriptions yourself," suggests People's Medical Society president Inlander, "and bring them with you to the hospital. [Make sure you bring them in their original containers.] You'll need to mention this when you're admitted, because the hospital will insist that you attest to the fact you will supply and administer those drugs."

Note: Before packing your own medication, check the practice with your insurer as well. For plans that cover all hospital costs, it is less expensive to let the hospital provide drugs— even at those inflated prices.

Make sure to ask your doctor about pain relievers as well. You may pay up to $8 for each hospital-administered tablet, whereas an entire bottle bought over the counter can cost half that amount.

Be hospitable to a "hospitalist." These doctors—part of the fastest-growing medical field in the United States—have expertise in managing a patient's entire hospital experience, from admission until discharge. According to a six-year study

A 2002 Consumer Reports survey found that patients whose out-of-pocket expenses exceed $2,000 are twice as likely to find billing errors as are those with lower bills. The survey also revealed that only half of hospital patients scrutinize their bills for possible overcharges.

of 11,750 patients published in the September 2004 issue of *The American Journal of Managed Care,* hospital stays for patients under the care of a hospitalist were 16 percent shorter and 8 percent less expensive than those for patients treated for the same condition by other practitioners.

"We found no difference in the quality of care received," says lead researcher George Everett, M.D. "Some patients worry they won't get as good care from hospitalists, who are now employed at many facilities, as they would from their regular doctors or other physicians with hospital visiting privileges. But our findings suggest that just isn't the case."

Far from practicing magic, hospitalists may simply be more skilled than other doctors at guiding patients through a hospital stay.

ID IVs. Some of the most common overcharges are applied to the saline or other nonmedicated solutions that intravenously deliver a variety of drugs—including anesthesia and pain medication. According to medical-billing expert Johnson, most hospitals pay only "spare change" for these solutions. Yet it is not uncommon for the patient's bill to show charges of $90 per bag.

How can you tell that you're getting scammed? "To be billable," says Johnson, "IV solution must be for a therapeutic or diagnostic purpose—treatment for dehydration, for example.

> ▶ **SCAM ALERT!**

Tabs on Your Time

It's no surprise that surgical costs are the single biggest expense on most hospital bills. But it's more than just surgery: Hospitals typically charge patients for the length of time they spend in the Operating Room. And that's just the facility's cut (so to speak), given that surgeons and anesthesiologists usually send separate bills for their services.

"The O.R. time that hospitals charge is usually on a per-minute basis, and can range from $20 to $90 for each minute the patient is in there," says medical-billing advocate Nora Johnson. "But you're often charged for more time than you're actually in the O.R."

How to keep tabs on your time? Compare the time your hospital says you spent in the O.R. with the time you were under anesthesia. "Many hospitals just match them up," warns Johnson, "but often you're under anesthesia before you're brought to the Operating Room." You will likely also still be "under" after you're wheeled out. A red-flag indication of a possible overcharge is if the hospital bills you for O.R. time that exceeds your time under anesthesia.

If it's being used for a drug delivery system, however, it's not supposed to be billable."

Why? Because when hospitals buy certain drugs, the IV solution is included in the cost. "But some hospitals routinely turn around and tack on an additional outrageous charge to the patient," says Johnson.

Address their dress. Charging for the scrubs, drapes, masks, and gloves worn by the surgical staff, says Johnson, is a favorite trick of the trade. But these items are included in the overall cost of O.R. time, so they should not be billed separately. The same applies to items used in your hospital room, such as sheets, pillows, and gloves; they too should be covered by your daily room charge, not billed as separate line items.

Don't pay if released by day. Some hospitals like to give a parting shot to their departing patients—charging them for the day they're discharged. "Unless you are discharged from the hospital at night, which is rare, you shouldn't be charged for your room or other expenses on the final day of your hospital stay," says Johnson. "Yet this is routinely done to unsuspecting patients."

Your protection: Doctors traditionally make their patient rounds in the morning. The day before you expect to be discharged, arrange to get your final checkup before breakfast—or, at the latest, by lunchtime. If the doctor's scheduling conflict makes this impossible, inform the staff you expect not to be charged as a result. Understand, however, that you will most likely be charged for the entire day if you are admitted to a hospital anytime before midnight.

Tests & Procedures

Get poked locally. Whether it's an annual cholesterol screening or a once-in-a-lifetime test for Lyme disease, you will probably pay more for blood drawn at your doctor's office than you will when you're tested at a local lab. "At the doctor's office," says Inlander, "you're charged for the office visit, as well as for drawing the blood and sending it to the lab for analysis." At a lab, by contrast, you're charged only for the blood work itself.

You may need your doctor to write a prescription or give you paperwork for a blood test done by a lab, but many physicians will call it in at no charge. As an added bonus, it's often easier to schedule an appointment at a lab than it is with your doctor. Look for these testing facilities in the Yellow Pages under "Laboratories—Clinical, Medical, Diagnostic" or Laboratories—Testing." Most accept medical insurance—but, as with your doctor, be sure the lab will take yours. Otherwise, your out-of-pocket costs will likely be higher.

Reject "no travel" referrals. Here's another excellent time to steer clear of your doctor's office: You're advised to see a certain specialist or get a certain test—and lucky for you, that doctor or equipment "just happens to be" on site at the time you get the news. "That's a red flag you're about to be duped with an unnecessary visit," warns cardiologist Evan S. Levine, M.D., author of *What Your Doctor Won't (or Can't) Tell You.*

According to Dr. Levine, some unethical general practitioners have been known to enter into "phantom rent" agreements with specialist colleagues or with companies that perform medical tests using portable equipment. This questionable relationship tends to be a patient hazard in bigger cities with more expensive rent. "In exchange for providing a certain number of referrals each month," says Dr. Levine, "these specialists or medical testing companies visit the GP's office half a day a week or once a month and pay a portion of that doctor's office-space rent."

But most good specialists are too busy to visit other doctors' offices to see patients. And "traveling" procedures such as echocardiograms are typically done by technicians, not physicians. So how can you figure out whether a referral is part of a true partnership? Some GPs and specialists legitimately share office space, so check the practice door or letterhead; everyone's name should appear there.

True partnerships aside, says Dr. Levine, "I always encourage patients to seek specialist care outside the GP's office. They should even avoid getting second opinions from someone recommended by the first doctor," he says. "Such a recommendation indicates that both doctors know each other or work together, so you may not be getting a truly unbiased second opinion."

To steer clear of such collusion, Dr. Levine recommends calling the appropriate department of a hospital or medical school where your primary-care physician does *not* treat patients and ask them to recommend a specialist.

▶ A BETTER WAY

Haggle for a Better Deal

If you're worried about big out-of-pocket expenses because you have no health insurance (or it's restrictive), ask the doctor for a discount. Only 13 percent of patients ever make this request—but when they do, proved a survey of 2,118 adults conducted by Harris Interactive, the majority secure a lower price. So if bartering is in your blood, try these hints to hone your haggling:

Before seeing your doctor, call a local health insurer to see what it reimburses area doctors for a similar visit or test. This figure often differs from the amount charged to patients for the visit or test—insurers typically pay doctors one-half to two-thirds of the billed amount. If you're paying out of pocket, you can offer to pay somewhere in that range when negotiating a lower price.

Before treatment is provided, try to negotiate a discount directly with the doctor, explaining that you are uninsured. When such requests are made by phone (or to office personnel) they rarely work, according to some experts.

Offer to pay cash or with a credit card, as opposed to paying with a check. This reassures the doctor that he or she will indeed receive payment.

Foil the follow-up fee. What does consumer advocate Inlander do when his doctor invites him back for a "follow-up visit" in six to eight weeks? "I ask why I need to be charged for that three-second check if my problem has cleared up by then. In 20 or so years, I've never been charged for a follow-up visit."

Before the return visit, Inlander negotiates the following deal with his doctor: If the rash or infection has cleared up and no additional treatment is needed, the follow-up visit is done at no charge. "But if there's a problem," he says, "I pay for the additional services. In my experience, most doctors are receptive to this because they want, and need, your business. If there's a problem, they know you won't be waiting another eight weeks to get it checked out."

Defend yourself from "defensive medicine." Although Pap smears are sometimes used to screen for uterine cancer, some 10 million women who have had a hysterectomy still submit to the test for its main purpose—to screen for cervical cancer, despite the fact that their cervix has been removed.

Why?

Because many doctors order or perform more tests than are medically necessary as a way of guarding against the possibility of a later lawsuit. Among practitioners, this is known as "defensive medicine." Among consumer advocates, it is known to saddle patients and insurers with an estimated $100 billion a year in unnecessary medical costs.

Your protection: Diagnose your doctor's motivation. Ask him or her whether the test is recommended for defensive medicine reasons. Does it fall under the guidelines of an authoritative body such as the U.S. Preventive Services Task Force? (This well-respected panel of experts assesses which preventive-care measures are necessary under the circumstances, and which aren't. To learn more, visit http://www.ahrq.gov/clinic/usptfix.htm.)

Also ascertain the doctor's personal knowledge of the value of the test: Specifically, what would the test confirm, reveal, or rule out as it pertains to you? Statistically, MRIs, CAT scans, and x-rays are the three tests most frequently conducted for defensive-medicine purposes.

Medications

Fill up on fabricator freebies. It's a no-brainer to ask your doctor for free samples. But let's face it, that handful of pill packets will get you through only a few days. For a 30- or 90-day supply—or an even longer steady supply—tap into the best-kept secret in the pharmaceutical industry: The more than 100 patient-assistance programs that provide free or cut-rate prescriptions from every major drug manufacturer in the United States.

You must contact the specific drug manufacturer to see if you qualify; each program is different and eligibility varies, but most are specifically geared for uninsured, underinsured, or low-income Americans—typically, $19,000 for an individual and $32,000 for a family of three. Most programs also require paperwork from your doctor, to whom the prescriptions are usually shipped.

Rx Warning From AARP

Although more than one million American consumers age 65 and over routinely receive 90-day supplies of prescription medications by mail order from Canada, you should be aware that importing drugs from Canada—especially on an individual scale—is illegal. The practice is unlawful, so AARP does not encourage consumers to purchase drugs from Canada. Nor does AARP endorse any pharmacy but its own.

"Even if you have insurance or a higher income," says Mark Grayson of the Pharmaceutical Research and Manufacturers of America (PhRMA), "you may qualify for certain higher-cost drugs or certain programs."

At least 10 million Americans do qualify, but only a fraction of those actually apply for and receive these free or low-cost drugs, which include many major brand-name products. Grayson's organization, which advances the interests of the drug industry, founded the Partnership for Prescription Assistance (888-477-2669) whose website at www.pparx.org lists hundreds of these pharmaceutical company assistance programs. Be aware, however, that with the rollout of the optional Medicare Part D drug benefit in 2006, some industry-sponsored assistance programs may soon be phased out. If you are eligible for coverage under Part D, signing up for a possibly short-lived patient assistance program instead of Part D could be a costly mistake.

You can also find out if you are eligible for state and local programs that offer assistance in obtaining prescription drugs by going to www.benefitscheckup.org. Another useful website for information on a wide range of programs is www.needymeds.com.

Slice costs with a simple request. When the doctor hands you a prescription, utter the following five-word mantra to cut its cost significantly: "Is there a cheaper alternative?"

"It's the easiest and most effective way to reduce your drug costs," says Dr. Levine, on staff at Montefiore Medical Center in the Bronx, New York. "But you'd be amazed how infrequently this is done."

It should be done more often, because outpatient drugs—that is, the ones your doctor prescribes in the course of an office visit—usually have a higher out-of-pocket cost than those administered in hospitals or other settings. "Unless you tell the doctor you want a cheaper alternative," says Dr. Levine, "in most cases you'll likely be prescribed the newer brand-name drugs, which tend to be the most expensive."

Studies prove he's right: Only a small minority of patients discuss price with their doctors when they receive a new prescription, yet 1 in 3 chronically ill people admit to underutilizing (or simply skipping) important medicines because they cannot afford them. When patients ask their doctors for cheaper alternatives, by contrast, research shows that they usually receive them. To learn about safe, effective alternatives for common conditions, visit www.aarp.org/health/comparedrugs/.

Schedule a medication review with your doctor or pharmacist. (There may be a small charge for this service.)

Put all of your prescription, nonprescription, and herbal medicines in a bag, then ask him or her to review the contents. This exercise may turn up duplicates, medicines that can be safely discontinued, or lower-cost alternatives that could work well for you.

Managing Medication Costs

Having prescription drug insurance is the best way to reduce medication costs. The Medicare drug coverage that began in January 2006, for example, offers just such insurance for people who are 65 and older or disabled. Most beneficiaries can cut their costs this way. The greatest savings go to those on limited incomes who qualify for the "extra help" part of the new benefit. But what about the estimated 45 million other Americans who are uninsured?

With prescription drugs so pricy in the United States, more people are buying them from abroad, usually via the Internet. This is still illegal under U.S. law, but that hasn't stopped some two million Americans from doing it anyway (they buy mainly from Canada). Meanwhile Congress dithers, endlessly debating whether to legalize the practice.

Licensed Canadian mail-order pharmacies have long been the most dependable bet in terms of safety and service. But with pharmaceutical companies stanching the flow of drugs to these pharmacies in a bid to cut off the cross-border trade, many legitimate Canadian pharmacies now give Americans the option of having their prescriptions filled in Israel, the United Kingdom, and other lower-cost countries at similar savings. Customers almost always receive these medications in "blister packs"—special manufacturer's plastic packaging designed to defeat tampering.

For brand-name prescriptions that must be taken regularly and long-term—for conditions such as high cholesterol, diabetes, or hypertension, for example—you can typically save 40 to 55 percent (and as much as 80 percent, in some cases) when you buy from abroad. That's the conclusion of Tod Cooperman, M.D., president of PharmacyChecker.com, which evaluates and compares prices of mail-order pharmacies.

Generic drugs, on the other hand, are usually more expensive abroad than they are in the United States. But there are exceptions. Thanks to differing patent laws, Canada and other countries sometimes produce generic versions of brand-name drugs long before they become available in the U.S. For that reason, certain new generics purchased from abroad offer substantial savings.

The online purchase of "lifestyle" (as opposed to life-saving) drugs such as Viagra is more hazardous, whether such medications purport to originate in the United States or abroad. "Our sister company Consumerlab.com bought what was sold as Viagra from websites all over the world," reports Dr. Cooperman, "and found that many had not been formulated properly. They usually contain the active ingredient—but not necessarily enough of it to be effective." In a separate 2004 study, British researchers found that half the Viagra sold on the Internet was phony.

In addition to aggressively marketing newer drugs to doctors, pharmaceutical companies promote them heavily on television. Thus the doctors have the newer (and, not coincidentally, costlier) drugs on hand, and their patients have been primed to request them. "The pharmaceutical companies say they no longer give trips or tennis rackets to doctors for prescribing their drugs," says Dr. Levine, "but plenty of 'training' seminars on these medications are still held at the local steakhouse."

Use location to locate a deal. Never dismiss the power of competition. The more pharmacies there are in a neighborhood, the likelier you'll be to find price discounts.

Pharmacies in pricy neighborhoods or those that pay expensive mall rent typically charge higher prices in order to cover their overhead. "If you make some calls in different neighborhoods, you'll often find substantial savings," says Tod Cooperman, M.D., of Pharmacychecker.com, a website that evaluates mail-order and online pharmacies. "Often there's a significant difference between branches of the same chain—CVS or Walgreen's, for example—in different areas of the same city."

Buying through pharmacy-sponsored mail-order programs is often even less expensive.

Rethink Net-bought bargains. Seeking lower drug prices, many people have turned to the Internet. That might sound like a savvy move, but it's not.

According to Bernard Bloom, Ph.D., professor of medicine and health-care systems at the University of Pennsylvania, "You'll usually pay at least 35 percent more for drugs purchased online than you would at your local pharmacy. Some drugs cost two to three times as much online as they do in a bricks-and-mortar pharmacy."

That doesn't even include shipping and handling costs, which average $15 for prescriptions purchased from most

Request a prescription for an older brand-name medicine rather than the new one you just saw advertised on television.

Request a generic medication—if one is available, that is, and if your doctor gives the okay that that it's appropriate for treating the symptoms in question.

e-pharmacies based in the United States (some offer free S&H on large orders). In addition, many e-pharmacies charge $55 or so—higher than the typical in-person doctor visit—for an "online consultation," in which a customer completes a questionnaire in order to obtain or verify a prescription. "Online websites that don't require these consultations," says Dr. Bloom, "just tack on more shipping and handling fees."

Excluding these charges from his calculations, Dr. Bloom compared prices of numerous drugs in two studies done five years apart. Between those two dates, the cost of purchasing medicines online increased 30 percent. "If you don't have easy access to a doctor or pharmacy, going online offers convenience," he says. "But to better ensure both safety and savings, you should buy only from legitimate online websites associated with a licensed U.S. chain."

Determine legitimacy by letters. How can you tell if an online pharmacy is legitimate? Look for a respected seal of

Generic drugs can cost a fraction of the price of their brand-name equivalents in the United States. U.S. generics also usually cost much less than those available from abroad.

Assessing the True Cost of Pricy Drugs

When health-insurance co-payments increase for prescription drugs, the resulting hike in out-of-pocket costs prompts many people to cut back on necessary medications—or stop taking them altogether.

In May 2004, the *Journal of the American Medical Association* published a study that tracked the pharmacy records of 529,000 working adults with company-provided drug coverage. The study revealed that when co-payments doubled—typically from $6 to $12 for generic drugs and from $12 to $24 for brand-name medications—the insured reduced their intake of prescribed drugs by 20 to 35 percent.

"What's really alarming," says RAND Corporation researcher and study co-author Geoffrey Joyce, "was that we saw a significant reduction in the use of medications for chronic conditions such as diabetes, asthma, and depression.

"What this says is that even in a well-insured, working-age population, people are still sensitive to medication prices—even for prescription drugs we think are necessary."

approval that appears on the home page of the pharmacy's website. As things stood in February 2006, only a dozen U.S. Internet pharmacies displayed the VIPPS seal, which denotes a Verified Internet Pharmacy Practice Site that has undergone voluntary review for endorsement by the National Association of Boards of Pharmacy (NABP).

To ensure the seal is authentic and not put there to fool customers, try clicking on it; when you do, you should be routed to the NABP website, says Ilisa Bernstein of the FDA's Counterfeit Drug Task Force. To view a list of VIPPS-approved pharmacies, visit www.nabp.net/vipps/intro.asp.

Split pills to save big. One easy way to protect your wallet from sky-high drug costs is to ask your doctor to double your prescription dose, then split the tablets (but not capsules) to make them last twice as long.

Warning: Although most scored pills and tablets can be cut in half, this practice should never be done with time-release or specially coated prescriptions. Not only that, but splitting certain pills—extended-release tablets, for example, capsules containing powder, and certain migraine drugs—can have fatal consequences. Engage in this practice *only after securing your doctor's approval to do so.*

Assuming you have your doctor's okay, you can buy pill-

PROTECTIVE DETECTIVE

Cheaper Than Canada?

Since Canadian mail-order pharmacies began selling to American consumers in 2000, some 80 percent of their clientele has been seniors seeking affordable prescription drugs. With the 2006 advent of Medicare drug coverage (Medicare Part D), many of these customers have asked if Canada is still the cheaper option. An investigation of this question by the *AARP Bulletin* revealed that many American consumers could save more through Medicare coverage in 2006 than they could by buying from Canada—provided, that is, that they chose the least expensive Medicare plan in their area that covered all their drugs. This favorable Stateside comparison holds true even when Part D expenses such as premiums and deductibles are factored in. The savings do not apply to everyone, but the lower drug costs under Medicare were still widespread enough to show the importance of carefully doing the math when choosing among competing drug plans, or when comparing them with the cost of drugs from Canada. See "The New Math," January 2006, at www.aarp.org/bulletin/prescription.

Generics: Cheaper *and* Safer

THOSE "NEW-AND-IMPROVED" drugs you see advertised on TV may be nothing of the kind. In 2002 the FDA approved 78 new drugs, of which only 7 were truly innovative—defined as containing new active ingredients and likely to be better than drugs already on the market to treat the same condition. Not one of these new drugs came from American drugmakers; all of them originated with European companies or biotech firms.

In most cases, these new approvals are simply modified versions of existing drugs—often those whose patents are about to expire, allowing other manufacturers to copy the formula and the medications for much less as generics.

When the patent for the heartburn drug Prilosec was about to expire, for example, its manufacturer developed Nexium by essentially splitting the Prilosec molecule in half. After securing FDA approval for its "new" purple pill, the manufacturer spent nearly $500 million in one year alone trying to persuade Prilosec users to switch to the costlier Nexium.

"As a consumer, you pay for that advertising," says consumer advocate and former Pennsylvania Insurance Commissioner Herb Denenberg. "Without that advertising, you save. That's why you may spend two or three times as much on a heavily marketed brand-name drug as you do on an identical generic drug that is just as effective."

Exclusive patents on brand-name drugs typically last 20 years, but the clock starts ticking as soon as a pharmaceutical research company begins working on the product. It can then take 10 years or more for that drug to reach the market, meaning most drug companies are lucky if they get eight years of exclusive marketing before a competitor can copy the formula and develop its own, similar version.

Many doctors recommend waiting at least two years before you use a newly approved drug. "Some experts recommend waiting seven years," says Denenberg, who is also affiliated with the Center for Proper Medication Use.

The extensive professional caution stems from the nature of the FDA approval process. Because approvals are not based on head-to-head comparisons with other similar drugs, a new drug faces a fairly low hurdle before being adopted: To win approval, the new drug must be proven only more effective than a sugar-pill placebo. Not only that, but patients selected for drug trials are carefully screened beforehand, meaning they are often healthier—and younger—than the average real-life patient. Once the drug undergoing that trial gets FDA approval, however, millions more people take it over a short time period, causing side effects to surface that may have gone undetected in the initial studies.

splitters at most pharmacies, or have your pills split for free at Veterans Administration pharmacies. But don't expect drug-company reps to cheer from the sidelines. "The reason why certain medications come in hexagon, teardrop, or other different shapes," says Dr. Levine, "is to make them difficult to split. Drug manufacturers don't want consumers to do this because it hurts their profits." Other drugs, however—including the statins widely prescribed to lower cholesterol—are scored specifically to ease such pill-splitting.

How much can you save by doing this? According to a study presented before the 2004 annual meeting of the American Heart Association, the average patient could pocket $850 each year by asking for a higher-dose Zocor prescription and splitting the pills. Imagine that you require a 20-milligram dose; you ask your doctor for a 40-milligram script, then cut each pill in half. "Doubling the dose of a statin costs only about 20 percent more," says Dr. Levine.

For brand-name prescription drugs taken daily for ongoing conditions such as high cholesterol, diabetes, or hypertension, you will typically save 40 to 55 percent by requesting a generic alternative—in cases where one is available, that is.

Buy generics at buying clubs. For the best day-to-day deals on most generic drugs, consider Costco, Sam's Club, or another warehouse club. "These clubs offer discounts of 70 to 80 percent compared to the same items at retail chains such as CVS," says Gabriel Levitt, research director at Pharmacychecker.com. "You might save even more buying online at www.costco.com, which has less overhead than the in-store pharmacy and offers free shipping and handling on most generics." Another low-cost U.S. Internet pharmacy, Drugstore.com, likewise offers free shipping on orders that exceed a certain dollar amount, and competitive prices on a number of popular medications.

Wherever you buy, it pays to shop for generics, which may cost as little as one-tenth the price of comparable brand-name medications. For an illustration of this strategy, consider the case of the anti-platelet (or "clot-buster") drug Plavix, which costs about $4 a day. An older suitable generic antiplatelet drug, by contrast, costs mere pennies per day.

Nursing Homes & Assisted-Living Residences

Gauge reactions along with the grounds. A one-year stay in a typical assisted-living residence in the United States averages more than $30,000. For the same sojourn in a nursing home, the cost can exceed $70,000. Either of those would be a severe financial burden for most families. (Generally, Medicare does not pay for long-term care; Medicaid covers nursing-home care for older people with low incomes and limited assets.) So how do such institutions justify their costs to prospective residents or their inspecting families? Usually with an invitation for a personal tour to "see firsthand the fine level of care" they provide.

"Of course they put on their best face when they're giving the tour," says eldercare advocate Eric Carlson, a Los Angeles attorney for the National Senior Citizens Law Center. "And they can do their sales pitch standing on their heads. But if you get them into unfamiliar or unrehearsed territory, you'll get a better idea of the type of care they really provide.

"The key is to approach the inspection with a sense of entitlement and a list of questions about how they will improve the resident's stay." Carlson elaborates. "Gauge their reaction to each question you ask."

Let's say the prospective resident is a die-hard Chicago Cubs fan. "Ask what the facility will do to ensure he gets to watch the Cubs on TV," advises Carlson, author of the *Nursing Home Law Letter*. "If they say, 'We have cable, so we can do that,' that's a good sign. But if they say, 'That's not a problem—but the television shuts off at 8 p.m.,' that's an indication that personalized care may not be a priority.

"Think aggressively about the resident's personal interests. Does she attend weekly religious services? If so, how will the facility get her there? If he enjoys dominos, how will the facility encourage this? If the facility reps look at you like you're from outer space when you inquire about these personal interests, keep searching.

A nursing home generally provides a higher level of care than an assisted-living residence.

This usually includes skilled nursing care, medical services, therapies, and a broad range of services that assist people who have functional or cognitive limitations in their ability to care for themselves or perform other daily activities.

"If, on the other hand, the reps act as if they are willing to work with you, that's a good omen. For the amount of money the facility will receive every month—several thousand dollars—it should be able to provide an impressive level of personalized care."

Make a surprise visit—at night. After that scheduled tour—or perhaps even before you take it—make a surprise visit to the nursing home or assisted-living residence to see if the sales pitch conforms to reality. "I recommend you drop by unannounced at night," suggests gerontologist Sandra Timmermann of the MetLife Mature Market Institute, which conducts research on long-term care.

By day, most residential-care facilities are fully staffed: They show clear evidence of good staff-to-resident ratios, an abundance of activities, and prompt custodial care.

By night, all that may change: The nighttime may be the right time to get a true sense of how things really are. Minimum standards recommended in 1998 by the National Citizens' Coalition for Nursing Home Reform require at least one employee to be on duty for every five residents—and one licensed nurse to be on duty for every 15—during the day. At night, according to the coalition, at least one employee should be on duty for every 15 residents and one nurse for every 30.

A nighttime inspection is a good time to check for certain other telltale signs that a facility may be a poor choice for you or a loved one: Residents milling around in hallways with no after-hours social events or activities; staff only at desks or other posts, as opposed to interacting residents; odors that may be hidden from daytime visitors but undisguised at night. "The staff doesn't like it when you make a surprise visit, especially at night," says Met Life's Timmermann. "If they don't let you in when you knock unexpectedly on the door, I'd be suspicious of the care there."

Keep in mind that whereas nursing homes are required to

Although there is wide variance in what is considered an assisted living residence in each state, most such facilities provide personal care and supportive services 24 hours a day, some health care, meals, and housing in a congregate residential setting serving primarily an older population.

have nurses on duty around the clock, assisted-living facilities are not. Another distinction between the two is that nursing homes must comply with federal standards, whereas assisted-living facilities are regulated only at the state level.

Use your senses for sage spending. A nose for clues is just one way to size up any long-term care residence. Use your other senses, as well.

Brightly colored artwork and walls painted in warm colors such as yellows, reds, and oranges can stimulate energy and improve mood—an edge over the more common white or eggshell colors. Houseplants such as spider plants, bamboo, ferns, and philodendrons purify the air by ingesting toxins from building materials and other sources.

Full-spectrum lighting has one advantage: Most nursing-home residents do not get enough exposure to sunlight to stimulate adequate Vitamin D production in the skin. But the flicker and glare of overhead fluorescent bulbs can fatigue the brain, giving the edge to incandescent lightbulbs (which also create an atmosphere more homey than institutional).

"You also want to listen," counsels Timmermann. "A high level of noise can be especially distressing to those wearing hearing aids, which amplify these sounds."

Don't submit to cosigner scams. When it comes time to review nursing-home contracts and discuss the cost of care received in these facilities, beware any contract that requires a "responsible party" to cosign a pledge to be responsible for any unpaid fees, advises attorney Carlson. This provision is illegal—but that doesn't stop certain nursing homes from trying to sneak it in. Make the mistake of signing this clause and the facility may well attempt to hold you liable for the resident's nursing-home expenses.

"When that happens—and frequently it does, given the expense of nursing-home care—the resident should be Medicaid-

Resources: **Info on Eldercare**

AARP
Materials on caregiving, long-term care, and other critical social issues.
800-424-3410
www.aarp.org/life/caregiving

American Association of Homes and Services for the Aging
Represents a continuum of aging services, not-for-profit nursing homes, and assisted-living residences; provides lists of accredited facilities.
202-783-2242 / www2.aahsa.org

Assisted Living Federation of America
Trade association for the assisted-living industry. Provides consumer information and an online directory of homes and services.
703-691-8100 / www.alfa.org

Caregiving Online
Website that provides information for caregivers about support groups and resources.
www.caregiving.com

Caregiver Resource Directory
Online guide by Beth Israel Medical Center on navigating the health-care system and managing illness symptoms.
www.netofcare.org

Children of Aging Parents
Membership organization for adult children. 800-227-7294
www.caps4caregivers.org

Eldercare Locator
This public service of the U.S. Administration on Aging identifies state and community-based organizations that serve older adults and caregivers.
800-677-1116 / www.eldercare.gov

Family Caregiver Alliance
Supports caregivers with online fact sheets, tips, and discussion groups.
800-445-8106 / www.caregiver.org

National Adult Day Services Association
Information on adult day services.
866-558-5301 / www.nadsa.org

National Association of Area Agencies on Aging
This umbrella group for 655 agencies provides local contacts and information.
202-872-0888 / www.n4a.org

National Association for Home Care & Hospice
Trade association for hospices, home-care agencies, & home-care aide groups.
202-547-7424 / www.nahc.org

National Association of Professional Geriatric Care Managers
Trade organization helps consumers choose and manage caregiving options such as long-distance caregiving.
520-881-8008 /www.caremanager.org

National Citizens' Coalition for Nursing Home Reform (NCCNHR)
Lobbies to improve care in nursing homes.
202-332-2275 / nccnhr.org

National Senior Citizens Law Center
Legal advocates for low-income and disabled elderly individuals.
www.nsclc.org

Well Spouse Association
Membership organization provides support to spouses and partners of people with chronic illnesses and/or disabilities.
800-838-0879 / www.wellspouse.org

eligible," Carlson says. "Nursing homes may not want to hassle with Medicaid, so they try to pin the burden of payment on family members beforehand. Unlike cosigning for a car, however, where you know you're on the hook for a set amount, the potential financial obligation to a nursing home is unknown—and it can be staggering. Family members can act as agents on behalf of the resident, but they are not obligated to

What Do Medicare and Medicaid Cover?

Don't assume that all long-term care costs will be paid by Medicare, the federal health-care assistance program for seniors, or by Medicaid, a joint federal-state venture for the poor. Medicaid often subsidizes nursing-home care and long-term stays after Medicare runs out). Here are some guidelines of what you can expect:

Nursing homes. To qualify for Medicare coverage, recipients must have had an in-patient hospital stay of at least three days before needing skilled nursing care, certified by a doctor.

For up to 20 days, as long as medical necessity continues, Medicare pays for the full cost of covered services— a semiprivate room, meals, skilled nursing care, medical social services, medical supplies and equipment, medications, and physical, occupational, or speech-language therapy (if needed to meet a health goal).

From days 21 to 100, as long as medical necessity continues, residents are responsible for co-insurance ($119 a day in 2006). After 100 days in any single benefit period, Medicare coverage ceases. To then qualify for Medicaid, residents must meet income and asset requirements and certain health-related criteria. (For direct links to State Medicaid Office websites, visit www.cms. hhs.gov/medicaid/statemap.asp.)

Home care. To qualify for Medicare coverage, recipients must be homebound, under a doctor's care, and in need of skilled nursing or home health-aide services on a part-time or intermittent basis. Coverage includes medical equipment and supplies, nursing care, therapy, and some home health aides.

Hospice care. To qualify for Medicare coverage, a doctor must certify that residents have six months or less to live. Coverage includes all medical services, supplies, counseling, and homemaker services in a Medicare-approved hospice. Some drugs costs may be charged.

sign any document a facility presents that would commit them to financing their relative's care."

Under federal law, nursing homes must provide residents with information on how to apply for Medicaid. No facility is allowed to discriminate based on a resident's source of payment.

Fight back when care falters. Some unscrupulous facilities attempt to refuse services or specialized therapy within a few weeks of a resident's admittance. Eldercare attorney Eric Carlson explains how the ploy unfolds: "After Medicare benefits stop for a typical resident, a dishonest nursing home may try to terminate therapy services, claiming that the Medicaid program does not cover therapy. But this is not true: Medicaid may not pay as much for that therapy, but the nursing home remains under contract to the federal and state governments to provide the best possible care, regardless of which reimbursement source is financing the resident's care."

If this occurs, Carlson suggests, remind the residence in writing that it is required by law to provide the same level of care as it would be if the bills were still being paid by Medicare—or by any other source, for that matter. "Your letter should be polite, but firmly written," Carlson recommends. "Inform the facility that you expect all care decisions to be based on what's medically needed, regardless of coverage." Close the loop by faxing, mailing, or e-mailing a copy of your letter to your state long-term care ombudsman's office; a complete list of these appears on pages 226-228.

Beware hidden costs... With daily care at the typical nursing home averaging $200 per day for a private room and $175 for a semi-private room, you'd figure that items used daily (catheters, for example) would be included in the total cost of care. Figure again. "It's fairly common for nursing homes to charge for all sorts of extra supplies," says Carlson, "but they shouldn't. Unless you've signed an attachment to the contract specifically authorizing additional charges, don't pay anything. It's easier to not pay than to pay now and seek a refund later on."

Exceptions: If a resident needs additional services—help in being fed special therapies or medications, housing in a dementia unit—those extras can carry extra charges. These should be itemized and detailed in the contract. "Assisted-living facilities essentially bill you à la carte," says Carlson, "so you will be charged extra for services beyond your room and board. With nursing homes, on the other hand, it's understood that the base rate is pretty much all-inclusive."

Advice: When discussing fees before admission, list the prospective resident's current and predicted needs, then ask how they might inflate bottom-line costs.

...And be aware of real-life needs. A few commonsense considerations will increase the safety and convenience of any resident of an assisted-living facility:

- Does the assisted-living residence provide *free regular shuttle service* so residents can get to supermarkets, doctors' offices, or other local services? If not, you may be looking at some hefty cab fares.

- *Is there a kitchen* on the premises, or are meals brought in from an outside service? The former may be a better choice for residents of nursing homes or assisted-living facilities who require special or restrictive diets, says Timmermann of the MetLife Mature Market Institute.

- *Is the residence fenced in and secure* enough to prevent Alzheimer's patients from wandering? Does every corridor have handrails and overhead sprinklers?

- *How close is the nearest hospital* and ambulance service—in minutes, not miles? What arrangements has the facility made with those services to ensure the quickest and most qualified care for its residents?

• *How often*—and how thoroughly—are residents examined on site by visiting doctors? Is there a doctor on hand each day, or from 2 to 4 p.m. on Wednesdays only? Is this physician compensated by the facility, or is the resident charged for medical checkups? Expect different answers in nursing homes versus assisted-living facilities; the latter offer less-intensive medical care.

• *Where are emergency medical devices* such as defibrillators kept? Are they within easy reach on every floor? Can they be used by anyone, or only by the staff? Are able-bodied residents instructed how to use them?

Kick out the "kick-out clause." When the administrator of an assisted-living facility deems a resident "too infirm" to continue living there, the resident may be forced to move to a nursing home or hospice—often with scant advance warning, and with little or no assistance in finding such new accommodations. "These kick-out clauses are usually written into the contract by the facility," Sandra Timmermann explains. "They usually give the child, spouse, or other guardian no more than 30 days—and sometimes as little as two weeks. That's nowhere near enough time for many families to locate an available quality nursing home."

Timmermann's tip: Ask about this oft-overlooked kick-out clause at the time you "audition" an assisted-living residence. If it has one in place, make sure the contract grants you enough time to locate alternative arrangements, should it come to that. "I'd want at least several months to shop around," says Timmermann, "and adequate advance warning of the resident's declining health or independence."

Resources: **Turn Here for Help**

UNDER THE FEDERAL Older Americans Act, every state is required to have an Ombudsman Program, whose mission is to advocate for the residents of nursing homes and assisted-living facilities—as well as to answer any questions their family members may have.

Ombudsmen such as those listed below are also authorized to investigate and resolve complaints about long-term health care. In addition to these state offices, some 800 other ombudsmen programs dot the country.

Alabama
Phone: 877-425-2243
Fax: 334-242-5594
www.ageline.net

Alaska
Phone: 800-730-6393
Fax: 907-334-4486
www.akoltco.org

Arizona
Phone: 602-542-4446
Fax: 602-542-6575
www.de.state.az.us/aaa/programs/ombudsman

Arkansas
Phone: 501-682-2441
Fax: 501-682-8155
www.arombudsman.com

California
Phone: 800-231-4024
Fax: 916-928-2503
www.aging.ca.gov/html/programs/ombudsman.html

Colorado
Phone: 800-288-1376
Fax: 303-722-0720
www.thelegalcenter.org/services_older.html

Connecticut
Phone: 860-723-1124
Fax: 860-566-4499
www.ltcop.state.ct.us

Delaware
Phone: 302-255-9390
Fax: 302-255-4445
www.dsaapd.com

District of Columbia
Phone: 202-434-2140
Fax: 202-434-6595 (no website)

Florida
Phone: 888-831-0404
Fax: 850-414-2377
www.myflorida.com/ombudsman

Georgia
Phone: 888-454-5826
Fax: 404-463-8384
www.georgiaombudsman.org

Hawaii
Phone: 808-586-0100
Fax: 808-586-0185
www2.state.hi.us/eoa/programs/ombudsman

Idaho
Phone: 877-471-2777
Fax: 208-334-3033
www.idahoaging.com/programs/ps_ombuds.htm

Illinois
Phone: 217-785-3143
Fax: 217-524-9644
www.state.il.us/aging/1abuselegal/abuselegal-main.htm

Indiana
Phone: 800-622-4484
Fax: 317-232-7867
www.in.gov/isdh/regsvcs/providers/
index.htm

Iowa
Phone: 800-532-3213
Fax: 515-242-3300
www.state.ia.us/elderaffairs/
advocacy/ombudsman.html

Kansas
Phone: 877-662-8362
Fax: 785-296-3916
da.state.ks.us/care

Kentucky
Phone: 800-372-2973
Fax: 502-564-9523
chfs.ky.gov/public/default.htm

Louisiana
Phone: 866-632-0922
Fax: 225-342-7144
louisiana.gov/elderlyaffairs/
LTC_ombudsman.html

Maine
Phone: 800-499-0229
Fax: 207-621-0509
www.maineombudsman.org

Maryland
Phone: 800-243-3425, ext. 10914
Fax: 410-333-7943
www.mdoa.state.md.us/services/
ombudsman.html

Massachusetts
Phone: 617-727-7750
Fax: 617-727-9368
www.mass.gov/elder

Michigan
Phone: 866-485-5939
Fax: 517-373-4092
www.miseniors.net

Minnesota
Phone: 800-657-3591
Fax: 651-297-5654
www.mnaging.org.

Mississippi
Phone: 800-345-6347
Fax: 601-359-9664
www.mdhs.state.ms.us

Missouri
Phone: 800-309-3282
Fax: 573-526-4314
www.dhss.mo.gov/Ombudsman/5

Montana
Phone: 800-551-3191
Fax: 406-444-7743
www.dphhs.state.mt.us/sltc/

Nebraska
Phone: 800-942-7830
Fax: 402-471-4619
www.hhs.state.ne.us/ags/
ltcombud.htm

Nevada
Phone: 775-486-3545
Fax: 775-486-3572
www.nvaging.net/ltc.htm

New Hampshire
Phone: 800-442-5640
Fax: 603-271-5574
www.dhhs.state.nh.us

New Jersey
Phone: 877-582-6995
Fax: 609-943-3479
www.state.nj.us/health/senior/
sa_ombd.htm

New Mexico
Phone: 866-451-2901
Fax: 505- 476-4836
www.nmaging.state.nm.us

New York
Phone: 800-342-9871
Fax: 518-474-7761
www.ombudsman.state.ny.us

North Carolina
800-662-7030
Fax: 919-715-0364
www.dhhs.state.nc.us/aging/ombud.htm

North Dakota
Phone: 800-451-8693
Fax: 701-328-4061
www.state.nd.us/humanservices/
services/adultsaging/ombudsman.html

Ohio
Phone: 800-282-1206
Fax: 614-644-5201
www.goldenbuckeye.com/ombudsman.htm

Oregon
Phone: 800-522-2602
Fax: 503-373-0852
www.oregon.gov/ltco/index.shtml

Oklahoma
Phone: 800-211-2116
Fax: 405-522-6739
www.okdhs.org/aging/

Pennsylvania
Phone: 717-783-7247
Fax: 717-772-3382
www.aging.state.pa.us

Rhode Island
Phone: 401-785-3340
Fax: 401-785-3391 (no website)

South Carolina
Phone: 800-868-9095
Fax: 803-734-9886
www.aging.sc.gov

South Dakota
Phone: 866-854-5465
Fax: 605-773-6834
www.state.sd.us/social/
asa/services/ombudsman.htm

Tennessee
Phone: 877-236-0013
Fax: 615-741-3309
www.state.tn.us/comaging/
ombudsman.html

Texas
Phone: 800-252-2412
Fax: 512-438-3233
www.dads.state.tx.us

Utah
Phone: 801-538-3910
Fax: 801-538-4395
www.hsdaas.utah.gov/ltco.htm

Vermont
Phone: 800-747-5022
Fax: 802-863-7152
www.dad.state.vt.us/ltcinfo/
ombudsman.html

Virginia
Phone: 800-552-3402
Fax: 804-644-5640
www.vaaaa.org/ltcop

Washington
Phone: 800-422-1384
Fax: 253-815-8173
www.ltcop.org

West Virginia
Phone: 800-834-0598
Fax: 304-345-5934
www.state.wv.us/
seniorservices

Wisconsin
Phone: 800-815-0015
Fax: 608-246-7001
longtermcare.state.wi.us

Wyoming
Phone: 307-322-5553
Fax: 307-322-3283
www.wyomingseniors.com/
ombudsman.htm

EVERYDAY PROTECTION

9

Halt Humdrum Health Hazards

THE KEYS TO A LONG and healthy life seem clear enough: Eat right. Don't smoke. Exercise regularly. Wear seatbelts. Avoid barroom brawls with anyone named Icepick.

Less obvious are some of the dangers standing between you and that extended existence. Consider your telephone receiver or desktop: Square inch for square inch, both are likely to be laden with 500 times more fecal bacteria and other disease-causing germs than the typical toilet seat. Then there's your food, which contains viruses, bacteria, parasites, and toxins known to cause at least 250 diseases that strike 76 million Americans each year, causing 325,000 hospitalizations and more than 5,000 deaths. There's also the air you breathe: When all else is considered, living in a high-pollution locale can raise your chance of dying from heart disease by 25 to 30 percent compared with residing in a clean-air community. That's roughly the same risk as living with a smoker.

Indeed, it seems, everyday life can be downright hazardous to your health. At work, the typical adult touches as many as 30 different objects per minute, many of them containing germs that remain active on metal, wood, and plastic surfaces for several days. At home, kitchen countertops, TV remotes, and other frequently used surfaces are bacterial incubators, even when wiped down regularly. Between those two places, you run the risk of picking up germs each time you push an elevator button, use an ATM machine, take your kids to the playground, ride public transport, or go shopping. It's enough to make you emulate germ-phobic TV detective Adrian Monk.

Infectious disease, reports the Centers for Disease Control and Prevention (CDC), is the underlying cause in the deaths of 160,000 Americans each year—nearly as many as those felled by stroke, the country's third leading cause. Worldwide, human-spread infections kill as many as 1 in 3 people.

How can you fend off this contagion? You can't always depend on germ-combating drugs: During the past 25 years, antibiotics initially hailed as the nemesis of many infectious diseases have proved to be ineffective against stronger, medication-resistant microbes in the environment. And even when these prescription and over-the-counter (OTC) drugs "work" against run-of-the-mill ills, they can be rendered useless by incorrect storage. (Hint: The most common places are among the worst.)

But there's a way—many ways, in fact—that you can protect yourself from the sort of day-to-day perils that threaten your health. Read on to learn what they are.

Medication Smarts

Keep meds high and dry. The two most common places to store medications—the bathroom medicine cabinet and the kitchen—are probably the worst for preserving their efficacy.

"Never keep medications any place that is humid or where there are extremes in temperature," says Cynthia LaCivita, Pharm.D., of the American Society of Health-System Pharmacists. "That makes the bathroom an inadvisable place to keep your drugs."

Humidity can quickly destroy a drug's effectiveness. That's one reason why you should always discard the cotton ball inside many drug bottles, both OTC and prescription, as soon as you open it. "It attracts humidity from the air and retains it inside the bottle, damaging drugs more quickly," says

No joke: "Laughter acts as the antithesis of stress, releasing beneficial chemicals to counter the detrimental effects of stress."

So says Michael Miller, M.D., of the Center for Preventive Cardiology at the University of Maryland Medical Center. Hearty laughter provides a mini-aerobic workout. Second for second, it can be just as effective as intense exercise.

Food & Drug Misadministration

Serious interactions can occur when you take certain over-the-counter (OTC) or prescription medications within several hours of consuming certain food, drinks, or other products. Ask your doctor or pharmacist which interactions may be triggered by each medication you are prescribed. The list of substances to avoid numbers nearly 400 and includes:

Grapefruit and grapefruit juice can interfere with more than 50 medications—including popular cholesterol-lowering statin drugs, antidepressants, and medications for high blood pressure, impotence, colds, and allergies. The vitamin C–packed fruit interferes with an enzyme in the intestines that normally metabolizes the above-mentioned drugs. That in turn keeps the drugs from being broken down the way they normally would be, says Amy Karch, R.N., of the University of Rochester School of Nursing. The effects of grapefruit or grapefruit juice remain in the body for up to 48 hours; grapefruit's interaction with a drug can cause a dangerously high (or ineffectively low) dose to be released into the bloodstream. Alternatively, it may cause too little of the drug to be released.

Milk and other calcium-rich foods block the absorption of some antibiotics, such as ciprofloxacin. Depending on the antibiotic, milk should not be consumed for at least two hours before or after dosing. However, notes Cynthia LaCivita, Pharm.D., a glass of milk *should* be downed with aspirin and other OTC pain relievers, such as ibuprofen, to avoid stomach irritation.

Green tea can increase your risk of blood clots. It should be avoided by those taking the blood-thinner warfarin.

Cranberry juice can also affect the absorption of many medications, because its acidity can temporarily alter kidney function. This is why pharmacologist Mary Ann Kliethermes of the University of Illinois warns that "chasing medications with cranberry juice may cause drugs to accumulate in the body—or to be prematurely eliminated."

Fiber supplements taken for intestinal and heart health can interfere with these medicines: tricyclic antidepressants, the diabetes medications glyburide and metformin, the heart drug digoxin, penicillin, and certain cholesterol-lowering drugs. Fiber supplements are usually safe if they are not taken within several hours of those drugs, but check with your doctor. Oat bran in its natural form can interfere with statin medications when consumed just before or after them.

Dietary supplements such as St.-John's-wort, echinacea, feverfew, garlic, ginger, and ginkgo biloba interfere with various drugs, from aspirin to high blood pressure. Tell your doctor if you're taking these or any other herbal remedy.

Dr. LaCivita. Telltale signs of humidity damage—an indication you should not take that medication—include any discoloration or change in "taste," capsules that clump together, or pills that crumble.

Sunlight, heat, and cold likewise destroy many medications, vitamins included. For that reason, avoid keeping medicines near a window (those amber-colored vials block some, but not all, ultraviolet light), in a car, or (unless directed to) in a refrigerator.

"One common mistake that many people make is to keep their vitamins over the stove so they remember to take them with their meals," says Richard C. Becker, M.D., a cardiologist at Duke University Medical School. "But many supplements—especially oil-based products such as fish oil—become unstable when exposed to heat."

Your protection: Provided that neither place is next to a window, explains David W. Bates, M.D., chief of general medicine at Harvard's Brigham and Women's Hospital, the ideal site to store medications is on top of your bedroom bureau or your dining-room table.

"Keep your drugs somewhere that is dry, not too hot, and perhaps more importantly, a place where you will remember to take them," advises Dr. Bates, who also directs one of the three national Centers of Excellence for Patient Safety and Research and Practice. Of course, medication should always be stored where it cannot be reached by children.

PROTECTIVE DETECTIVE

Safer Outdoor Exercise

Believe it or not, long-term exposure to air pollution poses a greater risk of death from heart disease than from respiratory ailments. One reason: Air pollution inflames blood vessels, which in turn accelerates atherosclerosis and alters cardiac function. As part of this inflammation response, plaques become more susceptible to rupture, increasing your risk of blood clots and heart attacks.

This is why, says researcher C. Arden Pope III, Ph.D., of Brigham Young University, people who live in the most polluted cities—among them Los Angeles, Houston, New York, and Atlanta—face an increased risk of heart disease that's comparable to living with a smoker.

Your protection: "In most communities, air and ozone pollutions tend to peak between noon and 4 p.m.—not during rush hour—so it's best to limit outdoor activities then," says Dr. Pope. "And whenever you exercise, the further you are from busy streets with a lot of traffic, the better."

Learn labeling language. Storing your drugs properly is a waste of time unless you also take them properly. What does that mean? Here's how to decipher some common prescription instructions:

- *"Take three times daily"* can be confusing. Unfortunately, it may be written more often than the more definitive "Take every X hours." Because there are 24 hours in a day, you might reasonably assume that "Take three times daily" means "Take one dose every eight hours." But as Dr. LaCivita explains, "For medications that require multiple dosing, such as three times a day, unless you are otherwise directed you should space the medication as evenly as possible over the *waking hours* of the day." (If you sleep six hours, take it every six.)

- *"Don't take with food"* means the drug should be taken at least one hour before eating—or at least two hours after eating.

- *"Avoid with"* instructions mean you should not consume the listed food or drink within four hours of taking the medication. At least 400 OTC and prescription medications are known to cause occasionally serious interactions when consumed within several hours of certain food and drinks. On the other hand, unless your doctor instructs you otherwise, you usually need not observe a total ban on the listed food or drink.

- *"Take with"* instructions note that the drug may be better absorbed, or at least cause fewer stomach problems, when taken with a meal. When there are no "take with" or "avoid" instructions, chase your medication with a full glass of water. "At the very least," says Mary Ann Kliethermes, Pharm.D., of the University of Illinois at Chicago College of Pharmacy, "this helps avoid stress on the kidneys and aids in absorbing the medication. Moisture also helps dissolve some medications

To track how much you trek— 10,000 steps daily is the ideal—wear a clip-on step counter and log your results online at http://aarp. stepuptobetter health.com/ default.asp.

Registration for the program is free; if you don't have a step counter, you may purchase one online. There is a discount for AARP members.

more easily, but the main benefit of drinking water is to pass the drug through the stomach more easily—especially if you have acid reflux or are elderly, when the gag reflex diminishes." (In some cases, pneumonia can result when pills lodge in the esophagus and migrate from there to the lungs.)

React when you have a reaction. Because the advertisements and labels for most drugs include a long list of common side effects, many people anticipate at least one of these reactions to be a "normal" part of taking the drug. This unreasonable expectation often leads them not to mention a side effect to their doctor or pharmacist when one occurs.

Bad move, says Harvard's Dr. Bates. His research reveals that early notification can prevent or reduce 1 in 5 of these adverse events—which sometimes lead to permanent problems. "At the first sign of any side effects," he emphasizes, "you really should alert your doctor—who may see fit to prescribe you a different dose or an alternative medication."

Fighting Germs at Home & in Public

Be dutiful about your digits. If you want to put your finger on the cause of most infections, look no farther than the end of your arm. About 80 percent of germs are spread through hand contact: Typically you touch an infected surface or person, then touch your own mouth, nose, eyes, or an open cut, inviting microbes to enter the body and cause problems.

The problem is, most people don't wash their hands often enough—at least 12 times per day. Nor do they wash them correctly, especially when in public. "To kill germs that cause illness, you must use soap and hot water, and you must wash your hands for at least 20 to 30 seconds," says University of Arizona environmental microbiologist Charles Gerba, Ph.D., the so-called "Dr. Germ" who has collected thousands of germ-concentration samples for dozens of medical studies. "Yet in

Researchers in France have discovered that the risk of heart attack in people with high blood pressure (but not others) doubles when the mercury dips below 25 degrees F.

The suspected reason: Exposure to cold weather constricts blood vessels, impeding blood flow and raising blood pressure even more.

studies we've conducted, we've found that only 65 percent of people wash their hands after using a public restroom. Of those, only half use soap—and of those, in turn, only half wash their hands for at least 20 seconds."

Your protection: Practice what is preached at many daycare centers: Sing "the alphabet song"—nice and slowly—to ensure that your handwashing session lasts long enough to be effective. If you finish washing before you reach the line "Next time won't you sing with me?," your wash was too short and you need to keep sudsing and rinsing. If you're not a fan of preschool ditties, you can also use store-bought alcohol gels, wipes, and other hand-sanitizing products. "They're actually a little more effective than soap and water alone," notes Dr. Gerba, a world-renowned authority on germs. "They are also probably your best defense against germs when you're out in public."

Round up unusual suspects. That coworker coughing in the next cube. That stranger sniffling on the bus seat behind you. They're both highly probable carriers of colds or other viruses. But can you guess when *any* person's hands are most likely to be infected with even more dangerous microbes, such as fecal bacteria and *E. coli*?

- *Make like Mrs. Macbeth.* "Right after you prepare a meal is when your hands are at their germiest," says Dr. Gerba.

BMI Countdown

Most medical experts now accept the body mass index (BMI) as the most reliable gauge of a person's level of overweight or obesity. A desirable BMI falls between 19 and 25. A BMI of 25 to 30 is considered overweight, while a BMI above 30 is deemed obese.

To calculate your own BMI, try this formula, suggests Robert Bonow, M.D., chief of cardiology at Northwestern University's Feinberg School of Medicine: First, multiply your weight in pounds by 703. Then multiply your height in inches by your height in inches, and divide the first answer by the second. For example:

A 5-foot-10 (70-inch) man weighing 160 pounds:
160 x 703 = 112,480.
70 x 70 = 4,900.
112,480 ÷ 4,900 =
BMI of 23 (desirable).

A 5-foot-3 woman (63-inch) weighing 155 pounds:
155 x 703 = 108,965. 63 x 63 = 3,969.
108,965 ÷ 3,969 =
BMI of 27.5 (overweight).

"Concentrations of *E. E. coli* and other microbes are highest when you handle raw meats." So wash or sanitize your hands both before and after you prepare a meal—and always before you eat.

- *Sanitize teeter tots.* Playground equipment—especially monkey bars—is the second germiest environment known to humankind. "They're primarily used by small children," says Dr. Gerba, "who run around with colds and rarely wash their hands." To stave off a viru-

▶ **A BETTER WAY**

Call 911 for "Nose to Navel" Pain

Time is of the essence in heart attacks, which claim some 460,000 American lives each year—half within one hour of the onset of symptoms. Is there a way to ensure quicker treatment at a hospital emergency room?

Yes, says Charles L. Curry, M.D., the former chief of cardiology at Howard University School of Medicine and the 1999 recipient of the American Heart Association's "Physician of the Year" award. Call 911 if you have *any* unexplained "nose to navel" discomfort, especially if you're statistically at risk for a heart attack—that is, if you're over the age of 40 and/or have high cholesterol, diabetes, obesity, or other risks of heart disease.

"When you arrive at a hospital by ambulance for a suspected heart attack," says Dr. Curry, "you will get quicker treatment than if you drive there yourself. In order to earn their accredi-

tation, hospitals must meet guidelines dictating that ambulance-delivered patients with heart-attack symptoms be given an EKG within 10 minutes of arrival, and that they be examined by a physician within 30 minutes." Those arriving under their own steam may not benefit from these treatment-timed requirements.

Why call 911 for any mysterious nose-to-navel problem? Because difficulty breathing or discomfort in the chest (ranging from mild tension to crushing pain) are just two of the many signs of a heart attack. Women having a heart attack often feel discomfort in the back rather than the chest, and therefore delay seeking treatment. Other sometimes-ignored symptoms, among both sexes, include an unexplained feeling of fullness; indigestion, gas, or nausea; lightheadedness; sweating; or pain in the arms, the jaw, or the neck.

lent case of Jungle Gym Fever, wash or sanitize every-one's hands—both your kids' and your own—immedi-ately after playground equipment has been used.

- *Revenge of Captain Underpants.* Believe it or not, laun-dry time gets the bronze medal for germ concentra-tions. Thanks to energy-conservation efforts—to say nothing of the popularity and efficacy of cold-water detergents—"only 5 percent of Americans regularly wash their clothes in water hot enough to kill fecal bac-teria," notes Dr. Gerba. In a cold- or warm-water wash cycle, he notes, bacteria can spread from one article of clothing to another inside your washing machine; then, when you go to remove that "clean" laundry, it infects your hands. To keep this from happening to you, wash underwear and towels in hot water—ideally at least 120 degrees F. If you use cold or warm water on a given load of laundry, sanitize your hands immediately after you take the wet items from the washer. Luckily, the dryer is hot enough to kill most germs.

In public, keep in mind that surfaces such as ATM and ele-vator buttons, shopping carts, telephones, airplane serving trays, computer keyboards, doorknobs, and desktops are rarely, if ever, cleaned. "Personally," recommends Dr. Gerba, "I use my knuckle—never my fingertip—to push elevator buttons, especially for the ground floor, which is the most likely to be germ-ridden." Other surfaces, such as telephones or keyboards, can be cleaned with alcohol wipes or cleaning products containing bleach before you touch them. "But wip-ing surfaces with a wet paper towel only spreads germs around; it doesn't kill them."

Rethink that picnic. Dining alfresco may be appetizing food for thought, but public picnic tables rank close to playgrounds as germ collectors, according to Dr. Gerba. "They are never cleaned or disinfected. Birds like to roost on them, especially

When shopping for your next toothbrush, con-sider this: Clear brush heads and bristles are less hospitable to disease-causing bacteria, fungi, and virus growth than those that are darker.

To reduce your risk of illness, replace your toothbrush every two weeks—or sooner, if you are recovering from a passing illness or any infection.

on picnic tables near a pond or in the shade. People often use them as diaper-changing stations (and worse). So never eat from a picnic table—don't even touch its surface—unless you've brought along your own tablecloth."

Fresh produce containing the highest levels of pesticide includes spinach, bell peppers, apples, green beans, peaches, raspberries, cherries, and imported grapes and celery.

Those with the lowest levels are pineapples, watermelons, plums, grapefruit, avocados, cauliflower, asparagus, broccoli, onions, cabbage, eggplant, and mangoes.

Left is the right choice. Because they are cleaned and disinfected regularly, public restrooms are freer of germs than the typical American home. Still, they harbor infections untold. Is there a way you can minimize your exposure the next time nature calls?

"Most people use the middle stall," says Dr. Gerba, "so that one tends to be the germiest. My advice is to use 'stalls with walls'—that is, one of the stalls at either end, which tend to be used the least often." Overall, the stall closest to the door is probably the safest, because many users want their privacy and janitors tend to tackle that unit first. But if you enter a bathroom with stalls on both sides of the door, head to the one farthest left: Most people travel to their right, making those left-end stalls statistically less frequented.

Left is also the right choice when it comes to choosing public restroom faucets, whose moist environment makes them even more septic than toilet seats. This is a key fact to know in airport bathrooms, whose janitors cannot effectively battle the relentless influx of germs from around the world.

Finally, when you dry your hands, opt for a paper-towel dispenser over an air-blowing hand dryer. Bacteria can thrive inside the dryer vents, then settle on your hands in that blast of hot air; you can also inhale these bacteria.

Food Safety

Chill to prevent ills. Unless you happen to be conducting an 8th-grade science-fair experiment in your kitchen, green dots or gray fur growing on your food should be seen as discouraging signs. Those perils are easy enough to avoid—you simply throw away the tainted food.

▶ **A BETTER WAY**

Trim Your Weight—and Tax Bill

If you are under doctor's orders to lose weight, you may be able to trim another heavy load: your tax bill. The Internal Revenue Service allows taxpayers to deduct certain expenses related to combating obesity and associated diseases.

The caveat: The expense has to be related specifically and exclusively to weight loss, says IRS spokeswoman Nancy Mathis. This makes your out-of-pocket expenses for gastric bypass surgery deductible—the procedure is done only to combat obesity—but disallows the cost of your gym membership.

The reason: You could attend a gym to build muscle, to enhance general wellness, or for other reasons not related to weight loss, says Mathis. Under these rules, detailed in IRS Publication 502 (www.irs.gov/publications/p502/index.html), the cost of Weight Watchers meetings or nutritional counseling is an acceptable write-off; the cost of food sold as part of a certain diet is not. (As Mathis explains it, you needn't eat *that particular food* in order to lose weight.) Smoking-cessation expenses are also allowed under Publication 502, but again restrictions apply: Prescription nicotine-replacement products (such as a nicotine inhaler) are deductible, whereas OTC products (such as a nicotine patch) are not.

Here are some conditions you must meet in order to claim the weight-loss tax deduction:

The therapy must treat a specific disease diagnosed by a doctor, such as obesity or a weight-associated ailment such as hypertension or diabetes.

The out-of-pocket costs must be itemized; when combined with other allowed medical deductions, they must exceed 7.5 percent of your adjusted gross income. For someone with an adjusted gross income of $50,000, this means that all allowed medical expenses would have to exceed $3,750; for a household earning an adjusted gross income of $80,000, the deductibility threshold would be $6,000.

Generally, expenses must be claimed for the tax year in which they were paid. It does not matter whether weight loss occurred or not.

The real danger stems from invisible infections. Indeed, foodborne illnesses cost American consumers an estimated $6 billion a year in medical expenses and lost productivity. The best way to prevent problems is to adopt the Raccoon Routine: Wash everything—including hands, utensils, countertops, and the food itself—before you prepare or eat any meals.

Temperature plays a key role, too. Like the mold that shows up uninvited on bread and cheese, many of the microscopic germs that cause bacteria grow most rapidly in temperatures above 40 degrees F. That might seem a bit chilly for you, but for disease-producing microorganisms it's an invitation to thrive: They can double their number at that temperature in just 20 minutes. Even if your refrigerator is set below that—and it should be—it may only slow, as opposed to prevent, the growth of dangerous microbes. On the next page, you'll find some cool rules to reduce your risk.

▶ **A BETTER WAY**

Learn Label Lingo

Would you throw out a potential dinner because you noticed at the last minute that its "use-by" date had expired? That could be wise—or it could be a waste of munchies and money. Except for poultry, infant formula, and certain baby foods, product dating is not mandated by Uncle Sam. (Twenty of the 50 states, by contrast, do require date stamping on some food packaging.) Here's a guide to what food labels really mean:

"Expiration" dates are the essential ones to watch. They indicate the last day on which the product can be consumed without jeopardizing your health. Eggs are the exception; they usually can be safely eaten three to five weeks after the expiration date.

"Use by," "Best if used by," and "Quality assurance" dates indicate freshness, not safety. They signal the last date on which the product is likely to retain its peak flavor and quality. "Guaranteed freshness" usually refers to baked goods; they can be safely eaten after that date, but they may taste stale.

"Sell by" or "Pull" indicates the date on which the retailer should remove the item from sale. You should buy it before this date, but you don't have to use it by then. Milk can be consumed up to one week after its sell-by date.

"Pack" or "Package" dates denote when the food was processed. Like "Use by" dates, they too signify freshness, not safety.

"Born on" may be a cutesy marketing ploy of Anheuser-Busch, yet the taste of any beer does begin to decline roughly 110 days after the "born on" date.

- *Refrigerate or freeze* any perishable or prepared food (including leftovers) within two hours of preparing it. When the temperature is above 90 degrees F, refrigerate or freeze the food within one hour.

- *Separate large amounts of food* into smaller containers for quicker cooling.

- *Defrost meat in the fridge*—not at room temperature. Place it on the lowest shelf to prevent its juices from dripping bacteria onto any foods below. Never submerge meat in cold water unless you change the water every 30 minutes; this should prevent bacteria from proliferating as the meat warms.

Be mindful of mold. When your food changes visibly before you get a chance to cook it, the likely culprit is mold—a form of minute fungi whose best-known manifestation is those splotchy green spots that attack your hoarded hunk of Cheddar just when you're in the mood for a grilled-cheese sandwich, or that downy coat of white that materializes on those last two slices of bread in the loaf. Despite their unearned reputation as "friendly" bacteria, some molds can cause serious allergic reactions and respiratory problems. A few can mutate into poisonous substances.

The United States Department of Agriculture (USDA) recommends that you discard most foods at the first sign of mold—including deli meats, casseroles, pasta, breads, soft cheeses, fruits, and vegetables. The exceptions: Hard cheeses and firm vegetables such as peppers and carrots can be eaten, if you first cut at least 1 inch around and below the mold. You can scrub mold off hard salami and dry-cured hams; surface mold is normal for them.

PROTECT YOUR RIGHTS

IDENTITY THEFT

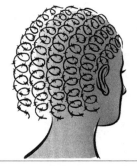

10

Armor-Plate Your Name & Reputation

To scan the Federal Trade Commission's yearly list of the Top 10 Consumer Fraud Complaints is to rediscover the wisdom of an adage: "The more things change, the more they stay the same."

In 2001 the FTC received 204,000 complaints from consumers claiming to be the victims of some type of fraud. Of those cases, nearly half—42 percent—involved identity theft. Not only was ID theft the nation's single most prevalent type of fraud, but it generated almost as many reported incidences as the next eight categories combined.

The following year, things changed—and stayed the same: Overall fraud reports to the agency's database nearly doubled, to 403,688. Again, identity theft took the top spot, with a 40 percent market share. In 2003 fraud complaints spiked to 542,378, with the number entailing identity theft remaining constant at 40 percent. In 2004 the FTC received 635,173 overall complaints (a threefold increase in just three years), and 39 percent concerned—you guessed it—identity theft.

What these numbers say is that scams have become a nationwide epidemic, and that identity theft leads the way.

But wait, it gets worse: Those FTC complaints represent only a fraction of the crimes taking place. Each year, almost 10 million Americans are robbed of their identities. At least 1 of every 6 adults in the United States had already been victimized by the time ChoicePoint, Bank of America, Time Warner, and nearly a dozen other large companies or employers sheepishly revealed in 2005 that they had "lost" or been relieved of sensitive data about millions of customers.

Identity theft occurs when someone hijacks details of your personal information to obtain goods, services, or money in your name. These events slam victims' credit-card accounts with $20 billion in bogus charges each year, and more than $17 billion to other active accounts. Another $16 billion is scammed annually by identity thieves who open new accounts or commit other fraud in their victims' names. The per-victim price tag totals some $5,700, according to the 2005 Identity Fraud Survey Report by the Better Business Bureau and Javelin Strategy & Research. And though your financial liability may be limited if you can prove that a scam occurred, it can take years to restore a credit score damaged by an identity thief.

How does identity theft occur? In nearly half of cases, it stems from bad luck or bad blood. About 30 percent of the time, according to the Javelin study—which surveyed thousands of known victims—identity theft begins with a lost or stolen wallet, checkbook, or credit card. In almost 12 percent of cases, victims are scammed by a relative, a friend, or an acquaintance who obtains their driver's license, Social Security number, credit card, or other account data, then uses it on their own or sells it to others. Other sources of this increasingly common crime include:

- *About 13 percent of cases* stem from the theft of account information during a "personal" or online transaction. This can result from a lost or stolen receipt or some other method. Frequently it occurs via "shoulder surfing" while you are standing in line at the checkout counter.

- *Corrupt employees* with access to personal data are responsible for about 9 percent of thefts. These workers may include waiters, cashiers, or employees of banks, mortgage companies, or any other business that processes checks and credit-card payments. The workers may use this information personally, or they may be acting as steady suppliers for entrenched identity-theft rings. (See "Portrait of an ID Thief," page 248).

• *Stolen mail* accounts for about 8 percent of cases. This includes the theft of incoming bills that contain account information, incoming credit-card applications, or incoming medical, tax, or other forms containing Social Security numbers. Once they get their mitts on these forms, identity thieves submit address-change forms in your name, then open new accounts. This leaves you none the wiser, because the bills for "your" purchases get sent to the new location.

ID theft via purloined letters also includes the pilferage of outgoing envelopes containing checks you have written to pay utility bills and the like. Unless you filled them out with the special pen described on page 251, the checks can easily be "washed"—dipped in an acetone bath to produce a blank check signed by you—and reused to deplete your account.

• *About 5 percent of cases* result from computer spyware—software installed remotely and invisibly in the victim's computer and designed to collect personal information (it also bombards you with spam e-mails and pop-up ads).

• *Almost 4 percent* of identity fraud results from online hacking or "phishing"—the illegal act of sending an email that directs responders to a look-alike website masquerading as that of their bank or other service provider.

• *Approximately 3 percent of cases* stem from "Dumpster diving" to retrieve discarded documents containing personal data.

About 1 in 8 Americans have been robbed of their Social Security number, birth certificate, or driver's license, says a 2005 survey. Of those, 1 in 10 say an unauthorized bank account was set up in their name; 1 in 7 report their stolen identity was used to open new credit-card accounts.

Portrait of an ID Thief

FOR NEARLY 20 YEARS, Ron Hemphill says, he was an identity thief, running a crime ring that bilked millions from thousands of Americans.

"It all starts with corrupt employees," reveals Hemphill. "The information I obtained all came from inside sources—mainly employees working for banks, credit-reporting agencies, and mortgage companies."

Hemphill, released from federal prison in 1999 after serving 18 months for mail fraud, says he bought customer information from "moles"—often temporary workers—who were contacted directly by himself or indirectly by his informants. "At the height of my career," he maintains, "I had 60 people on my payroll." He now counsels corporations on how they can avoid the ploys he used to pull, and has chronicled his exploits in *Rollin': True Confessions of an Identity Thief.*

Hemphill says he often paid $5,000 for a new "hookup"—who, in turn, gave him names, addresses, Social Security numbers, and account data for up to 50 customers at a time. "Bank and credit-card company employees were instructed to give me information on customers who had banked or had credit cards there for at least five years, had FICO scores of at least 700, and had a credit line of at least $10,000."

With that information, Hemphill created phony driver's licenses and employee ID badges in the victims' names. "I bought the same machine used at the DMV," he confides. "I would call the credit-card companies and tell them 'I' had moved, and they would send me a replacement card or one with a new account number—even though the new address differed from the one on file."

Initially, Hemphill says, he bought items on his victims' accounts for his own use. "But as my operation grew, I paid some employees with merchandise I illegally gained through identity theft." The scamsters in his pay even developed specialties: Some were buyers, others exchangers—people who would return newly purchased furniture, electronics, and other ill-gotten gains a few days later for cash back.

It ended in January 1998, when Hemphill was arrested and charged with mail fraud. In jail, he says, he underwent "a spiritual conversion" that now motivates him to educate the public about identity theft (see www.idtheftexposed.com).

"You can take every precaution to prevent identity theft," he reflects, "but it's for naught if an unscrupulous worker is handling your account. There's no shortage of people willing to sell your information. Until companies are held accountable for the actions of their workers, this crime will continue."

- *About 2 percent* of cases result from e-mails sent by criminals posing as legitimate businesses.

- *The remaining cases* result from unknown methods.

Alphonse Karr—the 19th-century sage who penned that line about things changing and staying the same—also noted, "Happiness is composed of misfortunes avoided." If you can sidestep the following catalogue of calamities, you can up the odds of protecting your own financial happiness—and safeguarding your good name and good reputation.

Simple Steps to Take Now

By now, the most basic ways to protect yourself from identity theft have been made known to virtually every American vulnerable to the crime. Those at risk include pretty much anyone with a bank account or Social Security card; anyone currently holding or eligible for a credit card or driver's license; and anyone who rents or owns a home. All of the following steps are worth taking:

- *Shred it.* Rather than throw it away, destroy with a cross-cut (or "confetti") shredder all incoming mail with any sensitive information—your name, address, account information, Social Security number, and especially "convenience checks" and new credit-card offers. This simple action makes it virtually impossible for Dumpster divers to read your personal data.

- *Check it.* Review your credit history at least once a year with each of the major credit-reporting bureaus to stay informed of inquiries and purchases made on existing accounts, applications made for new accounts, and the placement of any judgments or liens. By law, all Americans are eligible to get one free credit report annually from each of the major bureaus (Experian, Equifax, and Trans Union) at www.annualcreditreport.com. By rotating your requests, you can get a free credit history report every four months or so.

- *Post it.* Mail outgoing bills and other vulnerable correspondence from the post office or a secure mailbox, not from an unlocked mailbox in front of your house.

- *Opt out of it.* To reduce the risk of incoming-mail theft, opt out of solicitations for new credit cards, mortgages, or other loans. To do this, call 888-567-8688.

- *Rebuff it.* Hang up on "telemarketers" who request bank account numbers, Social Security numbers, or other sensitive data. Better yet, use an answering machine or caller ID to screen your calls so you never talk to them in the first place; many scamsters block the display of their numbers, making them appear as "Private."

- *Leave home without it.* Do not carry your Social Security card or PIN codes in your wallet.

- *Delete it.* Avoid opening "spam" or other e-mails from those you don't know. Never click on links in incoming e-mails from "banks" or "credit-card companies" urging you to "update your personal information." If you need to correct details of your account, type in the website address yourself—or, far better, call or write the company directly.

- *Scrutinize it.* Carefully check bank-account and credit-card statements as soon as they arrive. Take immediate action to fight any fraudulent activity.

These measures are all important—but they are not all-inclusive. What else can you do to keep the identity wolves from your door?

Shield your fortune with a $2 pen. All it takes to empty your bank account, says Frank W. Abagnale, the world's most

---

If you're the parent of an 18-year-old registering for the Selective Service System, tuck the SSS postcard in a sealed envelope before you mail it back. Otherwise the vital stats it bears—your child's name, address, birth date, and Social Security number—will be in plain view to identity thieves.

infamous check-forger, is a single signed check stolen from your unlocked mailbox and some acetone—the active ingredient in nail-polish remover. (Conveniently for criminals, pure acetone is also available in the paint department of home-improvement centers.) "These guys drive around neighborhoods while residents are at work and look for mailboxes with the flag sticking up, showing there's outgoing mail," says Abagnale, who chronicled his life as a young identity thief in an autobiography that was made into the movie *Catch Me If You Can.*

Here's how the scam goes down: The crook steals mail likely to contain a signed check—envelopes addressed to the phone or electric company are easy pickings. He or she then removes your check, puts a piece of cellophane tape over the front and back of your signature, and places the check in a pan of acetone. This process—known as "check-washing," says Abagnale—takes only about 30 minutes to rinse everything but the printer's ink from the check. Your tape-covered John Hancock and the printer-inked information, of course, remain intact. The check is then blow-dried and flattened in a book, the tape is carefully peeled away, and *voilà!*—a blank check signed by you, replete with your name, address, and bank-account information. "The bad guys then call the bank," explains Abagnale, "to find out how much money is in 'their' account. That tells them how much they can steal. And thanks to overdraft 'protection,' the crooks can get even more."

Your protection: One type of ink—the kind in gel pens manufactured by Uni-Ball—resists acetone or other chemicals used in check-washing, says Abagnale, who now counsels corporations and law-enforcement agencies on check fraud. The ink in pens such as the Uni-Ball 207, which sell for about $2 each, contains pigments that soak into a check's paper fibers, trapping the ink and making it withstand check-washing efforts. (These pens are specifically marketed to prevent identity theft, with Abagnale's "signed" endorsement on their packaging.)

Write four digits for more protection. Even when you fill them out with a washproof pen, your outbound checks may offer identity thieves another bit of primo booty: your complete account numbers for credit cards, mortgages, or other loans, which are routinely written (at the payee's insistence) on signed checks. "A check can be handled by dozens of people along the way," notes Abagnale, author of *The Art of the Steal* and a book designed to protect college students from identity theft. "These include people from the credit-card company; employees of their bank; employees of your bank; and all the various vendors who process checks before, during, after, and in between."

Your protection: Rather than obediently scribbling your entire account number on signed checks—often on the "Memo" or "For" line—list only certain digits, such as the last four numbers of your credit-card account. Or write down no integers at all. Firms routinely ask you to note your entire account number, but there is no need to comply. "Credit-card companies, mortgage holders, and others always include a stub that you return with your payment that has your entire account number," says Abagnale. "If you return that stub with your payment—and you always should—there's no reason to write your account number on checks."

Keep 'em guessing with new checks. If your current checks display your first name, order new ones showing only your initials. That's the advice of Mari J. Frank, a California attorney who became an identity-theft protection lawyer after being victimized herself. "That way, the fraudster won't know how you sign your name," notes Frank, author of *From Victim to Victor: A Step-by-Step Guide for Ending the Nightmare of Identity Theft.*

Your protection: To further guard your privacy, keep phone numbers off your checks. If you must list one, make it your work number, not your home phone. Another good move: Get a Post Office Box number and use it (rather than a street

Your Private Life Gone Public

Psst! Wanna buy a Social Security number? Look no further than the Internet.

More than a dozen websites offer an array of personal information for sale—including names, addresses, and ages. Even that Holy Grail of identity thieves—the "Open Sesame!" known as another's Social Security number—can be purchased for $15 to $35 at www.secret-info.com. An SSN will set you back $55 at www.iinfosearch.com. Despite public outcry, no law prohibits this sale.

Want an even better bargain? According to a November 2004 report by the Government Accountability Office, about 1 in 4 county governments throughout the United States still posted crucial records on the Internet. The data thus archived in open view included property deeds, tax liens, court records, birth certificates—and, in some cases, Social Security numbers. As of December 2005, several states—California, Florida, and Texas among them—had passed legislation limiting the listing of Social Security numbers on Internet sites accessible to the general public.

address) as your mail-delivery point. Of course, never display on any check your Social Security or driver's license number. To prevent new checks from being stolen from your incoming mail, specify that the delivery be sent not to your home but to your bank (for later pickup there).

Finally, seek out check styles that offer security features, such as a special substrate that stains during check-washing attempts. "To protect yourself even more," urges Frank, "I would suggest that you stop using checks altogether. Commonly available software programs allow criminals to create new checks bearing your bank's routing number and your individual account number. Then, thanks to the lack of adequate protective measures in place at most banks, the fraudster easily siphons the entire contents from your account. You are actually safer using a credit card, because federal law protects you from card fraud."

Say cheese. Stealing your identity isn't hard, but stealing your face is. Take advantage, therefore, of an option offered by certain credit-card companies and retail stores that sponsor their own plastic: Your photo can be affixed to your credit card. "You may have to ask for this," says Mari Frank, "but the issuer will often comply." For in-store plastic, some retail stores keep a camera behind the counter to capture your mug shot on site. For all-purpose credit cards, you may have to send in your own photograph at the same time you send in your payment. For added security, order business cards that include your likeness; a pictureless business card was the passkey to Frank's identity theft.

Avoid casual clues. You welcome trouble into your life when you use your birth date or your mother's maiden name as your clue password or PIN for bank and credit-card accounts. Savvy identity thieves are adept at obtaining this information, notes Frank. They simply ferret out birth certificates and other public records online, then use the significant dates they find there to guess passwords until they succeed in cracking your account.

Your protection: "If a company asks for your maiden name or your mother's maiden name," Frank recommends, "reply that you want to use an alternative password to that." Alternatively, fabricate a "maiden" name or pick a bogus birthday—one that you can easily remember, of course. The same goes for listing your phone number in the telephone directory (it can be changed with a quick call to your phone carrier): Having yourself listed under a name that is not your own will enable you to effortlessly spot telemarketing calls and junk mail. If your name is John Smith and you list yourself in the phone directory as J. Jones, for instance, any contacts targeting a "Mr. Jones" at your address or phone number clearly arose when a list broker sold names and contact info culled from the phone book. Better yet, opt for an unlisted number—the extra few dollars you'll pay for the privilege are well worth the cost.

Open bank statements quickly. Federal law gives you only 30 days from the postmark on mailed bank statements to notify your bank of any discrepancies in your account. After that time, you can be liable for lost or stolen funds.

Hire a spy. Your bank accounts can be drained in a couple of days. Your credit history can be damaged for months or even years. But if you detect identity theft at the very moment it occurs, you may be able to stanch the outflow of funds. (You could be liable for $50 in fraudulent credit-card charges, but most credit-card companies won't charge even that. Debit cards are a different story; you may be liable for all such fraudulent charges made on your account.)

Your protection: One way to spot identity theft as it happens is to subscribe to a service that alerts you when anyone checks your credit rating or tries to use existing accounts—or open new credit—in your name. A cottage industry of credit-monitoring services have hung out their shingles since identity theft reached critical mass in the early 2000s, but some take a week or longer to notify you. Worse still, some may supply you summary statements only quarterly. Sift through these services until you find one with "enhanced" features that monitor your credit record on a daily basis—and inform you of any developments immediately via e-mail. Such programs include PrivacyGuard (www.privacyguard.com) and Identity Guard (www.identityguard.com). Some credit-card companies also provide similar services for a lower monthly fee.

No matter how often a credit-monitoring system reports its findings to you, says former identity thief Ron Hemphill, the protection will be for naught if it is short-lived. "Sign up for at least five years of protection," he recommends. Many credit-card companies offer limited credit monitoring—as a marketing incentive for new business or for a small fee to existing customers—but it usually lasts only a year or so. "That really isn't enough," notes Hemphill, who claims to have run a criminal ring with some 60 "employees" until being caught, jailed, and reformed. (See "Portrait of an ID Thief," page 248.)

Here's why longer protection is better: Established identity thieves often buy, barter, or steal information on hundreds of potential victims simultaneously. "If you have a credit-monitoring system and someone like me tries to open a new account in your name, the red flags go off," says Hemphill, who now operates the Identity Theft Help & Information Network at www.idtheftexposed.com. "That's what we call a 'blow-up.' When a blow-up happens, that name goes to the bottom of the pile." Months later, however, the identity thief may revisit that person's information to check if the credit-monitoring shields are still raised. "An identity thief may wait a few months or as long as a year to try again," he says, "but not one of them will wait a full five years to steal from that person. It's much easier to move on to someone else who doesn't have credit-monitoring protection in place."

Stop Junk Mail & Telemarketers

Just say no. Each year, more than three million Americans discover that credit accounts have been falsely opened in their name; of these, at least 400,000 can blame the crime on stolen mail. But in the space of an hour, you can deter both direct mailers and telemarketers. To decline vulnerable mailings (such as credit-card applications) and put an end to most unwanted phone calls, contact the following:

- *Credit Bureaus Opt-Out Line.* Call 888-567-8688 (888-5-OPT-OUT) from your home telephone (so it can be checked against an address database) or visit www.optoutprescreen.com to stop preapproved credit-card and insurance offers from reaching you by mail or phone. (The source for these come-ons is lists sold to companies by the credit-reporting agencies Equifax, Experian, TransUnion, and the smaller Innovis.)

  If you call, you'll get an automated voice-response system that requests your name, telephone number, and Social Security number; don't worry, they have it already as part of your credit history. Whether you call or go online, you can opt out for five years or permanently; if you choose the latter, you'll be sent an additional form in the mail that must be mailed back. Your opt-out "vote" goes into effect in about five business days, but do not expect to see a noticeable reduction for roughly one month.

- *Do Not Call List.* If you haven't done so already, by all means register your phone number with the National Do Not Call Registry, maintained by the FTC. Once you have registered your telephone numbers at www.donotcall.gov or by calling 888-382-1222, most telemarketers are barred from calling you. (They're subject to steep fines if they do call, so casually ask them to supply some identifying details.) You will still receive calls, however, from any charitable organizations, pollsters, or even commercial companies with which you have "an existing business relationship."

- *List Brokers.* Pooling information gleaned from phone books, public records, and other sources, these companies prepare and sell mailing lists to businesses. To remove yourself from all of their lists, you'll have to contact each one individually. (Preprinted mailing labels to ease the task are available at www.fightidentity theft.com/junkmail_labels.html.) Details on reaching the four largest list brokers appear at right.

- *Direct Marketing Association.* The DMA is a trade group whose

The "A List" for Getting Delisted

They don't exactly make it easy for you, but if you send a written request to each list broker below, your tide of junk mail should eventually ebb.

Dun & Bradstreet
Customer Service
899 Eaton Avenue
Bethlehem, Pennsylvania 18025

R. L. Polk & Co. / Name Deletion File
List Compilation Development
26955 Northwestern Highway
Southfield, Michigan 48034-4716

Database America
Compilation Department
470 Chestnut Ridge Road
Woodcliff, New Jersey 07677

Acxiom U.S.
Consumer Advocate Hotline
Phone: 877-774-2094
www.acxiom.com/us

Junk Mail: None for Me, Thanks!

Perhaps hoping to upgrade its image as the nation's leading source of shredder fodder, the Direct Marketing Association has graciously devised all manner of means by which you can just say no. Try one of these:

To stop receiving mailings, go to www.dmaconsumers.org/cgi/offmailinglist and complete the online opt-out form. Then click the "Register Online" button. This is the fastest way of adding your name and address to the DMA's Mail Preference Service (essentially a "do-not-mail" list), but it costs $5, payable by credit card.

Alternatively—and at no charge other than the cost of a postage stamp—you can complete the online form, then click the "Register by Mail" button instead. A tracking number will be generated for the Mail Preference Service (MPS). You'll have to print out the completed form, then mail it to the address listed on the form.

If you don't want to go online, send a postcard or letter including your name, address, and signature (and a request to opt out) to:

Mail Preference Service
Direct Marketing Association
P.O. Box 643
Carmel, New York 10512

This option is also free of charge, but it is the slowest; a minimum of two months will be required before your name and address have been added to the MPS opt-out list.

To stop telephone solicitations from DMA members with whom you do not have a current or past business relationship, visit www.dmaconsumers.org/cgi/offtelephone and complete the opt-out form you will find there. Here again there is a $5 charge to register online, or you can print out the form and mail it in at no charge. You can also send a letter or postcard with your name, address, telephone number (with area code), and signature to:

Telephone Preference Service
Direct Marketing Association
P.O. Box 1559
Carmel, New York 10512

To reduce e-mail solicitations from DMA members at up to three e-mail addresses, visit www.dmaconsumers.org/consumers/optoutform_emps.shtml. To confirm your submission, the Direct Marketing Association will send an acknowledgment to each address you submit; you must reply to each one within 30 days in order for your registration to take effect.

To remove the names of deceased loved ones from commercial marketing lists, visit https://preference.the-dma.org/cgi/ddnc.php and complete the form you find there. There is a $1 charge to verify your credit-card information.

5,200 member companies use the telephone, mail, and the Internet to pitch their products directly to consumers, bypassing such intermediaries as traditional bricks-and-mortar retail outlets. The DMA offers half a dozen ways for you to opt out of receiving solicitations from its members. According to DMA spokesman Louis Mastria, this should stop about 80 percent of such offers within several months. To take him up on his offer, try one or more of the remedies detailed in the sidebar on the opposite page.

In most states, if you have already signed up on your state's registry, your telephone number should appear on the national registry as well. Of the 25 states that maintained state registries as of January 2006, 17 had shared their lists with the national registry. If you live in Indiana, Louisiana, Mississippi, Missouri, Tennessee, Texas, Wisconsin, or Wyoming, you may want to add your number to the state registry as well. For a list of state "do-not-call" registries, visit www.ataconnect.org/GovernmentAffairs/StateDoNotCallLists.html. The federal registry is free; some states charge a small fee to delist you.

Don't snub those stuffers. The opt-out contacts listed above primarily deal with unsolicited mail and telephone calls from companies you have nothing to do with. But what about stopping the spread of your personal information from companies with which you already do business?

Your protection: Once a year, financial institutions are required to inform their customers how they use their personal information, and what opt-out rights those customers have. "The trick is that these notices often come in envelopes stuffed with other correspondence," notes Eric Gertler, author of the landmark *Prying Eyes: Protect Your Privacy from People Who Sell to You, Snoop on You, and Steal from You.* "Because of this, many people unknowingly discard them."

These notices sometimes provide a mailing address (or,

Identity thieves often use a victim's information to get new phone service.

According to the FTC's Identity Theft Clearinghouse, 10 percent of victim complaints involved a fraudulent wireless phone account opened on their dime. Six percent of complaints involved new landline accounts.

more rarely, a phone number or a website address) that permits customers to stop their financial institutions from sharing their personal information with unaffiliated third parties. This is that rare offer you truly should not refuse: Taking them up on it may halt junk mail that originates from totally unsuspected sources. Even if you don't take this step, you can always stop the spread of your personal information the good old-fashioned way: Contact your bank, credit-card issuer, or insurer and inform them you are opting out of sharing.

As you may have come to suspect by now, that will constitute only a partial solution. Opting out stops a company from supplying your personal information to third-party firms, but that company can go right on furnishing the data to its subsidiaries or affiliates. Gertler, the former CEO of Privista—an identity-theft protection and credit-management company—cites the hypothetical example of a customer who banks with Citibank: "Even if you opt out, your information may be passed to any of Citibank's affiliate companies, such as its credit-card division or its mortgage component."

Waive that warranty card. When you buy a new toaster, it's easy to get burned long before the bread pops up. The source of the tsuris is the warranty card included in the packaging.

"Warranty cards are primarily used by the product's manufacturer to profile you," explains California identity-theft attorney Mari Frank. "They will then sell that information to others, who in turn send you mailings for their own products and services. That's why warranty cards so often ask you for your household income, how many kids you have, what your hobbies and interests are. But you should know that unscrupulous employees can easily get their hands on your warranty-card info, then use it to steal your identity."

Your protection: Provided you keep the receipt, a product is under warranty for the designated period whether you return the warranty card or not. If you unwisely choose to "register" your purchase with the manufacturer, submit the

Who'll Stop the Mail?

The U.S. Postal Service delivers—but don't expect it to deliver you from the mountains of junk mail it dumps on your doorstep. Direct marketing mailings—which have increased by some five billion pieces since the National Do Not Call Registry went into effect in October 2003—generate billions of dollars in revenue for the USPS.

Maybe that's why some seemingly obvious steps for refusing these mailings don't really work. For instance:

Writing "Return to Sender" or "Refused" on the envelopes of unsolicited letters and placing them in your outgoing mail will not remove you from the sender's distribution list. The USPS does not forward third-class bulk mail; postal regulations require that it be thrown away instead.

Placing unsolicited mail in a return envelope with postage due is another futile attempt to stop future mailings. In all likelihood, the United States Postal Service will simply return the envelope to you for the correct postage. If you omit your return address and the Post Office is unable to return it to the sender, the envelope will go to the USPS's mail recovery center.

warranty card bearing nothing more than your name, address, and date of purchase. (If required, enclose a copy of your receipt.) In the same mailing, specify that your personal information is not to be distributed to others. There's no need to answer any other questions.

Shore Up Online Security

Get the down-low on downloading dangers. In May 2005, the privacy software company Webroot revealed a startling statistic: At any given time, said the company's "State of Spyware Report," 2 of every 3 personal computers in the United States are infected with spyware that raises your risk of identity theft. What's more, the firm reported, the typical computer scanned for the survey was infected with an average of 25 different spyware programs.

Password Dos and Don'ts

Need another reason to guard your computer passwords? It's possible they could be cracked by eagle-eared identity thieves using a high-tech microphone that detects sound through glass.

"Depending on its keyboard location, each key emits a different sound—in much the same way a bongo drum does," says computer scientist Doug Tygar of the University of California at Berkeley. These differences go unnoticed to the untrained ear, but Dr. Tygar and his colleague Li Zhuang used a $10 microphone to record keystrokes, then ran the sound of each through a software program originally designed to recognize human speech. By the third try, the program identified 96 percent of typed characters.

When assigned to decipher the keyboard recording of a 10-digit password, Dr. Tygar's doctored software came up with 75 possibilities. "That means if we tried all 75 passwords, we could break into that user's account.

"I cannot say this is being done, only that we have done this in the lab. We hope our experiment persuades manufacturers to produce keyboards that mask these sounds." Given the easy availability of laser microphones that can record sound through windows across the street, Dr. Tygar is already tackling that task himself.

To keep your passwords unknown—and unknowable—follow these pointers:

• **Do combine** parts of two unusual, unrelated words, such as "gastrocumulus" or "cytoplasticity." The longer and stranger the better.

• **Do mix** capital and lowercase characters, as well as symbols and numbers, in the middle of the password: *f2reeDoMeYe#wTness*, not *freedomeyewitness*.

• **Do use** words from a foreign language in combo with an English word. Many hackers try to crack passwords with common words, or with those pooled from the dictionary database of a single language.

• **Don't use** anything that can be easily guessed by neighbors, coworkers, or strangers who get their hands on your wallet—a nickname, child's name, pet's name, or your favorite sports team or hobby.

• **Don't use** slightly different versions of the same password on different websites, such as ABCebay, ABCmortgage, and ABCvisa.

• **Don't pair** a common word or your name with a different character at the beginning or end, such as $user or johnsmith7.

• **Don't use** the same password from one application to another. "It's fine to have a simple, short password on a news website," says Dr. Tygar. "But use a different, longer, more complicated password on a site with sensitive information."

Spyware is a catchall phrase for software covertly installed on your computer to track your activities online. Some versions monitor your every keystroke and send it back to a waiting attacker. Other variants, often called "adware," examine your past Internet activity to determine which rotating banner ads to display. In the workplace, employers use "overt" spyware to gauge their workers' on-the-job computer use.

When it comes to identity theft, however, the primary purpose of spyware is to capture sensitive online data: user names, passwords, and account numbers.

How does spyware infiltrate your computer? It can piggyback on other applications, hiding inside the "install" commands of Internet software such as music-download programs. It can lurk inside that free screen saver of a dancing gecko that your preteen found so cute online. It can even worm its way into your machine when you visit certain websites or open certain e-mails.

Your protection: "The first rule of preventing spyware is to be careful about what you download on your computer," says Doug Tygar, Ph.D., a computer-science professor at the University of California, Berkeley. "Think twice about installing freebie software, no matter how enticing it appears." Topping the list of virtual verbotens should be "agent" or "personal assistant" software such as Gator, BonziBuddy, or Comet Cursor. Forbidden landing zones should include any website offering sexy photos of your favorite starlet. And never open unsolicited e-mails promising discount products.

"The second rule," adds Dr. Tygar, who specializes in computer security, "is to scan your computer once a week or more often with a good anti-spyware program." But the number of commercial spyware-detection or -protection products tops 350—and includes some that have been known to install spyware themselves rather than uproot it. So how do you pick a reputable program to install on your own Mac or PC?

"My recommendation is to use Ad-Aware," suggests Dr. Tygar, who has no financial interest in the product and no affiliation with its manufacturer. "It's free—and, based on my experience, it's among the best anti-spyware programs available." (In an impromptu test by a certain scam reporter, Ad-Aware detected and quarantined more than 10 spyware entities that had escaped the notice of a brand-name, $50 anti-spyware program.) For a free Ad-Aware download, visit www.lavasoftusa .com/software/adaware.

Consider a different browser. The most popular browser—that gateway to the Internet—is Internet Explorer, which comes preinstalled on most personal computers. Small wonder, then, that most viruses and spyware programs target Windows-based PCs rather than Macintosh computers.

"If you have not updated your browser recently or you are using an older version of Windows," says Dr. Tygar, "I recommend using alternative browsers such as Firefox or Opera to address identity-theft or online-privacy concerns. Internet Explorer is used by nearly 95 percent of the Web population, so that's the one everyone tries to attack."

These alternative browsers can be downloaded free of charge. To learn more, visit www.getfirefox.com or www. opera.com. Although Macintosh computers are generally safer, Dr. Tygar recommends that Mac users download the browser named Safari on their machines. Safari is a browser included for free in recent versions of the Macintosh OS X operating system. For more information about Safari, visit www.apple.com/macosx/features/safari.

Get a second (or third) e-mail account. Never use your real e-mail address in online chat rooms. Never use it when shopping online. And never use it to register at any website. "If you have ever done business online," says John Hambrick, an FBI supervisory special agent with the Internet Crime Complaint Center, "you have to expect that your e-mail address will be compromised; there is [then] the potential for that account to be stolen or sold."

So do what the G-man does: Establish a separate e-mail account—free on MSN's Hotmail, Yahoo!'s Mail, or Google's Gmail—and use it specifically and exclusively for online purchases. "I keep my primary e-mail account very private and never use it to make online purchases," says Hambrick. "When I'm doing nonprivate correspondence or purchasing online, I use another."

The Hambrick trick should make your private accounts less vulnerable. Why? Because spammers and phishers often target online retailers and auction sites. Using widely available software, these identity burglars automatically harvest the e-mail addresses of previous visitors to those sites. And truly

PROTECTIVE DETECTIVE

Tips for Tight Technology

Here are some additional ways to safeguard your online security, suggested by UC/Berkeley computing professor Doug Tygar and other privacy experts:

Upgrade your operating system. If you use Windows XP—the mainstay for PCs purchased in recent years—enable the automatic Windows Update feature (if you have not done so already) by visiting www.microsoft.com/protect, where you can download Service Pack 2 and anti-spyware software. To check your Windows system, hit the "Start" tab, then make your way to "Control Panel" and finally to "Security Center."

Build a firewall. Most new computers have a built-in firewall. For older systems, however, you may need to purchase and install one—especially if you have a high-speed connection to the Internet.

If a router links two or more computers in your home, it probably has a built-in firewall. To keep hackers from gaining control, though, you still need to take two additional steps: 1) change the router's default password and 2) disable "remote administration."

Employ multiple protection. In an August 2005 product test, not a single anti-spyware program tested by *Consumer Reports* caught every intruder. It therefore makes sense to adopt a multipronged approach: You can combine a free service such as Ad-Aware with commercially available products such as McAfee or Norton, which typically cost $25 to $50.

lazy scamsters, for their part, simply buy lists of website visitors directly from those retailers—it's legal, and you agreed to it when you first registered to gain access to that site.

Often, though, spammers gain access to e-mail addresses by brute-force luck. They send out mass e-mails using methodical sequences of name-and-number combinations, such as "JohnDoe1," "JohnDoe2," and so on. Or they utilize a "dictionary attack," trying e-mail addresses built on words commonly found in the dictionary.

Your protection: When choosing a "free" e-mail address for online shopping, some people opt for a pseudonym or non-identifier. As long as you have valid payment information, most retailers won't care whether or not it matches your real name. But which free service is best? "Currently, Gmail probably gets the edge," says Dr. Tygar. "It is excellent at detecting spam and phishing, though Hotmail and Yahoo are improving quickly." You can also establish multiple e-mail addresses with most Internet service providers, including AOL and telecommunications companies that offer broadband and cable service.

Watch your e's for cues. Likewise be wary of any incoming e-mails, to any of your accounts, from unrecognized names— especially strange-sounding ones. Spammers often send e-mails using first names only, misspelled ones, or the simply absurd. "A large amount of spam and phishing attacks come from foreign countries and can easily be detected by their poor command of English," notes Dr. Tygar. "If you read just the names and subject lines of incoming messages, you can often tell they're counterfeit because they are riddled with misspellings and grammatical errors. Real banks never send e-mails asking you to give your account information online—but if they did, they would probably spell the message correctly. Of course, sophisticated phishers now take the time to proofread their messages."

Your protection: Assuming you don't really know "Dai,"

"Petter Parrker," or "Hudson Fabergé," why bother opening e-mail from them? At the very least, strangely titled or misspelled e-mails are likely to be spam pitches. Yet the mere fact of clicking such an e-mail open can alert the sender that your e-mail address is active—and therefore ripe for attack or sale. Worse, opening unknown e-mail may automatically admit spyware or viruses into your computer.

Look for signs of security. The real dangers in online identity theft typically result from two scams:

- *Phishing,* in which fraudulent bulk e-mail messages guide naïve users to legitimate-looking but fake websites—where they are prompted to reveal personal information such as account numbers or passwords.

- *Pharming,* an even more insidious maneuver, in which the domain-name server is tampered with to reroute legitimate website traffic to a bogus site. (You have no clue you've arrived at a sham site because its URL appears to be correct in the Web-address field.)

Phishing attempts are such dead-on mimics—hard for even Internet security experts to detect—that scrutinizing the Web address itself may be the best way to spot them. The phonies closely resemble the authentic address, with the exception of a single letter. Here are two examples: You receive an e-mail from ebay-billing.com; on closer examination, you realize a capital "I" is masquerading as the second lowercase "l." Or you receive an e-mail that lacks the indication of a "secure" website; rather than starting with "https," it starts with simply "http."

Phishing addresses may also consist of a series of numbers, as opposed to a company name. And then the text contains those telltale spelling errors and other mistakes. Phishers often pretend to be from banks, online retailers or auction sites, or companies such as PayPal.

Online Auction Ripoffs

Online auctions such as eBay are a likely target of phishing and pharming scams, but the trouble for shoppers doesn't end there.

"For instance," says John Hambrick of the FBI's Internet Crime Complaint Center, "you might get an e-mail saying, 'You aren't the winning bidder, but I have one more of those items to sell.' They're trying to circumvent the auction system and get you to send them a cashier's check. Trust me, they will not send you anything in return."

Other signs that an online rip-off awaits you include sellers who:

• *Don't accept standard* third-party payers such as PayPal; instead, they ask you to use their own escrow service.

• *Ask for payment* by Western Union.

• *Ask for your* bank account number, Social Security number, or any other information not required.

• *Ship from,* or are registered in, Andorra —a country in the Pyrenees known to be a haven for phony eBay vendors.

• *Ship merchandise from* an address or area other than the seller's address.

Pharming scams are more difficult to detect. One clue, says Dr. Tygar, is to look for valid certificates of authority, such as a locked padlock icon or the VeriSign indicator that matches the site's name. "Also look for the security lock icon on the bottom bar of your screen," advises Dr. Tygar. "It should be part of the actual window surround—in an outside frame, not part of the page itself." Although savvy pharmers can dummy up a convincing-looking illustration of a secure-lock icon, "it's much harder to do this on the frame of the window than it is to do it somewhere inside the actual Web page. And the latest version of the Firefox browser displays certificate information right next to the lock icon."

The bottom line: Assume that most e-mails requesting sensitive information are bogus; the keepers of your credit-card and bank-account numbers never request e-mail "updates" of your customer information. If they do, they'll provide a phone number that can be easily cross-checked. Even if such a number is provided, however, look up the company's number independently, then call it yourself. "Verification" numbers given by phishers and pharmers will simply be answered by a party to the scheme. Except for a few isolated incidences, such as FAFSA forms to apply for student aid, it's the rare government agency that will ask you to supply your Social Security number via e-mail. If you receive an e-mail that requests your SSN and claims to originate inside a government agency, don't respond until you have called that agency directly and received both verbal and written confirmation that the e-mail is authentic.

Trash files on old computers. If you're buying a new computer and plan to discard or donate your old one, consider this: As many as 150 million computers are trashed each year, often without having their hard drives erased. You might as well do the identity thief's job for him. Scammers routinely retrieve old machines from curbside trash or buy them for less than $50 at thrift stores, salvage yards, or auctions.

"A friend of mine examined a discarded computer," reports Dr. Tygar, "and found all kinds of personal information from the owner—including password and account information. If someone gets access to your old computer, make sure that doesn't also grant him access to your information." In one experiment, MIT students retrieved sensitive information from up to half of the discarded computers they tested.

Your protection: Deleted files are easily retrievable by anyone with a larcenous streak and a modicum of tech savvy. To wipe your hard drive clean for good, purchase special hard-drive shredding software from a computer supply store. Better yet, physically remove—or have a techie friend do it for you—the hard drive from inside the machine, then use a hammer to destroy it. Or, if you prefer, simply contact a local shredding agency and have them shred the hard drive for you.

You've Been Victimized—Now What?

Here's what to do if you are victimized by identity theft—or merely suspect you may have been:

Contact a law enforcement agency. It's unlikely that your local police department will solve the case—or even investigate it. Still, filing a police report may help you regain your good name—and your good credit rating—with creditors and credit-reporting bureaus. After contacting your local police, you may also need to notify the police department that oversees the location where the identity theft most likely occurred. (You should also contact your state Attorney General's office, which may direct you to other agencies.)

If the identity theft occurred from online activity, contact the Internet Fraud Complaint Center (a partnership between the FBI and the National White Collar Crime Center) at www.ic3.gov.

If you believe the identity theft resulted from mail theft, report it at www.usps.com/websites/depart/inspect.

If you suspect you were victimized by ATM skimming (pages 290 and 302) or crime involving your debit card, notify the local Secret Service field office; a contact list is available at www.secretservice.gov/field_offices.shtml.

If you believe your credit card number (or the little plastic rectangle itself) has been stolen, notify the fraud department of your credit-card company.

Among Americans who have had their credit card or bank numbers stolen, 62 percent report unauthorized charges on their existing plastic; 54 percent report unlawful withdrawals from their bank accounts.

Shut 'em down. Close the accounts that you know or believe have been tampered with and notify the sponsoring institution(s) of the theft. You usually have to provide the company with two documents: 1) a report filed with the local, state, or federal law enforcement agency and 2) an identity-theft report. Some companies provide their own forms for the latter, but most accept the Federal Trade Commission's Identity Theft Affidavit, which is available online at www.consumer/gov/idtheft. There, you can also find a link to file your complaint with the FTC. Or you can call the FTC's Identity Theft Hotline at 877-438-4338, or write to Identity Theft Clearinghouse, Federal Trade Commission, 600 Pennsylvania Avenue NW, Washington, D.C. 20580.

Place a fraud alert on your credit reports. Contact one of the three major credit-reporting bureaus (they are listed in the sidebar at right) and request that a fraud alert be placed on all your credit accounts. (The initial bureau you notify is required to contact the other two, which should then place alerts in their systems.) This signals creditors that you've been victimized by fraud. In theory, it should also block any new accounts from being opened in your name unless someone contacts you first and obtains your express consent.

There are two types of fraud alerts:

- *An initial alert* lasts about 90 days. It is placed by a credit-reporting bureau if you suspect that you have been—or simply are about to be—a victim of identity theft. If your wallet has been stolen or you've been hoodwinked by a phishing scam, for instance, you should instruct at least one of the three major credit-reporting bureaus to place an initial alert on all your accounts. Taking this action entitles you to one free credit report from each of the Big Three.

- *An extended alert* stays on your credit report for seven years. It should be placed if you know you've been victimized. To have an extended alert placed on your accounts, you will need to provide an identity-theft report (generated by your local police department) to at least one consumer-reporting company. Placing an extended fraud alert entitles you to receive two free

Let These People Know

Your first act of damage control if you think you've been hit by ID theft is to file a fraud alert with one of the credit-reporting agencies below. Whichever one you inform is legally obligated to notify the other two.

Equifax Fraud Division
P. O. Box 740241
Atlanta, Georgia 30374-0241
800-525-6285; www.equifax.com

Experian
P. O. Box 9532
Allen, Texas 75013
888-397-3742; www.experian.com

TransUnion Fraud Victim
Assistance Division
P. O. Box 6790
Fullerton, California 92834
800-680-7289; www.transunion.com

credit reports from each of the three main consumer-reporting companies within 12 months. In addition, those firms must automatically remove your name from marketing lists for prescreened credit offers for five years (unless you opt back in). Getting the credit reports allows you to examine them quickly, then notify the appropriate agency (such as retailers, credit-card companies, and the like) of any fraudulent charges—or of any changes that a scammer may have made to your address, Social Security number, or other personal data.

In 2004, the federal government reports, 29 percent of identity-theft victims were aged 18 to 29; 25 percent were in their 30s, 20 percent in their 40s, 12 percent in their 50s, and 9 percent were older than age 60. Only 1 in 3 reported the crime.

Contact your bank and creditors. Notify credit-card companies (including retail stores for which you have credit accounts), the mortgage company, and the issuer of your car note or other loans. Your credit-card companies will likely close your existing accounts and issue you new plastic with a different card number. By law, you will be liable for only $50 in fraudulent charges (and it's unlikely you'll be charged for even that amount). You may also want to close your existing savings and checking accounts, and move the funds they contained to new accounts. If your financial company isn't helping you as much as you'd like, contact the agency that oversees your bank. To find the name of this agency, call your bank or go to the "Institution Search" section of the National Information Center of the Federal Reserve System at www.ffiec.gov/nic.

Respond quickly to debt collectors. If a debt collector contacts you about new accounts opened in your name or unauthorized charges made to existing ones, respond immediately in writing—and keep a copy of your letter. Explain why you don't owe the money in question. Enclose copies of any supporting documents, such as an official identity-theft police report or an FTC affidavit. Also ask the debt collector for the name of the business trying to collect the debt, and the amount allegedly owed. Then contact that business—also in writ-

PROTECTIVE DETECTIVE

Get Your "Other" Consumer Reports

You know the importance of regularly reviewing your credit-history reports, now available three times a year to all Americans at no charge under federal law. Far less publicized is another government-mandated freebie: "specialty" consumer reports that detail your check-writing history, insurance claims, residential or tenant history, or even your medical conditions.

"The same law that allows for the free credit reports gives consumers the right to one free 'specialty' report each year," says Tena Friery of Privacy Rights Clearinghouse, a consumer advocacy group in San Diego. "If you're shopping for a new car or homeowner's insurance, you might want to get your C.L.U.E. report [Comprehensive Loss Underwriting Exchange] detailing insurance claims you've made in the past." For that, call ChoicePoint at 866-312-8076 or visit www.choicetrust.com. ChoicePoint al-

so maintains tenant and residential reports.

Interested in reviewing your medical history report? Contact the MIB, a nationwide consumer-reporting agency that compiles records concerning individual life, health, long-term care, and disability insurance. About 1 in 5 adults have a MIB file. For advice on how to get yours, call 866-692-6901 or visit www.mib.com/html/request_your_record.html.

To see the specialty report on your check-writing history, contact Chex-Systems at 800-428-9623 or Shared Check Authorization Network (SCAN) at 800-262-7771 (the two share the website www.consumerdebit.com), or contact TeleCheck at 800-825-3243 or www.telecheck.com.

For more on specialty reports, read Fact Sheet 6(b) of the Privacy Rights Clearinghouse at www.privacyrights.org.

ing—and request copies of the credit applications or any other documents linked to transactions you believe were made by the identity thief. Send these letters by registered mail, and get an acceptance receipt from the post office.

Contact the Department of Motor Vehicles. This step, often overlooked, must be taken to guarantee that the identity thief has not applied for a new driver's license in your name. These bogus licenses take two forms: a replacement license that pairs your license number with the thief's picture, or a new license with a new number. Ask that a freeze be placed on your license until you can get a bona fide replacement (to simplify this process, bring along your Social Security card and other identifiers). And if your state is one of the 19 that still allow your Social Security number to double as your license number, ask to have another number substituted.

A little preparation now will make all of these steps much easier to take later on, should it come to that. Therefore, make photocopies today of all your credit cards and identifying documents. Include your driver's license, Social Security card, birth certificate, and even a business card. Keep these facsimiles in a safe spot in your home, workplace, or a safe-deposit box. And don't forget to follow the Prime Directive of foiling identity thieves: Never, ever carry your Social Security card in your wallet!

ON THE JOB
Your Rights at Work

11

REMEMBER THE GO-GO 1990s? The recession officially ended in March 1991, and then came nine straight years of solid job growth. Layoffs occurred here and there, but with a robust economy generating some 300,000 new jobs each month during the latter part of the decade, opportunities for new employment abounded.

Now it's the gone-gone 2000s. Since January 2001, nearly three million jobs have vanished from the U.S. private sector. Another three million-plus are expected to be shipped overseas or rendered obsolete by 2015. Although monthly unemployment rates have averaged 5 to 6 percent through most of this decade, today's rehiring forecast is nowhere near as rosy as it was for those handed pink slips in the 1990s. Thanks to years of anemic new-job creation, 1 of every 5 unemployed workers remains that way for at least six months.

As of March 2005, an estimated 13.6 million Americans were unemployed or underemployed—that is, forced into a part-time job status that confers few or no workplace benefits. Four years earlier, the number was 10.6 million. And every month, reports the U.S. Bureau of Labor Statistics, brings at least 1,000 new "mass layoffs"—those affecting 50 employees or more.

So where's the scam in all this? Despite the alleged corporate belt-tightening that has left millions of Americans

275

jobless, layoffs customarily make stockholders and top brass fat and happy. Fewer employees mean fewer company expenses, yielding upticks in pay for those who orchestrate a downsizing. During the recession of 2002, reports the Institute for Policy Studies in Washington, D.C., median pay skyrocketed 44 percent for CEOs of the country's 50 companies with the most layoffs. At companies announcing fewer or no layoffs, meanwhile, the average salary hike for chief executives was a comparatively paltry 6 percent.

The net result has been to render "job security" a 21st century oxymoron. Forty-nine U.S. states and the District of Columbia recognize "at will" employment. (The lone holdout, Montana, protects employees from being fired without cause once they have completed a six-month "probationary period.") Plainly put, "at will" means that workers or their employer may end the employment relationship at any time. The good-news aspect of this arrangement is that workers may quit whenever they want. The bad-news side of the "at will" doctrine is that most employers can terminate employees for virtually any reason; they do not even have to say why.

Gazing out upon today's layoff-laden corporate landscape—and considering the fact that most wrongful-termination lawsuits tend not to favor litigating employees—you may find cause to employ the following tips for protecting your job sooner than you think.

Avoiding a Layoff

Pave a paper trail before you need it. Although most employees can be terminated without reason, marshaling evidence for why you shouldn't lose your job is the first step in keeping it. "It's a good idea to retain copies of any and all documents that show good performance," says Ellen Simon, a Cleveland-based attorney who specializes in employment law. "Make copies of all favorable job-evaluation reviews, any laudatory e-mails you received from supervisors or customers, and any awards or certificates you've gotten. Anything and everything that establishes a record of good performance makes it harder for employers to justify down the road why you were selected for termination, because often the instructions for a reduction in the workforce are to keep the best people. You want to be able to prove—with documentation—that you're among them."

This paper trail of past praise is especially important in avoiding a common scenario: The charge that an employee's performance is not up to snuff. One exception to the "at will" doctrine practiced in 49 states and the District of Columbia is a firing due to discrimination based on age, race, gender, or pregnancy. Any one of these can trigger a successful lawsuit against the company—something every firm on Earth avidly wants to avoid.

"There are two major types of evidence that courts recognize in an employment-discrimination lawsuit," says Paula Brantner of Workplace Fairness, a San Francisco-based advocacy group that educates employees on their workplace rights. "One is direct evidence—incidences of flat-out bias, such as comments or actions that show discrimination. The other is circumstantial evidence so when you put all the pieces together, it raises an inference of discrimination that makes a layoff harder for the company to do. And included in that category is when employers say that you've been underperforming for years, but they have no documentation of that fact."

Your protection: When you receive a favorable performance evaluation, ask your supervisor if you can keep a copy. Many companies allow this; some may not. If your employer has a Human Resources department, you may also be able to copy the contents of your employee file. Obviously, all congratulatory e-mails, "atta-boys," and "atta-girls" should be printed out and squirreled away—not just stored in your computer. These documents alone are unlikely to prevent a layoff, but they could be used as leverage to negotiate a better severance package should you face termination.

If your employer tries to demote you to a lesser job, fear not: "You usually have the right to get paid at the same rate, even if your job responsibilities or title decreases," notes employment attorney Steven Mitchell Sack.

If you are fired for refusing to accept a demotion, you have the right to file for unemployment compensation. Employees terminated "for cause" lack that option.

Recognize red flags. When a company faces layoffs, smart employers usually stifle news of the impending doom to head off worker unrest. But often there are warnings signs: "Traditionally, HR is in an administrative role," says Nancy Collamer, author of *The Layoff Survival Guide.* "As a former HR director, I can say that Human Resources is not always consulted about key corporate decisions. When it comes to layoff decisions, however, HR is almost always included because they hold employee files and records."

Your clue that trouble may be brewing: "Your antennae should go up if you notice Human Resources personnel suddenly burning the midnight oil, or if HR is, out of the norm, now spending more time with higher-level executives."

You might consider yourself on the hit list if your day-to-day duties suddenly change, adds Steven Mitchell Sack, a New York employment attorney and author of *Getting Fired: What to Do If You're Fired, Downsized, Laid Off, Restructured, Discharged, Terminated, or Forced to Resign.* "Some common signs that you're a candidate for layoff are when you are suddenly asked to train new hires, denied visits with customers, kept out of meetings you would normally attend, or unexpectedly receive a poor performance review. And those are your cues to take preventive measures."

Your protection: In addition to a paper trail of performance highlights, Sack recommends you discreetly make copies of information that is important to you as well as to the company. (This advice applies whether you anticipate getting laid off soon or not.) If you're in sales, for instance, you might take home your Rolodex of key clients—or at least make a disc of those names stored in your computer. "Do those things now," Sack advises. You may not get the chance later." Laid-off employees are often escorted from the premises immediately, preempting theft or sabotage but leaving them unable to access their desk, computer, or other "company property." However, discretion is paramount. You never want to tip your hand that you are taking these defensive measures, lest they unleash

Only 40 percent of 3,233 workers surveyed by Harris Interactive in the spring of 2005 rated their office morale as "good" or "excellent." At the same time, the majority of bosses reported that their employees are happy.

the mother of all self-fulfilling prophecies: They may increase your odds of being let go.

Lie low, except to socialize. What else is likely to land you on the hit list? Reacting impulsively to layoff rumors—with anger, resentment, or fear. "Many times," says Collamer, now a career counselor in Old Greenwich, Connecticut, "the company knows it has to lay off X employees. But the decision of who gets laid off is sometimes made at the very last moment." In other words, this is probably the worst possible time to be spotted dawdling at the proverbial water cooler,

"At Will" Employment

Most workers in the United States are considered "at will" employees, meaning they or their employer can end the employment relationship at any time, without giving notice or citing a reason. In reality, this favors employers, not staff. Yet certain exceptions to state laws, detailed below, benefit that endangered species, the clock-puncher:

Union members and others working under the provisions of a labor contract can be terminated only as that contract allows. In some cases, a company handbook or personnel code may effectively serve as a "contract" for non-union workers. In those instances, however, the company is usually savvy enough to have a disclaimer on file stipulating that company rules and procedures are just that—and that they do not serve as an employment contract.

If a plant or office closes and the resulting layoffs affect at least 75 employees, workers must be given a minimum of 60 days' advance notice of their impending termination. If that notice is not given two months beforehand, the workers affected by the shutdown must be paid at least 60 days' worth of severance pay—whether or not they are unionized, and whether or not they have a contract.

Federal employees are exempt from "at will" laws in cases where their termination would violate the United States Constitution or the constitution of the state in which they work. A federal worker's rights to freedom of speech, association, and religion, for example, can be at issue when he or she is dismissed, as can his or her freedom from unlawful search and seizure.

or to be discovered passing e-mails to other employees. (Assume that the message traffic to and from your machine is monitored.) "Being seen as the company gossip or office agitator can very well target you at the 11th hour," Collamer warns. "When the rumors start to fly, the smart thing is to lie low—except to show the company your professionalism, your loyalty, and your contributions."

How?

One obvious way is to copy the brass on correspondence that reflects positively on you.

Another is to contribute more in meetings—provided you have something significant to say.

Either move, of course, may be seen as brown-nosing born of desperation. If that thought makes you uncomfortable, try stressing another important trait—good old team spirit—instead, especially when layoffs loom. Painful as it may be when you or your colleagues are facing the unemployment line, make sure to attend that company picnic, office birthday party, or other social event. To show their distaste for the rumored sharpened ax, many employees unwisely "boycott" such festivities. But that's precisely where certain employers keep a sharp eye on the troops. There's no need to feign allegiance, but your presence will be noted—and your absence even more so.

Mind the seasons. Historically, layoffs have heated up as temperatures cool, says John A. Challenger, chief executive officer of Challenger, Gray & Christmas, Inc., the nation's oldest international outplacement firm. Of the more than 10 million corporate jobs slashed from 1993 to 2004, 38 percent were eliminated from September 1 to December 31; in 2004, forty-one percent of layoffs were carried out during those four months. The second most active downsizing period is the stretch from January to April.

"In such scenarios," says Challenger, "the best way to save your job is to become a franchise player—someone too valuable to be let go. You have a small window of opportunity to build a reputation as someone who is willing to do things others are not." How can you do that during this critical time?

- *Put in face time.* Although your company may allow telecommuting—and your productivity may soar when you work from home—employees who are out of sight are also likely to be out of mind when the higher-ups compile their MVP lists. At the very least, telecommuters are more apt to miss key impromptu meetings such as "brainstorming" sessions, when rising stars are most likely to shine in the eyes of supervisors. So-called "face time" also outweighs phone calls or e-mails in providing favorable updates that lodge in the boss's mind. Even on-the-road salesmen are encouraged to deliver person-to-person reports on their activities.

- *Finish what you start.* Volunteering for extra duties is a fail-safe strategy for securing your job, right? Not necessarily. Workers with a reputation for completing current projects are seen as more valuable than those with a tendency to bite off more than they can chew.

- *Be a generalist.* Specialists in one area are prime candidates for cutting should a corporate restructuring affect that particular area. Instead, during this vulnerable time, try to learn other people's jobs and responsibilities so you can easily transition to another area, should it come to that.

- *Consider postponing vacation.* Workers who recognize that a company is struggling to reach year-end or quarterly objectives, then play their part in achieving those goals, are viewed as team players—an image that sticks in managerial memory banks. Cancun will still be there when the dust settles; if you must take some R&R, make sure supervisors know you're also packing your laptop or cell phone.

Forty-three percent of employers say their company is loyal to its workers— a belief shared by only 1 in 4 employees.

• *Dress for survival.* Like it or not, says Challenger, appearance affects your perceived skill level or work ethic. At the very least, it conveys your commitment to professionalism. So forget about Casual Friday for now. As the day when many layoffs occur, it should properly be dubbed Casualty Friday.

Can you guess the main reasons why 4 in 10 workers plan to change jobs within a year?

According to a Yahoo! Hotjobs survey, 44 percent of workers feel there is no potential for job growth in their current job; 29 percent want to move to a company with higher morale; 25 percent believe they are undervalued.

Get More When You Say Goodbye

If you're pulled into an office to be given a pink slip, no doubt you'll have plenty to say. Don't say it. There's no more certain way to sabotage your own case than to blurt out the anger-fueled "You can't fire me—I quit!" With those six words, you relinquish your rights to any departure benefits from the company or state-issued unemployment compensation. "Never quit a job," advises employment attorney Sack, who also wrote *The Employee Rights Handbook: The Essential Guide for People on the Job.* "Always make them fire you."

If that's the company's intention, there's probably precious little you can do to save your job. But with the right mindset—and with that all-important paper trail documenting your past performance—you don't have to walk away with nothing more than a hollow thanks and a patronizing pat on the back. Here's what you should know:

Say little, especially now. Assuming you're being terminated through no fault of your own—that is, you've violated neither company policy nor the law—it's perfectly understandable to express shock and dismay, considering your years of top performance and dedication. But most of your "talking" should be done wordlessly; instead, make detailed notes of what the ax-wielder is saying. This move signals the bearer of bad news that you're not about to surrender, thereby boosting your chances of a better departure package later on. Of course, if you're terminated "for cause"—illegal or inappropriate behavior—you likely won't be entitled to any parting compensation, no matter what you do or don't say.

"You don't want to negotiate a severance package or parting benefits at the termination meeting," says Sack. Nor is there any need to do so. Although the company may present you with a prepared separation agreement for your signature, you are legally allowed to take at least a few days—and sometimes several weeks—to review it.

At that initial meeting, the company may also offer you an opportunity to sign a letter of resignation "to save face." Don't fall for this ploy. Because of the "at will" doctrine, signing such a document will be considered a voluntary resignation, thus eliminating any chance you had to collect severance pay, unemployment compensation, or other termination benefits. The company will simply say, "Sorry—you quit, so you're not entitled."

Let your signature be your leverage. Once you've been told you're being terminated, the company wants you out quickly—with your signature on its papers. But your best defense is to delay. Say something like, "This comes as a shock; I need time to think about it and will contact you in a few days before I sign anything." Then walk out.

After a few days, request an appointment to "discuss matters" with a key decision-maker—not necessarily your direct supervisor or the HR representative.

Why would your employer agree to such a meeting? First of all, they understandably want an amicable separation, explains Paul H. Tobias, founder of the National Employment Lawyers Association (NELA) and an employment attorney in Cincinnati, Ohio. They fear negative publicity from disgruntled former employees contacting board members, the Internal Revenue Service, current employees, or the media. They also want to banish any possibility of a wrongful-termination lawsuit and minimize the motivation for ousted employees with insider information to actively seek new jobs with a competitor out of spite. That's why your signature is so critical, because the company will likely want you to sign:

- *A release* that waives your right to later sue the company for wrongful termination.

- *A "noncompete" clause* that forbids you to seek employment with a competitor—and, more important, that bars you from passing along proprietary information or "company secrets."

- *A "nondisparagement" promise* that you won't bad-mouth the company or its management to active workers or anyone else.

When Buyouts Go Bust

The first step taken by many companies facing mass layoffs is to offer buyout or early-retirement packages—usually to older, longtime workers, who tend to earn higher salaries.

On one hand, these arrangements commonly offer a better separation package than do general layoffs. The formula for calculating severance pay may be more generous. Pensions or stock options may vest at a faster rate. And the lure of extended medical benefits may be dangled under your nose.

On the other hand, warns employment attorney Steven Mitchell Sack, author of two books on the rights of employees facing termination, "Some early-retirement offers and buyouts promise lifetime medical benefits for employees who volunteer to be laid off. But the company may renege on that

promise a few years later, or change its policies." And, says AARP attorney Mike Schuster, "The courts have generally held that in the absence of a written agreement, the company can do that."

Another potential problem with life-time medical benefits comes if the company you worked for is sold after you leave it: The new owners may be held not liable to honor promises made by the previous owners.

Your protection: If you believe you'll be laid off whether you take that buyout offer or not, consider accepting it. "Have an experienced employment lawyer draw up the agreement," urges Sack, "including a written caveat that you'll receive guaranteed benefits in the event the company is sold or there's a policy change later on. By not doing that, many people get screwed down the road."

These may be separate documents or simply clauses in the separation agreement itself. Either way, you'll want to carefully examine all papers before adding your John Hancock. Far better yet, hire an experienced employment lawyer to scrutinize this paperwork on your behalf. (Qualified employment attorneys typically charge $150 to $300 an hour.)

Negotiate for more. "Once a company decides whom to lay off," notes Sack, "it's very difficult to prevent those people from getting fired." What's *not* as difficult, he points out, is to get more than just the sharp edge of the terminator's ax.

"Few people realize that the terms of your termination are negotiable," says Sack. "The vast majority of people who are laid off accept whatever the company offers them, bow their heads, and shuffle out the door."

In your post-announcement meeting with a decision-maker, try to negotiate a better departure package for yourself. To accomplish this, make it clear you speak on your own behalf, not that of a larger group. The company will be likelier to raise the parting ante on an individual basis. (Even in this solo capacity, of course, you may wish to have an attorney present to represent you. Be aware, however, that showing up at that first negotiation meeting with a lawyer in tow will put your newly former employer on the defensive.)

So precisely which deal points should you try to negotiate—ideally *before* signing any separation documents the company offers?

- *Severance.* Unless stipulated in an employment contract, firms are not legally obligated to furnish severance pay to parting workers. Many do, however—and the formula for calculating the amount is usually spelled out in the company's personnel handbook. At many workplaces, one to two weeks' pay for each year of service is the typical severance ratio for laid-off rank-and-file employees and mid-level managers. That certainly should not stop you from requesting more, though. "Ask for four weeks' severance pay for each year of employment," suggests Sack, "noting the tough job market and the difficulty you'll face finding a new job. Although that's pretty rich for those who are not in top management, you stand a relatively good chance of getting three weeks per year. If the standard severance at your company is one week per year, shoot for at least two."

The key, says Sack, is to be calm yet forceful. Resist threatening a lawsuit or any other form of retaliation; that only makes the company dig in its heels.

• *Medical benefits.* Most terminated employees never ask for what can be the most important company "benefit" of all, says Sack, "even though employer-paid medical insurance is probably the easiest thing to get in a layoff." That's because employers are quick to mention that (except for those fired for "gross misconduct") most terminated workers and their dependents are eligible for temporary continuation of their health coverage through COBRA—the federal Consolidated Omnibus Budget Reconciliation Act, passed in 1986.

Although group health coverage for COBRA participants is less expensive than individual health insurance, it is still far costlier than health coverage for active employees: COBRA coverage can cost some terminated workers with children up to $2,000 a month. That's because COBRA participants pay the entire premium themselves, whereas the employer pays part of the premium for active employees at discounted group rates. Sack recommends that you ask for your old health insurance rates to remain in effect for as long as your severance pay lasts—and for the company to pay such benefits on your behalf. If you're entitled to six months of severance pay, for example, ask for six months of extended medical coverage. "When it comes to medical benefits," he says, "companies tend to be more sympathetic to valued employees who are laid off—partly because it's goodwill on their part, and partly because their contribution is a drop in the bucket compared to what workers would have to pay on their own or through COBRA."

• *Bonuses.* There's a good reason why more employees are laid off during the last three months of the calendar year than at any other time: At many companies, year-end bonuses are paid to eligible recipients who are on the payroll as of December 31—and the company may be under no legal obligation to pay an annual bonus if you're laid off. If your layoff occurs within a few months before you were scheduled to receive it, however, you stand a decent chance of getting something.

"If you are laid off within two months before a bonus is to be paid, you should never relinquish it," says Sack. "At the very least, ask that it be prorated based on the number of months you were employed in the eligible year." This tactic may succeed if you were employed for at least six months of bonus eligibility; if you're laid off within a few months of the beginning of your bonus eligibility, though, you'll likely receive bupkus.

• *Stock options.* Unvested options typically lapse when you're terminated, but some companies will agree to vest your stock options in exchange for your accepting lower severance pay. If you believe your company stock will rise and you're willing to shoulder the risk, stress that the company will save money by giving you less severance but more stock.

• *Pensions.* This is a trickier one. Federal law forbids any company from changing its pension rules just for you. But if you're over age 40 when terminated—raising the employer's fear of an age-discrimination lawsuit—take note of what the law does allow: A company can legally

The pay gap is widening: In 2004, the average total yearly compensation for the CEOs of 367 large U.S.-based corporations was nearly $12 million per person—about 430 times the annual pay of their typical production worker.

That ratio is 10 times higher than the 42-to-1 disparity that existed between top bosses and line workers in 1982.

keep you on its payroll as a consultant or in some other capacity, sending you a small paycheck for a few years, to "bridge" you to vesting in its pension program. Of course, this works only if the vesting date is slated to occur within those few years. It is a negotiating tool best suited to workers near retirement.

- *A reference.* Ask and you may receive a glowing written reference for future employers. This nets the company goodwill at no cost. Seek permission to approve the wording. Better yet, draft your own recommendation for signature by a higher-up. (Apply the same strategy to internal corporate memos announcing your departure.) Also ask to review your personnel file; if it contains unflattering or derogatory remarks about you, request that the documents in question be destroyed as part of your separation agreement. Although future employers will not be able to access your personnel file, it will likely be reviewed by any HR representative who is asked to provide a reference to a prospective employer.

- *Other perks.* Most companies want to see laid-off workers land on their feet. It eases their guilt and defuses their fears of retaliation. This is why many cheerfully pay job-hunting expenses for terminated employees, including the cost of outplacement counseling. Some will also reimburse you for tuition or retraining costs. A few companies provide office space and equipment for once-valued employees in their job search (if only

What Do *You* Care What I Weigh?

In a survey cited in *Tipping the Scales of Justice: Fighting Weight-Based Discrimination* by attorney Sondra Solovay, 16 percent of employers admitted they would not hire an obese woman "under any condition." Another 44 percent confessed they would hire one "under certain conditions."

Only four places in the United States have regulations in place to fight such weight discrimination: Washington, D.C.; San Francisco and Santa Cruz, California; and the state of Michigan. Other states, however—Massachusetts is one—are considering such legislation.

for a limited time), saving them phone, copier, and mailing costs. Finally, employers may allow terminated workers to buy their company-issued mobile phones, laptops, or PDAs at discounted rates.

Fighting an Unlawful Dismissal

Both federal law and most states prohibit discriminatory discharge based on an employee's race, religion, gender, national origin, age, pregnancy, or disability. In addition, 16 states and the District of Columbia ban discrimination because of a worker's sexual orientation. Most states also forbid discharge for employee "whistle-blowing," such as the retaliatory firing of a worker who alerts officials that the company is guilty of dumping toxic waste or some other episode of corporate chicanery.

Despite these laws, it's tough to prove that discrimination or whistle-blowing per se sparked a termination. Each year, some 80,000 charges of discriminatory dismissal are brought before the U.S. Equal Employment Opportunity Commission. In the vast majority of those cases, the federal agency effectively rules in the employer's favor. In 2004, for example, the EEOC found "no reasonable cause" for allegations of age discrimination in 61 percent of cases made by older workers who lost their jobs. A mere 3 percent of cases were shown to have reasonable cause for the allegations. (Most of the others were dropped or resolved.)

"The burden of proof," notes Workplace Fairness director Paula Brantner, "is always on the employee to prove their charges of discrimination." Most companies now train their managers to avoid saying or doing the sorts of things that might land them in the muddy waters of such allegations. Furthermore, the discrimination usually must directly affect the "terms of employment" (explained below), not just the workplace atmosphere, and it must have been perpetrated or condoned by supervisors or decision-makers.

Additionally, not every employee is protected. Some discrimination laws exclude small businesses, applying only to workers at larger companies—those firms with at least 20 employees. Not only that, but the majority of nondiscrimination statutes protect only those workers who fall within a "protected class." So even if he or she was the oldest person let go in a mass layoff, for example, a 35-year-old employee could not charge age discrimination under federal law; that particular "protected class" comprises workers age 40 and older.

"No matter the type of discrimination," says Brantner, "it's always better to have a paper trail documenting the discriminatory or unlawful actions by the company." For instance, your boss may make discriminatory comments only in a one-on-one conversation with you, with no one else present to witness them. To strengthen your case, document and date each instance as it occurs: Send yourself an e-mail from a private account (not via the company system, which is monitored), then print out that e-mail to capture its official date.

If you detect workplace discrimination, by all means consult an experienced employment attorney. To find one, visit www.nela.org or contact your local bar association for referrals. The following seven categories describe garden-variety discriminatory actions and suggest how best to shield yourself from them, according to Brantner's Workplace Fairness website.

Age discrimination. The federal Age Discrimination in Employment Act (ADEA) applies to workers in companies that regularly employ 20 or more workers; many states also have minimum employee requirements. (For information on your state, visit the Age Discrimination section at www.work placefairness.org.) These laws protect age-40-and-over workers fired—or not hired—because of their age.

"Examples of potential age discrimination," says attorney Ellen Simon, who has won age-discrimination lawsuits brought by terminated employees, "include singling out older workers for different treatment—such as termination when younger workers with similar or lesser qualifications (or less favorable performance records) are not being fired—and/or evidence of derogatory age-related remarks, such as referring to older workers as 'old timers,' 'dinosaurs,' or 'dead wood.'"

Other possible examples include:

- *Receiving a poor performance review* because you weren't "flexible" in taking on new projects or because you were allegedly "unable to keep up" with other employees.

- *Getting fired* because your boss wants younger employees who are paid less.

- *Being turned down* for a promotion that went to a younger employee because the boss wants "new blood."

- *Being among a majority group* of older employees who get terminated in a layoff when those retained are younger workers with less experience or seniority.

Age-discrimination laws may not apply to police and fire personnel, tenured university faculty, and some federal employees, such as air-traffic controllers, whose jobs have age restrictions. They also may not apply to executives expected to retire at age 65 if they receive retirement compensation exceeding $44,000 a year.

Disability discrimination. State laws and the federal Americans with Disabilities Act (ADA), passed in 1990, make it illegal for private and government employers or labor organizations to discriminate against qualified workers with physical or mental impairment. In addition to covering those who are deaf, blind, or in wheelchairs, the ADA may protect employees with physical conditions such as diabetes, HIV infection, severe arthritis, hypertension, or carpal tunnel syndrome.

Tax Tips for Job Hunters

Whether you are currently employed or not, certain job-search expenses are deductible.

The rules: You need to be seeking a new position in your current field, and the total amount of all itemized "unreimbursed employee expenses" deducted on your Schedule A tax form must exceed 2 percent of your adjusted gross income.

Here are half a dozen items you can legitimately claim:

Nonreimbursed travel costs incurred specifically for interviews with prospective employers. This includes airfare, hotels, and 50 percent of the cost of meals. Sorry, but visiting a prospective employer while on vacation does not constitute a lawful write-off.

Résumé-preparation costs, including typing, postage, and telephone calls made in the course of a job search.

Fees you paid to employment agencies or career counselors.

Newspapers and periodicals purchased for their help-wanted ads.

Legal fees paid to an attorney to review an employment contract.

Moving expenses to relocate to a new job, whether or not you itemize your other job-search deductions.

These employees, however, must meet the job requirements—possessing the necessary education, experience, skills, and licenses—and be able to perform the job with or without reasonable accommodation.

Disability discrimination means treating otherwise qualified workers differently because of their disability or perceived disability, or associating those workers with a disability. Examples include:

- *Harassment* based on a disability.

- *Questioning job applicants* about their past or current medical conditions, or requiring only those applicants to take medical exams (an employer can require a medical exam only if all applicants must take it).

- *Creating or maintaining* a workplace that includes sub-stantial physical barriers to the movement of the physi-cally disabled.

- *Refusing to provide* a reasonable accommodation to employees with physical or mental disability when such an adaptation would allow them to work.

Sex/gender discrimination. Title VII of the Civil Rights Act of 1964 protects individuals in companies with 15 or more employees from discrimination based on their sex. Most states also have sex-discrimination laws, some of which are like-wise subject to minimum-number-of-employee provisions. These laws make it illegal to not hire workers (or to fire them) based on their gender, or to treat them differently because of gender. Examples of potentially unlawful sex/gender dis-crimination include:

- *Not hiring female candidates* because the company believes its clients are more comfortable dealing with men, or vice versa.

- *Laying off* an overwhelming percentage of one gender during company cutbacks while those of the opposite sex with less seniority or experience keep their jobs.

- *Failing to provide equal pay* for equal work performed by those of the opposite sex.

- *Offering benefits to one gender* that differ from the bene-fits offered to the opposite gender. An example of such bias might be a company health plan that covers female spouses of employees but not male spouses.

Six states—California, Illinois, Maine, Minnesota, Rhode Island, and New Mexico—also have antidiscrimination laws that protect transgender employees and those who are about to undergo, or have already undergone, a sex-change operation.

Pregnancy discrimination. Both the Civil Rights Act of 1964 and the Family and Medical Leave Act of 1993 (FMLA) protect employees against discrimination on the basis of pregnancy, childbirth, and related conditions such as doctor-prescribed bed rest or mandatory recovery time from a Caesarean operation. The FMLA covers male and female employees who have been working at least a year for employers with 50 or more employees, allowing them to take unpaid leave to care for a newborn or newly adopted child (as well as to recover from their own illness or to care for a seriously ill member of their immediate family).

Pregnancy discrimination includes actions by an employer such as refusing to hire a pregnant applicant; firing or demoting a pregnant employee; denying the same or a similar job to an employee upon her return from a pregnancy-related leave; treating pregnant employees differently than other "temporarily disabled" employees; or failing to extend a male employee's health-insurance coverage to his wife's pregnancy-related conditions when the husbands of female employees of that company qualify for comprehensive health-insurance coverage through the same company plan.

Some other examples of potentially illegal pregnancy discrimination:

- *During an interview,* a female applicant is asked how many children she has or whether she plans to get pregnant. The applicant responds that she is four months pregnant, whereupon she is directed to come back after she has had her baby and is ready to work.

- *Upon informing her boss* that she is pregnant, a female employee is fired—even though she is able to work for several more months.

- *A pregnant worker is forced* to quit a job after being required to do heavy lifting or other physically exhausting duties not required of other workers recovering from surgery.

The nadir of workplace productivity occurs during the two-week NCAA basketball tournament each year. During "March Madness" of 2004, says outplacement firm Challenger, Gray & Christmas, $1.5 billion in productivity was lost as workers tracked games and played office betting pools on company time.

- *A pregnant worker is docked pay* or is disciplined for missing work for doctor visits when other employees needing ongoing medical treatment are not.

Race discrimination. Title VII of the Civil Rights Act protects employees and applicants from racial discrimination on the job. Basically it says that you cannot be denied hiring, promotions, or equal treatment and pay—nor can you be fired—based on your race, color, or national origin. Title VII covers employers with 15 or more workers. Many states have laws that offer similar protection.

Title VII further holds employers accountable for their failure to deal with harassment. This covers sins of omission—neglecting to discipline workers who continue to make ethnic jokes or slurs after they've been reported—as well as sins of commission, such as an employer exhorting aggrieved workers to ignore such remarks or to "get a sense of humor."

Federal laws likewise make it illegal to discriminate against an employee married to a spouse (or simply friends with someone) from an ethnic minority, such as a white worker married to (or friends with) a Native American or an African American. These statutes also ban discrimination against an employee for belonging to a minority-based organization or group. In the same vein, it is unlawful to discriminate on the basis of a condition that affects a certain race. An example of such unfair treatment: citing a company's "no beard" employment policy to terminate an African-American man with pseudofolliculitis barbae (severe shaving bumps). Such policies can legally be enforced, however, in cases where the company is able to prove that the policy in question is "job-related and a business necessity."

Religious discrimination. As with other forms of discrimination, workers cannot be treated differently because of their religious beliefs or origin. If some employees are allowed to wear baseball caps or scarves, for example, others cannot be terminated or disciplined for wearing yarmulkes, turbans, or hijabs (head scarves). If some workers are allowed to display personal items such as photographs or knickknacks in their work spaces, others cannot be forbidden from displaying religious icons. Finally, no company may require employees to work on the Sabbath—be it Friday, Saturday, or Sunday—or another religious holiday if other workers will trade shifts to spring that employee.

Marital/parental status discrimination. This type of discrimination results from different treatment or benefits because of marital or parental status—or the lack thereof. Examples include being expected to work longer hours because you're single, or getting bypassed for a promotion because you have children or expect to start a family soon.

For private-sector workers, marital- and parental-status discrimination are not covered by the federal laws that prohibit other forms of discrimination. Some states, however, have laws on their books to protect workers against these types of discrimination. Many employees of the federal government are shielded from marital/parental status discrimination by the provisions of the Civil Service Reform Act of 1978.

For more information on other types of discrimination, state-by-state laws, and the steps required to file a complaint, visit the Discrimination section of the Workplace Fairness website at www.workplacefairness.org.

Starting Over

Reconsider the résumé. Most job-seekers put too much emphasis on the résumé, says outplacement firm CEO Challenger. "A résumé does not get you a job, but it may keep you from getting one. Employers primarily use it to eliminate candidates from consideration."

Because of that, he recommends that you present your résumé as a sales document, not a chronicle of your work his-

Your money or your time? When Salary.com posed that question in a 2001 survey, 2 in 3 respondents wanted a higher salary, while 33 percent preferred more vacation.

By 2004, however, a slight majority of respondents said they would prefer more down time.

▶ A BETTER WAY

Food for Thought at the Interview Meal

Be careful not to cook your own goose when being wined and dined by a prospective new employer.

That's what can happen, says etiquette expert Jacqueline Whitmore, to job candidates who display improper table manners during a business meal. Whitmore, author of *Business Class: Etiquette Essentials for Success at Work* and founder of the Protocol School of Palm Beach, offers these pointers for the protocol-challenged:

Patience at the venue. Wait for your host to sit down before you do. Wait for him or her to remove his or her napkin and begin eating before you do likewise.

Hold your horses. Don't initiate any business-related conversation until everyone present has ordered.

Ban the wolf. "Don't go to a business meal hungry. You're there to talk and listen." So order a smaller entree—something that requires utensils. (Sandwiches may be cut into quarters and eaten with the fingers.)

I'll have the cheap skate. Never order the most expensive item on the menu. It implies you're wasteful with money.

Too much info. Don't mention that you're following a special diet. Instead, simply order food that conforms to your eating regimen as much as possible and "eat around what you're served."

KYMS. Don't chew with your mouth open may seem to be an obvious dining decree, but Whitmore reports that it's the pet peeve among CEOs she has surveyed. Other decorum-busters cited by executives include eating too quickly and speaking while chewing.

The Beemer mnemonic. Utensils are used from the outside in. Your bread dish is to your left, your glasses to your right. If you need a reminder, recite the initials "BMW": B for bread (on your left), M for meal (in the middle), and W for water (on your right).

Teetotality. Never drink alcohol in the course of a mealtime job interview, even if your host is imbibing.

tory. "Getting a job is similar to making a major sale," notes Challenger. "A résumé should be treated as a brochure— something that employers can use to highlight your benefits and advantages over those of other candidates." His advice:

• *Focus on achievements, not responsibilities.* "Chances

are you're competing with others who have had the same responsibilities as you," notes Challenger. "So talking about the duties you've handled in the past won't make you stand out from the crowd." Instead, detail how you parlayed opportunities into achievements: Note increased sales, instances where you saved the company money, or specific steps you took to boost efficiency or market presence.

In 2004, displaced workers over age 50 required an average of 4.35 months to find a new job— only a few weeks longer than younger employees, who typically needed 3.75 months.

- *Use keywords.* With so many applicants applying for jobs online, it's more important than ever to employ the sort of keywords that will invite a closer examination of your résumé. In you're in Human Resources, for instance, critical catch phrases include "employee relations," "compensation and benefits," and "recruiting." If you're in Production, the keywords to trot out include "just-in time," "inventory control," and "distribution." For Sales personnel, specify "customer service," "new account development," and "exceeded sales objectives."

- *Don't list personal objectives.* Many résumés kick off with a catalogue of the applicant's "career goals" or "objectives." Bad move, says Challenger: "By doing that, you place yourself in a concrete, inadaptable form. The employer may get the impression you're more interested in yourself than you are in the company. And if your objectives do not mesh tightly with those of the company, listing them can quickly exclude you from consideration."

- *Spotlight the last five years.* "Employers want to know what you've been doing lately, not 15 or 20 years ago," advises Challenger. It's fine to recount your entire work history, but the bulk of your bullet-point achievements should be in jobs you've held recently.

  And don't omit your education—with graduation dates—in a bid to conceal your age. Most employers will

Cover Your Assets

With the résumé losing its luster as a job-seeking tool, says career consultant Nancy Collamer, the cover letter is growing ever more powerful as a way to package yourself—and your capabilities—for prospective employers.

Each letter should target the job you're seeking. In no more than three paragraphs, it should detail why you're applying for a particular job and why you believe you are best qualified for it; what makes you interested in that company; and how you propose to follow up for an interview.

It's a no-brainer that the cover letter must be syntactically squeaky-clean— free of spelling or grammar mistakes. Those that work best, says Collamer, include a few punchy bullet points (see below) that itemize your expertise.

Your Specifications

- 5 years experience with a consumer products company.
- Proven track record in both sales and marketing.

My Qualifications

- 3 years with X Inc., 4 years with Y Inc.
- Exceeded sales objectives by 15 percent at X Inc., where I was named "Outstanding Sales Executive" the last two years.

assume, correctly, that you're trying to hide something. "Actually, many employers these days are actively seeking older workers because of their experience and strong work ethic." For information on firms considered ideal for employees older than 50, visit www.aarp.org/bestemployers.

- *Avoid going through HR.* A company's Human Resources department typically serves as the gatekeeper for collecting résumés; rarely does it make the final hiring decision. To contact a decision-maker directly, call the company switchboard. If you're applying for a sales job, for instance, ask the switchboard operator for the name of the sales director. (Don't disclose the reason for your inquiry—you'll only be transferred to HR.) Then, using that name, contact the person directly to request a brief, face-to-face meeting to introduce yourself and explain what you can do for the company. To avoid running into the protective wall some assistants build around their bosses, Challenger recommends calling before 9 a.m. Many executives and managers begin work earlier than that, making them likelier to answer their own phones by dawn's early light.

- *Review your "unwritten" Rolodex.* Many new jobs are landed via networking—knowing someone who is a current employee, intern, temp, consultant, customer, or client of that company. "Think of anyone and everyone you know who may have some access to a decision-maker," says Challenger, "or someone else with access to that person. This can facilitate your approach to that decision-maker."

THE DIRTY DOZEN

12

A Roundup of Common Scams

LIKE THE SUCKERS who fall for them, new scams are born every minute. Yet some classic cons never die. Although the frequency of individual scams varies—by area, by season, by victim demographics—the most common and devious schemes remain remarkably constant. Here in alphabetical order are the 12 most prevalent scams being perpetrated today: The Dirty Dozen.

1 Advance-Fee Loans

The scam: You've heard the pitch: You are "guaranteed" a loan or credit card, regardless of your income, job status, or past credit history. The catch: You must pay an up-front fee before receiving the money or plastic. The result: The loan or credit card never materializes, and your advance fee is lost.

Although legitimate lenders may charge for applications and credit reports, these scams differ in that they require an advance payment for the promise of a loan—an illegal act, according to the Federal Trade Commission. (Credit-card companies do not charge customers to secure a card.) These loan sharks often claim that their fees will go to a third party for credit insurance or a related service; sometimes they even fax materials using stolen or forged logos and letterheads from legitimate companies. The loan and credit-card contracts they provide are fake; they are interested only in the advance fee, which can be hundreds—even thousands—of dollars. These scams are often solicited via phone. Many advance-fee loans are also promoted in the classified sections of newspapers and magazines, or through direct-mail advertisements.

Ripoff tip-off: When was the last time Citibank or another leading bank advertised its loan services in a small classified ad in the local newspaper? Another clue: Many advance-fee scams provide contact information with the area codes 416, 647, 905, or 705—all from Canada (although sometimes U.S.-based toll-free area codes 800, 866, or 877 are used). Some scammers require that advance fees be sent via Western Union, or that personal checks be made payable to an individual rather than a business.

Your protection: Ignore any request for up-front payment for the promise or "guarantee" of a loan. Many advance-fee scams originate in Canada; to investigate advance-fee phone solicitations, call PhoneBusters in Canada at 888-495-8501.

2 ATM Skimming

The scam: A small, portable card-reading device—similar to those used to make credit- and debit-card purchases in stores—is placed over the mouth of an Automatic Teller Machine (ATM) to create an unobtrusive false front; sometimes it's placed on the card slot that unlocks a door to gain entrance to the ATM. This "skimming" device, which can be purchased on the Internet, reads and stores information encoded in the magnetic strip of debit cards. Sometimes, a miniature camera is mounted nearby to capture customers entering their PIN access codes. The skimmer and camera are later retrieved—perhaps to be installed at other ATMs. Duplicate cards are produced and sold on the black market (with their access PINs supplied), often overseas, to make fraudulent withdrawals.

Ripoff tip-off: Although skimming devices can be hard to detect, be suspicious of often-used ATMs that suddenly sport new equipment protruding from the card slot. Avoid using machines bearing signs denoting "new equipment," a common ruse to fool customers—especially if the sign has spelling errors. This scam is often pulled by Russian organized-crime members, say officials.

Your protection: Cover your hand whenever you punch in your PIN; this will reduce the chance of its being stolen and used to access your money. If your debit card can also be used as a credit card—and many can—ask to have it converted to a "debit only" card; this helps block fraudulent online credit transactions.

Notify your bank to set a daily ATM withdrawal limit on your accounts. Although there may be a per-withdrawal limit of, say, $200, skimming scammers easily avert that: They simply make numerous withdrawals in a single day. Also, keep close tabs on your day-to-day account balances. Banks will often reimburse victims of ATM skimming, but some require customers to report the money as missing within 60 days.

3 Charity Cheats

The scam: You receive a telephone call, letter, e-mail, or home visit soliciting a donation for a charity—be it hurricane relief, medical research, a police or fire department, or some other cause. Sometimes the request is made at the behest of a bona fide charity, such as the American Red Cross or the American Cancer Society, but scammers often claim to be collecting money for a sound-alike name, such as the American Cancer Research Society. Or they may invent new charities reflecting the latest crisis: In the wake of Hurricane Katrina, the FBI reported that at least 2,300 websites dealing with hurricane relief popped up. Most of them were fraudulent.

If contacted by telephone or e-mail, you may be asked to provide your bank account, PIN access code, or credit-card number for an electronic donation. Some scammers may also request your Social Security number for "tax-deduction purposes." Door-to-door solicitors may ask for an on-the-spot donation in cash or by personal check.

Ripoff tip-off: Be suspicious of any charity appeal that requests for your bank account, credit card, or other personal information—especially by e-mail or telephone. The Better Business Bureau's Wise Giving Alliance (www.give.org or 703-276-0100), which tracks legitimate charities, reports that e-mail solicitations are nearly always scams.

Likewise be wary of solicitations you receive in the wake of a natural disaster—tsunami or hurricane relief, for example—that claim to be from new charities allegedly associated with church or civic associations.

Police and fire-department charity solicitations are another popular ruse. To spot the legitimate fund-raisers amid all that chaff, look for mail solicitations that include a return envelope whose address can be easily verified.

And when out and about during the holiday season, beware of apron-wearing Salvation Army "volunteers" at shopping centers who seek donations in a large can or any other type of receptacle besides the trademark red kettle on a tripod. (Some scammers have been known to try using a large coffee can painted red.)

Your protection: To check the authenticity of a charity—especially those that sound unfamiliar—contact your state or local consumer-protection agency. Most states require charities to register with them and file annual reports indicating how they use the funds they collect. A list of such watchdog agencies is available at http://consumeraction.gov/state/shtml. The BBB's Wise Giving Alliance also provides information on both legitimate and questionable charities—and tells you which is which. Another website, www.charitynavigator.org, lets you match your interests with a specific, licit charity.

Of course, never offer an impromptu donation without personally checking the source. If you receive any solicitation claiming to be from a charity, contact that organization yourself. But don't rely on the contact info provided by the solicitor; instead, to make sure it's a legitimate request, call directory assistance yourself, or do an online search.

④ Door-to-Door Deception

THE PHONY INSPECTOR

The scam: Unscrupulous handymen aren't the only hucksters who come knocking. One common scam involves an impromptu visit by a phony inspector from your local utility company. These guys may claim there are service problems in your area, then ask to inspect your fuse box, furnace, or water meter. Don't let them! They will only inform you that regulations are being violated or repairs are necessary to continue your water, natural gas, or electricity service. The inspector then gives you the name of someone who—miraculously—is available to do the job at short notice and low cost. The inspector and his conveniently available repairman split any profit from your "repairs"—or use entry into your house to case it for a later burglary.

Ripoff tip-off: Phony inspectors may have an authentic-looking identification badge, uniform, or tool belt, but it's unlikely they managed to score a van or a truck from your local utility company. Additionally, no utility company or other service provider would send out inspectors or repair personnel without notifying you first. Even if you receive a notice-of-service call, authenticate it by dialing the customer-service number listed in your phone directory or on a utility bill.

Your protection: Unless you have contacted a utility company—or made an appointment for service—err on the side of financial and personal security: Keep the door locked.

THE GOOD NEIGHBOR GUISE

The scam: There's also the Good Neighbor Guise, in which a stranger comes knocking at your front door. Claiming to be the friend or relative of a neighbor (having learned their name—and yours—from the phone directory or property ownership records available at the local courthouse), he or she enlists your help under the pretense of car trouble—a breakdown or accident a few blocks away—or some other excuse, and asks to use your phone to call a tow truck because the neighbor isn't home. A bogus call may be made and you're asked to front the money for the tow—and the neighbor will pay you back. Do so and you'll likely find that your neighbor has never heard of the visitor. Plus you're out of money and it could be a set-up for a burglary a few days hence.

Ripoff tip-off: Usually, the car in need of service is said to be blocks away—not on your street. That's your first clue of a possible ruse. But if the scammer can point you to a car claimed to be inoperable, and you want to be a Good Samaritan, offer to call a tow truck yourself.

Your protection: Don't allow the stranded stranger into your home. Don't tender any up-front money.

5 Employment Scams

Remember when the most prevalent work-at-home schemes were those opportunities to "make big money" and "be your own boss" by stuffing envelopes or assembling magnets? If you're a nostalgia nut, you'll be thrilled to hear those come-ons still exist. Here's how they work: For an initial "registration" fee of $100 or more, "employees" typically receive a pittance of supplies (such as one box of envelopes or one sample magnet and a small bottle of glue, paint, or glitter). Then comes the real scam: To get enough supplies to "go into business," you need to pay more money. But after you do, lo and behold, those supplies never arrive: The alleged "inspection department" of the supposed supplier purportedly rejects the so-called shipment because of bogus quality-control issues (or some equally lame excuse).

Today, that classic has been supplemented with more sophisticated employment scams that cost victims even more:

WIRE-TRANSFER TANGO

The scam: Victims respond to postings on job-search engines or in help-wanted e-mails. The pitch is from self-proclaimed "top high-tech firms overseas" in need of American representatives to serve as "financial agents" to process payments for their U.S. orders. The work: These "agents" receive checks from the firm, typically ranging from $2,000 to $100,000, via express mail; all they have to do is deposit them in their own bank accounts, then wire-transfer the check amount to a foreign bank allegedly holding an account for the recruiting company. For each cleared check, the story goes, agents receive a 5 percent commission. The incoming checks are counterfeit, so any money wired to that foreign account will be your own. The overseas scammer also gets your bank account information—and, if you submitted employment forms, your Social Security number as well.

Ripoff tip-off: Truly great work-at-home opportunities seldom need to be advertised. Also, scrutinize the sender: These "leading firms" claim to be based in Russia, yet their names sound suspiciously American: Delta Soft Labs, International Health Care, Future Tech, V-Tech Sendit Software. In reality, officials say, they are fronts with little more than a website.

THE RE-SHIP RIPOFF

The scam: This is similar to the wire transfer, but deals with receiving and then re-shipping merchandise that has been ordered online—usually to locations overseas. Typically, re-shipper victims are recruited via job postings or help-wanted e-mails to unknowingly ship merchandise that has been paid for with stolen or fraudulent credit cards. This makes the shipper susceptible to fraud charges (as well as federal mail-fraud crimes if the re-shipping occurred via the U.S. Postal Service). But it only gets worse: For their participation, the scammers usually pay these "employees" with a third-party cashier's check—typically in excess of the designated amount. Employees are then instructed to cash the check and electronically forward the excess amount to an overseas bank account. Alas, the check is bogus—and the employee is liable for the total amount.

Ripoff tip-off: Re-shipping scams should be detected by the fact that legitimate companies use FedEx, UPS, and other international shipping companies; they have no need for middlemen to expedite shipping.

VENDING MACHINE VOODOO

The scam: In exchange for your investment—these machines can cost $5,000 or more each—you're assigned a location where they will remain: All you need to do is stock them and collect the coins.The assigned locations—like the devices themselves—are usually anything but choice: Often vending machines are placed in rural gas stations, deserted strip malls, or other locations hard up for foot traffic. (And the machines themselves may be in poor operating condition.) A similar ploy is used with pay-phone investments. Both of these scams often recruit victims by inviting them to be-your-own-boss "informational seminars" that travel from town to town like the snake-oil salesmen of old.

Ripoff tip-off: While the promise of collecting coins in perpetuity may be tantalizing, installing machines in the Last Chance Gas Station or on the edge of the desert may not be the wisest way to invest your hard-earned thousands. (Besides, who uses pay phones these days, anyway?)

Your protection against employment scams: If you want to work at home or earn extra money, consider reasonable alternatives within your proven skill set: Withdrawing money from your bank account and handing it over to strangers, as all of these employment scams encourage you to do, has never been the quickest path to career success. And with all the recent advances in automation, is there a human left on Earth who can outperform machines at stuffing envelopes or assembling trinkets?

6 Financial Account Updates & Alerts

Most of the attention in this category goes to "phishing" and "pharming" scams. These involve e-mails claiming to be from your bank, credit-card company, mortgage holder, or Internet provider, asking you to "update your account information."

PHISHING FOLLIES

The scam: These e-mails include an attachment that directs you to an authentic-looking website that asks for your account numbers, passwords, or Social Security number. By obliging, you provide these scammers with all the information they need to access your financial accounts—the first move in identity theft. You may even download software that disables your firewall protection and provides phishers and pharmers access to personal information for other accounts you maintain online.

Ripoff tip-off: Spotting a phishing website used to be straightforward. You simply scanned its URL to see if it lacked the "https" (indicating a secure website) before the "www." Or you looked to see if its address was misspelled ("www. wellfargo.com" instead of "www.wellsfargo.com," for example) or if its Web pages themselves contained misspellings and grammatical errors. Nowadays such detection is not so easy. Sophisticated scammers can replicate an authentic website down to its last detail, including a bona fide Web address. Although you may occasionally receive informational e-mails about new products and services from legitimate banks, loan holders, and credit-card companies, these companies never ask for online "updates" or "verification" of passwords, account numbers, or Social Security numbers.

Here are some other common scams that may target your financial accounts:

MISSING CARD MAYHEM

The scam: Someone calls you claiming to represent the fraud department of your credit-card company. The caller gains your trust by reciting your account number—pilfered, no doubt—and says that a "suspicious" charge has been made. Now here comes the scam: Under the guise of "verifying that you are still in possession of your card," the caller asks you to read off the three- or four-digit security number (usually on the back of the card; it's on the upper-right corner of American Express cards). This number gives the scammer the final piece of the puzzle she or he was missing, for it is needed to make online and telephone credit purchases without showing your piece of plastic.

Ripoff tip-off: Credit-card companies may call you to alert you of suspicious activity on your account, but to make sure you are in possession of your card, you'll be asked if you have it—not asked to provide the security digits.

LOWER-RATE LURES

The scam: The caller claims to be from your current or another mortgage company, and says he can offer lower-rate refinancing. To "determine if you qualify for that lower rate," however, you're asked to provide your Social Security number, bank account numbers, or other personal information "required to run a credit check." Provide any one of these and you will almost certainly fall victim to identity theft.

Ripoff tip-off: Phony phone calls alleging to be from banks and mortgage companies, like other telemarketing solicitations, often come in the evening—when most of these companies are closed.

THE BOGUS BANK EXAMINER

The scam: As you leave your bank, you're accosted by someone claiming to be a detective, a bank official, or a Federal Deposit Insurance Corporation (FDIC) representative investigating a crooked bank teller. You're asked to withdraw money from your account so the phony investigator can "look it over"; it is then replaced with counterfeit cash. Or in exchange for your withdrawal, you may be given a "receipt" and informed you'll be contacted to collect your money. You won't be, of course. You'll never see that money again, because you've just been robbed blind.

Ripoff tip-off: With closed-circuit televisions monitoring every move of bank tellers and customers alike, banks have absolutely no need of "examiners" to solicit your help in nabbing shady tellers.

Your protection against financial scams: To protect your finances from all of these scams, keep your account information private. If there's a problem with your savings, checking, or credit accounts, you'll be notified by mail—and the only time you are ever asked for personal information is when you call.

If, for whatever reason, you are contacted by phone, simply hang up and call the company yourself—using the phone number listed on your account statements or in the Yellow Pages. Telephone calls made by scammers often result from their buying lists compiled from public records (such as deed records from your county courthouse) or pooled from phone directories. To thwart these approaches, have your telephone number delisted, or put the account under another name, with no address. Get caller ID to weed out bogus calls.

You can minimize bogus e-mail attempts by conducting all online transactions and account maintenance with a separate e-mail account that makes no mention of your real name; free ones are available from Yahoo!'s Mail, MSN's Hotmail, and Google's Gmail.

7 Foreign Lotteries

The scam: Congratulations! Via a phone call, letter, or e-mail, you're informed that you've won a lottery held in another country—even though you never entered the contest nor set foot in that country. Sometimes these messages earnestly "explain" that disparity: A relative or a friend of yours happened to be visiting Australia, Spain, England, or some other foreign country and generously bought a lottery ticket in your behalf. At other times, you may receive an authentic-looking check in the mail. No matter the method, there's always a catch: "In order to avoid unnecessary delays," you are directed to pay a fee of several thousand dollars for "processing charges," "shipping and handling," "insurance," or "taxes."

You will usually be instructed to send this fee abroad via Western Union, or via a personal check. Don't do it. Once you do, that money is beyond the jurisdiction of U.S.-based law enforcement—and beyond recovering. Oftentimes, "winners" who send money are contacted a second time with—incredibly—more "good" news: Their prize is larger than originally thought, they are informed, so more money is needed for additional insurance, taxes, or whatever.

If you receive a check, it usually is for a portion of your total prize—say, the first $10,000 on your "million-dollar" award. The instructions are to deposit it in your bank account, then send back a portion of that amount to cover expenses. But that check is counterfeit—a discovery that will likely not be made for days or weeks after the check has been deposited. And the portion you sent to cover "expenses" is very real—and really lost.

To Report a Scam

If you think you've been scammed, contact your state attorney general's office or local police agency. You can also file complaints with any of the following:

Consumer Sentinel
This partnership among the Federal Trade Commission, the FBI, and other agencies has received more than one million consumer-fraud complaints that were then passed onto federal, state, and local law-enforcement agencies. www.consumer.gov/sentinel

National Fraud Information Center
The NFIC accepts complaints about Internet and telemarketing scams, but not other types. Its website also gives consumer-protection advice.
www.fraud.org
Phone: 800-876-7060

Better Business Bureau
Locate your local office, get tips, and file complaints. www.bbb.org

Internet Fraud Complaint Center (IFCC)
File a complaint with this partnership between the FBI and the National White Collar Crime Center if you suspect you've been victimized by Internet fraud. www.ic3.gov

And if you mailed a personal check, the scammers now have your bank-account information in hand; you have obligingly furnished them with the numerical keys they need to make fraudulent withdrawals at their leisure in the future.

Ripoff tip-off: Authentic lotteries never require up-front fees (other than the cost of a ticket) in order to be claimed. What's more, it's illegal for U.S. citizens to play—much less win—a foreign lottery; this should be a dead giveaway of the falsity of claims alleging to originate with the Federal Trade Commission, the Internal Revenue Service, or the U.S. Customs Service.

The real clue: Bona fide lotteries are typically managed by governmental entities within a particular state or nation. Yet foreign-lottery scams often note that your "winnings" will be paid out by a bank in another country. Claims of a bogus Australian lottery, for example, may indicate that a bank in the Netherlands will process your winnings.

Your protection: Never respond to any claim that you've won a foreign lottery (and be aware of any domestic come-ons—especially from states where you don't live.) These scams are among the most prevalent nationwide, especially among older Americans. (Indeed, complaints about foreign-lottery scams account for five times more mail to AARP's "Scam Alert" column than any other ruse.) Once you respond—whether by e-mail, letter, or phone—your contact information is placed on a "sucker list." This roster of rubes is then traded or sold to other scammers, flooding you with many more phony come-ons.

8 Gift Grift

The variations in this category are all on a common theme: You receive word that you've just won a "valuable gift" or a "catalogue shopping spree." But what you mostly receive is hype. Some common scenarios appear on pages 314-315.

"CLAIM AND WIN" CON

The only thing you need to do to claim your prize, you are informed by an obliging stranger whose existence you were unaware of until he came tap-tap-tapping at your computer screen, is to pay "shipping and handling" for its delivery to your home. In reality, natch, those costs exceed the value of the award itself. And that vaunted shopping spree? The value of the items you're allowed to choose from is grossly inflated, meaning that "$800 camera" may in fact be worth only $15— yet to claim it you're obligated to pay $50 or more in shipping and handling charges.

TEASER PRIZE LIES

This "guarantees" you will be awarded one of several prizes— provided you purchase another, more expensive item first, of course. When your actual "teaser award" arrives, it falls far short of its description—and you've overpaid for the more expensive "sucker" item.

ZENO'S PARADOX

You're "eligible" for tempting prizes after completing puzzles, games, or surveys. These "qualifiers" require an entry fee—typically $5 to $35 apiece—and entrants are then bombarded with a series of tantalizing "next step" actions required to get ever closer to the Big Prize. By the time you do finally reach the ultimate level of the contest, you may have been manipulated into spending thousands of dollars in entry fees—and the final-level test is so difficult that not even a national-lab supercomputer could crack it.

PROVE YOU ARE YOU

You're told that to claim your prize, you must confirm you are the "real" winner by divulging some vital piece of data— your bank account number, perhaps, or your Social Security number. As usual, it's another ruse to access the sort of sensitive info that facilitates identity theft.

THE GUILTY PARTY GRAB

You may receive an unsolicited gift—a pen, a book, a key-chain—with attached instructions that you are under no obligation to keep it. Hoping to make you feel guilty, the sender gives you the opportunity to return the freebie. The intent here is to get your contact information for a sucker list that can then be sold to other prize marketers.

Ripoff tip-off: Scammers aren't known for their "truth in advertising," but you may be able to detect subtle signs of deception in the product descriptions: A "beautiful diamond-like watch" translates to a $5 timepiece encrusted with bits of shiny glass. A "computer system" may be nothing more than a giveaway pocket calculator. Or a "new car" may be just that—duplicitously suppressing the fact that it's a toy. In "shopping spree" awards, "value" is a subjective term: An item vaunted as having a retail value of $1,000 may, in truth, be worth but a tiny fraction of that amount.

And, of course, contests that force entrants to jump through multiple hoops in a race to the jackpot are typically an exercise in futility—especially when they are sponsored by companies with names such as Treasure Express or Puzzles N' Prizes, whose emotion-driven appeals string you along: "You've worked hard and qualified for this Official Playoff Puzzle" or "You're so close to the grand prize, why stop now?"

Your protection against gift grift: Ignore tempting offers—especially those that require any action on your part, whether it's submitting an entrance fee or qualifying in some other way. Responding will only bring you more such offers.

9 Government Cons

Uncle Sam wants you—to update your records? Scams purporting to be official business transacted on behalf of the federal or local government include those exposed on pages 318-319.

What's Age Got to Do with It?

PEOPLE OVER AGE 60 make up only one-eighth of the U.S. population, yet they constitute 1 of every 3 scam victims. It's clear why they are targeted: After a lifetime of hard work and responsibility, older Americans are more likely to hold the financial brass rings sought by con artists—liquid funds, free-and-clear home ownership, excellent credit ratings.

When it comes to why older Americans actually fall for scams, the received wisdom often cites age-induced memory loss, the supposedly more "trusting" nature of seniors, or the loneliness factor. All of these are appetizing traits for hungry wolves in sheep's clothing, but what medical research reveals is this: The aging process causes changes in both mind and mindset that increase vulnerability to some scams while boosting resistance to others. People over 65 represent the fastest-growing segment of computer users, for example, yet they are least likely to fall for "faceless" Internet scams.

Gray matters. "There's great variability in individuals," says psychologist Larry Jacoby of Washington University in St. Louis, "but age declines in certain aspects of memory make older adults more vulnerable to many scams." It's not that an aging brain necessarily "loses" memory; instead, it simply processes those memories differently.

Studies by Dr. Jacoby and others indicate that when people 65 and older are given misleading cues—and especially when those clues are repeated—they are more likely than others to remember falsehoods as truth. "It comes down to recollection and familiarity," Dr. Jacoby explains. "Whereas young adults are better at recalling information they have already been given, age-related declines in frontal-lobe function (which controls recollection) mean that older people rely more heavily on familiarity."

In other words, the aging brain is more likely to remember false statements as true if they sound familiar or are repeated often. The aging brain is also less likely to recall what was originally said.

This could explain why seniors are more vulnerable to home-repair scams, as well as to other scams in which the victims overpay for services or are repeatedly charged for the same service. "A workman may quote you one price to get the work," notes Dr. Jacoby, "but right before handing you the bill he may cite a higher price or say you forgot to pay him. When you can rely on recollection, you are more likely to remember the original, lower price—or that he was already paid. When you have to rely on familiarity, however, what likely comes to mind is that later misinformation."

Your defense: Get everything in writing—estimates, receipts, background checks, your handwritten notes. Keep this documentation handy to backstop your recollection of it later on.

Another brain change could explain why seniors get duped in telemarketing and door-to-door scams: "Older adults tend to process information in a systemic way. They get the 'big picture' and move on," says Stacey Wood, Ph.D., a neuropsychologist at Scripps College in Claremont, California, who researches how age influences scam vulnerability. But as the day progresses, she says, older individuals grow less capable of processing fine-print details such as contract terms—especially under act-now pressure. "There is not much difference in this capacity between older and younger people in the morning," Wood notes. "But as circadian rhythms change, there is a noticeable decline among older people after about 2 p.m."

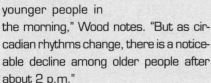

Your defense: Be aware that late afternoons and evenings are prime crime times for scammers. Mornings are the best time to review paperwork and other detailed information.

Words' worth. Then there's the popular notion that older people get scammed more often because they are somehow more trusting. Yet studies have found that people 62 and older are more adept at detecting lies than those aged 18 to 35.

"Seniors are no more trusting than anyone else," says Dr. Wood. "But they tend to be more patriotic and more religious, and that translates to increased vulnerability to charity and other scams that play on these emotions."

This faith in God and country, says William Arnold, a scam researcher and Arizona State University gerontologist, may explain an Achilles heel that commonly afflicts the older American consumer: sweepstakes scams. "When a sweepstakes offer arrives in the mail bearing that familiar 'Do not tamper under federal penalty' stamp," says Dr. Arnold, "seniors are more likely to respond because it appears to have come from the U.S. Postal Service. As a matter of fact, in one study we found that the majority of seniors think sweepstakes are a waste of time—but 40 percent admitted responding because of their trust in the government."

Your defense: The Postal Service cannot vouchsafe the contents of any envelope. Chances are you're not a winner—yet sweepstakes scams bilk the elderly of some $40 billion a year.

Older Americans are less likely than their younger counterparts to detect the signs of a scam ahead. In tests, seniors react just as strongly to positive images and actions, but younger people are "more reactive" to negative situations. "Seniors may not be as attentive to negative cues as younger people are," says Dr. Wood. "But that may be because older adults tend to have a more positive outlook."

TAX MAN TRICKERY

An e-mail, allegedly from the Internal Revenue Service, shows up in your in-box with the news that you are entitled to a tax refund, are exempt from paying taxes, or must pay back taxes. The message directs you to a link that requests personal information such as Social Security, bank account, or credit-card numbers.

THE BIG BROTHER BAMBOOZLE

An e-mail claiming to be from the FBI or the CIA warns that you are being investigated for visiting "illegal" sites, or that your help is needed to solve a crime. Often, recipients are then asked to answer the questions in an attachment. But when the attachment is opened, it downloads a computer virus that disables your firewall or other security software, giving hackers access to passwords, account numbers, and other personal information stored in your machine.

HERE WITH AN UPDATE...

An in-person visit from someone claiming to represent the Social Security Administration or the U.S. Census Bureau leads to a request for you to assist the interviewer in "updating your personal records." The scammer then asks you to produce a photo ID or some other proof of your existence, including a verification of your Social Security number. It's all an elaborate but phony back story, meant to steal your identity for fraudulent activities.

THE JURY JUMBLE

Someone claiming to be an agent of a federal, state, or local court calls to say you have been selected for jury duty—or that you have failed to appear as scheduled. The caller then asks for personal information, such as your Social Security or driver's license number. Some jury scammers are so bold as to ask for your bank account number or credit-card information as a way of "verifying your identity."

Ripoff tip-off for government cons: No federal agency or government bureau would ever ask for personal information via e-mail or telephone. They already have it on file, and nothing could have alerted them that it might somehow need "updating."

Social Security personnel do not appear in person to update your vital stats. Typically, government entities send only mailed correspondence, in which they ask you to contact the local office of that agency or department.

Jury-duty candidates are invariably summoned by mail, and they are the ones who must contact the court system to confirm their attendance. In summation, the courts don't care about your Visa card—only about your presence.

Your protection: Do not open any e-mail claiming to be from a government agency. Activating the caller ID feature of your telephone will verify the authenticity of any incoming caller, be it a government agency or a private solicitor. Any incoming calls marked "Private" do not originate within taxpayer-funded agencies; they should therefore be considered suspect.

🔟 "Kid" Candy & Magazine Sales

The scam: It's one thing when a neighborhood kid you recognize knocks on your front door, selling candy, pizza, or other items as a fund-raiser for the local sports league, school play, or good cause. But when a stranger shows up, you should assume that his appeal to your heartstrings is really aimed at loosening your purse strings.

In these scams, teams of children are recruited—often from the inner city—to go door-to-door (or at shopping centers) selling candy, magazine subscriptions, or other merchandise under the pretense of collecting for scholarship funds, drug-prevention programs, or other noble causes. The efforts they "represent" may not, in fact, exist. Or they may claim to be collecting for authentic charities but lack any real affiliation with them. Sometimes the children themselves are exploited, earning a paltry "commission" of pennies from the sale of each $2 candy bar. Meanwhile the crew chiefs who chauffeur these half-pint hawkers to various neighborhoods enjoy the bulk of the profits, having bought the items at a steep discount.

Ripoff tip-off: Assume it's a scam if an unfamiliar salesman asks you to make a payment by cash, check, or credit card at the time you place an order—especially if you do not receive the goods on the spot. Typical items "sold" this way include candy bars or coupons for local stores. Check for any unfamiliar vehicles—especially cargo vans—parked on or near your street. You can also look for adult strangers shadowing the door-to-door sellers. Magazine sales are a frequent vehicle for door-to-door scams by child or teenage vendors: At best, the subscriptions are overpriced; at worst, they are simply never processed.

And don't be fooled by any ID badges or other documentation these salesmen brandish as proof of their legitimacy; such certificates are easy to fabricate using a basic computer graphics program and a high-end color printer.

Your protection: Legitimate fund-raisers will leave behind printed information that cautious donors can use to verify the soundness of the cause being promoted. Do not, however, rely on any contact information a solicitor provides. If the seller claims to be selling items for the American Red Cross, for example, contact that organization's local office to verify that it has authorized a door-to-door campaign. Magazine orders should also be checked out, but not through the "clearinghouse" listed on the promotional brochure. These businesses—two to watch out for are All-Star Promotions and Subscriptions Services, Inc.—have a long history of nondelivery of placed orders. And never allow unfamiliar salesmen, no matter what their age, into your home: These door-to-door children and teens could be casing your home for a later burglary or other crime.

🔢 The Nigerian Letter

The scam: This is perhaps the granddaddy of all scams—a classic but bogus appeal that starts with your receipt of a letter, a fax, or an e-mail from someone claiming to be a current or deposed official of a foreign government (historically, Nigeria or another African nation) in the throes of political unrest. Or it may come from His Majesty's spouse, attorney, or even a "friendly" American official allegedly associated with the U.S. Department of State. The sender varies, but the pitch never does: If you help the hapless victim recover his millions, recently and unjustly impounded by an overseas bank, you will be handsomely rewarded.

How? You're encouraged to provide the sender your bank's name and account number for a "safe" transfer—a move that gives the scammer instant access to your own fortune. Or you may be asked for advance payment via personal check or Western Union wire to pay taxes and other costs to "free" the trapped funds.

Why would anyone be this gullible?

Because sometimes the scammer gains your confidence by sending you a cashier's check. Again, the check is counterfeit—a fact you likely won't discover until after you have transferred your own precious ducats overseas.

A newer twist of the Nigerian Letter Scam—known internationally as the 419 Scam, after the Nigerian criminal statute for fraud—is made through Internet seduction. Scammers lurk in chat rooms for the lovelorn, where they persuade their prey (sometimes after sending them gifts) to help transfer funds from a bank. Some of these con artists claim to be cancer victims in need of costly medical care. Others represent themselves as homeless from a recent job loss, natural disaster, or other misfortune. (Intriguingly, all managed to retain their Internet access.)

Ripoff tip-off: According to the Internet Fraud Complaint Center, the most commonly used names in Nigerian Letter scams are Mariam Abacha, Kayode Adeyemi, Isa Mustapha, Oliver Kabila, and Tonye Green. These bogus letters supposedly come from "barristers" or "bank auditors." They ask you to include in your response your telephone or fax number, your complete address, and your bank account information. Banks typically named in the phony correspondence include the ARB Apex Bank, Togolaise Bank, Standard Trust Bank, Ecobank Nigeria, United Bank of Africa, or the African International Bank. Also keep in mind that the jobless, the homeless, and the cancer-stricken usually have more pressing concerns than chat-room encounters.

Your protection: Assuming you're unrelated to royalty, it makes no sense that your help would be sought—yet thousands of Americans fall for this scam every year. To protect yourself, don't reply to any Nigerian letter. Don't respond to any request for personal information. Be leery of any and all hard-luck e-mails, letters, or other requests from strangers or new beaus.

12 Pyramid Schemes

The scam: Remember the chain letter? To get rich quick, all you had to do—supposedly—was send $1 to the name at the top of a list. Then you'd cross out that name, add yours to the bottom, and forward the letter to six friends. If they too followed the instructions, the story went, your name would eventually reach the top of the list—and you would reach Easy Street.

So, did you ever move?

Although the time-honored chain-letter scam still exists, today's pyramid schemes—also known as chain-referral schemes, matrix-marketing schemes, or binary-compensation schemes—are more elaborate. They demand the payment of costly "membership fees" that hypothetically reward participants for inducing others to join the program. (Ponzi schemes, by contrast, operate by paying early investors with money deposited by later investors; there is no emphasis on recruitment, and no awareness of the participation structure.)

The difference between pyramid schemes and legitimate multilevel marketing programs is that sales reps from the latter make money when they (and those they've recruited) sell products. In a pyramid scheme, however, there may be no sign of a product whatsoever. If there is, the "product" is usually a sham—bogus Internet service, for example, or nonexistent telephone calling plans.

The real money in a pyramid scheme comes from membership fees. These benefit only the initiators because of the following simple math: After paying their own membership or investment, new members are required to enlist several new members; the new recruits, in turn, must do the same. A nine-level pyramid built on each participant getting six others to join—a common pattern—would require the participation of 10 million people before you ever reached the top. But that never happens; those on the bottom-level rungs inevitably wise up and pull out.

Ripoff tip-off: If you've ever supervised anyone (kids or employees), you know that managing others is hard work, especially when the gratification is not immediate. That explodes the pyramid-scheme promise of "having to do little or no work because the people below you will." Also consider the product (if there is one): If it's all it's cracked up to be, why isn't a big company already selling it?

Your protection: Let a cliché be your mantra: "You can't get something for nothing." "There's no such thing as a free lunch." "If something sounds too good to be true, it's neither good nor true." Avoiding anything that smacks of a pyramid scheme is an excellent way to protect your wallet and your freedom. Whether you design one or merely help build it, the pyramid scheme is illegal—and a magnet for state Attorney General offices.

ABOUT THE AUTHOR

SID KIRCHHEIMER is an award-winning investigative reporter who has written or edited more than a dozen books devoted to empowering ordinary people to make the most of their time, money, and health. He has appeared on *The Oprah Winfrey Show* and other nationally syndicated TV programs, and covers medical and consumer issues for AARP Publications. Kirchheimer's popular "Scam Alert" column appears monthly in the *AARP Bulletin*. He is also a contributing editor to *AARP The Magazine*.

ACKNOWLEDGMENTS

FIRST AND FOREMOST, I am grateful to the nearly 170 consumer guardians interviewed for this book. Although the contributions of some were not used, all were generous with their time and advice. I am especially indebted to those listed on the following pages.

Special thanks to Allan Fallow, the Managing Editor of AARP Books, whose editing wizardry is surpassed only by his dedication to, and unstinting support for, this book and its author. Allan's vision prompted my article for *AARP The Magazine* in 2004 to evolve into this work, which has consumed the last 18 months of both our lives.

Others who deserve a gracious tip of the hat: At AARP Publications, there's Editor-in-Chief Hugh Delehanty, Cathy Ventura-Merkel, and Theresa Rademacher; *AARP Bulletin* editors Susan Crowley and Jim Toedtman; and at *AARP The Magazine,* I thank Steve Slon and Ed Dwyer for the opportunity to write the article that birthed this book, as well as for their continuing support afterward. I'm also appreciative to AARP consumer-advocate attorneys Sally Hurme, Deborah Zuckerman, Barbara Jones, and Jean Constantine-Davis.

A particular note of gratitude to this book's diligent fact-checker, Abby Contract, creative director Carl Lehmann-Haupt, designers Dorrit Green and Melissa Farris, and illustrator Alex Nabaum. At Sterling Publishing, a special thanks to Charles Nurnberg, Steve Magnuson, Andy Martin, and Leigh Ann Ambrosi.

On a more personal note, my heartfelt appreciation and love to Carol Svec, a brilliant author and true-blue friend; Gito, Hoo Bear, and Josie, my "most excellent" cheerleaders and offspring; and Gunther and Ilsa Kirchheimer, unsuccessful in their attempts to sway me toward a more lucrative profession than journalism but otherwise never failing as parents. Also thanks to the ever-supportive Nini.

And, of course, there's my wife, Chris, for being my always amusing muse, for spending endless hours poring over this manuscript when she had her own towering mountain of high schoolers' essays to grade . . . and for about a million other reasons.

PANEL OF EXPERTS

Frank W. Abagnale, former teenage identity thief turned check-fraud prevention consultant whose life was chronicled in the movie, *Catch Me If You Can*; author of *Catch Me If You Can* and *The Art of the Steal*

Bob Arno, world-renowned expert on pickpocket techniques and street crimes; author, *Travel Advisory: How to Avoid Thefts, Cons, and Street Crimes While Traveling*

William Arnold, Ph.D., director, Arizona Geriatric Education Center, and professor emeritus of social work, Arizona State University, Tempe

Chris Basso, spokesman, CarFax Vehicle History Reports (www.carfax.com)

David W. Bates, M.D., chief of general medicine, Brigham and Women's Hospital and professor of medicine, Harvard Medical School, Boston

Richard Becker, M.D., cardiologist and director, Duke University Cardiovascular Thrombosis Center, Durham, North Carolina

Jordana Beebe, communications director, Privacy Rights Clearinghouse, San Diego, California (www.privacyrights.org)

Matthew Bennett, publisher, www.firstclassflyer.com

Leo Berard, founding president, National Association of Exclusive Buyer Agents and the Massachusetts Association of Buyer Agents; real estate agent, Cape Cod, Massachusetts

Robert Blendon, Sc.D., professor of health policy and management, Harvard School of Public Health, Boston

Bernard Bloom, Ph.D., research professor of medicine, University of Pennsylvania, Philadelphia

Robert Bonow, M.D., chief of cardiology, Northwestern University's Feinberg School of Medicine, Chicago; former president, the American Heart Association

Paula Brantner, Esq., employment rights attorney and program director, Workplace Fairness, San Francisco (www.workplacefairness.org)

Eric Carlson, Esq., attorney, National Senior Citizens Law Center, Los Angeles

John A. Challenger, founder and CEO, Challenger, Gray & Christmas, Inc. (employment outplacement firm), Chicago

Nancy Collamer, president, Collamer Career Consulting, Greenwich, Connecticut; author, *The Layoff Survival Guide*

Tod Cooperman, M.D., president, pharmacy checker.com and ConsumerLab.com, White Plains, New York; co-author, *2005 Guide to Low-Cost Canadian and U.S. Pharmacies.*

Charles L. Curry, M.D., professor of medicine emeritus, Howard University School of Medicine, Washington, D.C.; 1999 recipient of American Heart Association's "Physician of the Year" award

Austin Davis, auto mechanic and owner, Master Auto Service, Houston; author, *What Your Mechanic Doesn't Want You to Know* (www.trustmymechanic.com)

Mary Lorrie Davis, former nurse and author, *How to Survive a Stay in the Hospital Without Getting Killed*

Herb Denenberg, former Pennsylvania Insurance Commissioner; board member, Center for Proper Medication Use; consultant to numerous federal agencies

Douglas G. Duncan, Ph.D., chief economist and senior vice president, Mortgage Bankers Association, Washington, D.C.

George Everett, M.D., internist and assistant director of medical education, Orlando Regional Hospital, Orlando, Florida

James Fisher, spokesman, Sprint, Washington, D.C.

Mari J. Frank, Esq., identity theft-protection advocate and author, *From Victim to Victor: A Step-by-Step Guide for Ending the Nightmare of Identity Theft*

John W. Frenaye, Jr., travel agent and director of marketing and business development, Capital Travel Center, Annapolis, Maryland

Charles Gerba, Ph.D., world-renowned authority on germs and professor of environmental microbiology, University of Arizona, Tucson

Eric Gertler, former CEO, Privista, an identity theft protection and credit management company; author, *Prying Eyes: Protect Your Privacy from People Who Sell to You, Snoop on You, and Steal from You*

Jack Gillis, author, *The Car Book;* public affairs director for the Consumer Federation of America, Washington, D.C.; advisory board member, Consumers for Auto Reliability and Safety; executive director, Certified Automotive Part Association

Mark Grayson, spokesman, The Pharmaceutical Research and Manufacturers of America (PhRMA), Washington, D.C.

Peter Greenberg, chief correspondent for Discovery's Travel Channel; travel editor, the *Today* Show; author of *The Travel Detective* series and other travel books

Jack Guttentag, Ph.D., professor of finance emeritus, Wharton School of the University of Pennsylvania, Philadelphia; founder, mtgprofessor.com; author, *The Pocket Mortgage Guide* and *The Mortgage Encyclopedia*

John Hambrick, supervisory special agent, Federal Bureau of Investigation's Internet Crime Complaint Center, Washington, D.C.

Alan J. Heavens, author, *What No One Ever Tells You About Renovating Your Home* and real estate columnist, *The Philadelphia Inquirer*

Ron Hemphill, former identity thief turned consultant on identity-theft prevention; author, *Rollin': True Confessions of a Former Identity Thief* (www.idtheftexposed.com)

Chuck Hughes, former admissions officer, Harvard University; president, Road-to-College, Inc. consulting service, Boston; author, *What It Really Takes to Get into the Ivy League and Other Highly Selective Colleges*

Peter Humleker, former car salesman and dealership sales manager; author, *Car Buying Scams* (www.carbuyingscams.com)

Charles Inlander, president, People's Medical Society (patient-advocacy group), Allentown, Pennsylvania

Larry Jacoby, Ph.D., professor of psychology and director of the Aging, Memory and Cognitive Control Lab, Washington University in St. Louis

Nora Johnson, medical bill auditor, Medical Billing Advocates of America, Salem, Virginia

Ben Kaplan, author, *How to Go to College Almost for Free;* founder, www.scholarship coach.com

Mark Kantrowitz, publisher, FinAid (www.finaid.org); director of advanced projects, FastWeb (www.fastweb.com)

Amy Karch, R.N., assistant professor of clinical nursing, University of Rochester Medical Center, Rochester, New York

Mary Ann Kliethermes, Pharm.D., assistant professor, University of Illinois at Chicago College of Pharmacy

Tom Kraeutler, home inspector, Oakhurst, New Jersey; host, *The Money Pit,* nationally syndicated radio show about home repairs and improvements

Bruce Kushnick, telephone bill auditor and founder of TeleTruth (www.teletruth.com), a telephone service advocacy group, New York City

Cynthia LaCivita, Pharm.D., director, Clinical Standards and Quality; American Society of Health-System Pharmacists, Bethesda, Maryland

Anna Leider, author, *Don't Miss Out: The Ambitious Student's Guide to Financial Aid*

Mel Leiding, Esq., attorney specializing in traffic cases; author, *How to Fight Your Traffic Ticket and Win*

Evan S. Levine, M.D., clinical assistant professor of medicine, Albert Einstein College of Medicine and Montefiore Medical Center, Bronx, New York; cardiologist; author, *What Your Doctor Won't (or Can't) Tell You*

Gabriel Levitt, vice president for research, pharmacychecker.com and Consumer. Lab.com, co-author, *2005 Guide to Low-Cost Canadian and U.S. Pharmacies*

Vincent Marchello, M.D., medical director, Metropolitan Jewish Geriatric Center; assistant professor of medicine, Mount Sinai School of Medicine, New York City

Tom Marshall, spokesman, California High Patrol

M. Thomas Martin, founder, National Mortgage Complaint Center, Seattle (www.nationalmortgagecomplaint center.com)

Bill Mason, former jewel thief and cat burglar; author, *Confessions of a Master Jewel Thief*

Nancy Mathis, spokeswoman, Internal Revenue Service, Washington, D.C.

Doug Mayer, producer, *Car Talk,* nationally syndicated radio show about auto repairs

Robert McKinley, founder and CEO of CardWeb.com (www.cardweb.com), a leading payment card research firm, Frederick, Maryland

John Midgley, guidance counselor, Methacton High School, Norristown, Pennsylvania

Ed Mierzwinski, credit card industry watchdog and consumer advocate, the U.S. Public Interest Research Group (PIRG), Washington, D.C. (www.uspirg.org)

Myrna Milani, D.V.M., veterinarian and animal behaviorist, Charlestown, New Hampshire; author of nine nonfiction pet ownership guides

Michael Miller, M.D., cardiologist and director, Center for Preventive Cardiology, University of Maryland Medical Center, Baltimore

Duane Overholt, former car salesman turned consumer fraud consultant, Gaithersburg, Maryland (www.stopautofraud.com)

Liz Palika, dog trainer, Vista, California; founder, Love on a Leash pet therapy program; author of 46 pet books

Barry Paperno, manager of consumer services, Fair Isaac Corporation, Emeryville, California

C. Arden Pope III, Ph.D., professor of economics and epidemiology, Brigham Young University, Provo, Utah

Norie Quintos, senior editor, *National Geographic Traveler* magazine

Philip Reed, consumer advice editor, Edmunds.com; author, *Strategies for Smart Car Buyers*

Alan Reiter, president, Wireless Internet & Mobile Computing, Chevy Chase, Maryland; founder, www.cameraphone report.com

Ira Rheingold, executive director and general counsel, National Association of Consumer Advocates, Washington, D.C.

Michael Royce, former car salesman and author, *Beat the Car Salesman* (www.beatthecarsalesman.com)

David Rowell, travel consultant and publisher, www.thetravelinsider.info

Steven Mitchell Sack, Esq., employment attorney, New York City; author, *Getting Fired* and *The Employee Rights Handbook*

Warren Sam, investigator, California Bureau of Automotive Repair, Sacramento

Rich Sayers, telephone rates consultant and founder, www.1010phonerates.com

Marc-David Seidel, Ph.D., co-founder, www.tollchaser.com; assistant professor of organizational behavior, University of British Columbia, Vancouver, Canada

David Sherer, M.D., physician director of risk management, Kaiser Permanente Mid-Atlantic division; author, *Dr. David Sherer's Hospital Survival Guide;* anesthesiologist, Falls Church, Virginia

Linda Sherry, editorial director, Consumer Action, Washington, D.C.

Marc Siegel, M.D., internist and associate professor of medicine, New York University Medical Center, New York City

Tom Silva, master carpenter and co-host, *This Old House* public television show

Ellen Simon, Esq., employment attorney, Cleveland, Ohio

Eric Skrum, spokesman, National Motorists Association, Waunakee, Wisconsin

Howard Strong, Esq., author, *What Every Credit Card User Needs to Know;* attorney, Los Angeles

Sandra Timmermann, Ed.D., director, Met Life Mature Market Institute

Paul Tobias, Esq., founder, National Employment Lawyers Association; author, Job Rights and Survival Strategies; employment attorney, Cincinnati, Ohio

Doug Tygar, Ph.D., professor of computer science and information management, University of California, Berkeley

Jacqueline Whitmore, founder and director, the Protocol School of Palm Beach; author, *Business Class: Etiquette Essentials for Success at Work*

Joel Widzer, travel consultant and author, *The Penny Pincher's Passport to Luxury Travel*

Stacey Wood, Ph.D., neuropsychologist and associate professor of psychology, Scripps College, Claremont, California

James Wysong, flight attendant; author (writing as A. Frank Steward), *The Air Traveler's Survival Guide* and *The Plane Truth: Shift Happens at 35,000 Feet*

Mitchell Zelman, owner, Mitchell's Auto Repair, Brooklyn, New York; author, *What the Experts May Not Tell You About Car Repairs*

INDEX